A LYNCHING

in the

HEARTLAND

A LYNCHING

in the

HEARTLAND

RACE AND MEMORY IN AMERICA

James H. Madison

palgrave

for St. Martin's Press

First published 2001 by
PALGRAVE™
175 Fifth Avenue, New York, NY 10010 and
Houndmills, Basingstoke, Hampshire, England RG21 6XS.
Companies and representatives throughout the world.

Palgrave is the new global publishing imprint of St. Martin's Press LLC Scholarly and Reference Division and Palgrave Publishers Ltd (formerly Macmillan Press Ltd).

ISBN 0-312-23902-5 hardback

Library of Congress Cataloging-in-Publication Data

Madison, James H.
    A lynching in the heartland : race and memory in America / James H. Madison.
    p. cm.
    Includes bibliographical references (p.) and index.
    ISBN 0-312-23902-5
    1. Marion (Ind.)--Race relations. 2. African Americans--Indiana--Marion--Social conditions--20th century. 3. Lynching--Indiana--Marion--History--20th century. 4. Cameron, James, 1914- 5. African Americans--Indiana--Marion--Biography. 6. Racism--Indiana--Marion--History--20th century. I. Title.

F534.M34 M33 2001
305.896'0730772'52--dc21   2001021826

Design by planettheo.com

First Edition: November, 2001
10 9 8 7 6 5 4 3 2 1

Printed in the United States of America.

To Jeanne

CONTENTS

ACKNOWLEDGMENTS

Many people generously helped me gather sources, make sense of complex issues, and communicate more effectively with readers.

I begin with Larry Conrad, an Indiana lawyer and politician who grew up not far from Marion, fascinated by stories of the lynching. In the late 1970s he devoted considerable time to gathering sources and interviewing Grant County residents. Some of those items are unique, particularly the tapes of the oral history interviews with people no longer alive. I am thankful that Larry Conrad's widow, Mary Lou Conrad, and his colleague Claudia Prosser turned over to me the several boxes of material I label in the notes as the Larry Conrad Papers. Another Hoosier with interest in the Marion lynching was Emma Lou Thornbrough, the premier scholar of Indiana's African American history. Emma Lou shared with me her deep understanding and notes that pointed me in important directions early on.

Many people in Grant County were welcoming and helpful even though some doubtless were uncertain whether an outsider stirring up these memories was a good thing for their community. I owe great debts to several Grant Countians with a passion for history and for their community. William Munn teaches history at Marion High School and heads the Community History Project at the Marion Public Library. Bill's curiosity and intelligence about his community's past and present are among its great treasures and were very important to many of the insights of this book. Dick Simons is the official Grant County historian; he offered many kindnesses in sharing his knowledge, not just from duty but from the generosity of his heart. Ed Breen was for many years the editor of the Marion newspaper. He knows nearly everyone and everything. Ed helped me see connections. Early in this project I called Tom Wise, then still a member of the Marion police force, now retired. We met several times over the years. His knowledge has been exceedingly helpful. Barbara J. Stevenson has made important contributions to Grant County history, particularly in gathering photographs and in conducting oral history interviews, which she has transcribed and published. Barbara generously shared unpublished material and also her own understanding of people and events. And at the Marion Public Library I had great assistance from Barbara Love, who makes the Indiana Room and history museum there a wonderful and welcome place to study the community.

I thank those Marion folks who spent a Saturday morning around a conference table discussing issues of race: Oatess Archey, Ed Breen, Harley Burden, Jr., Dr. Joe Casey, Carl Gulliford, Alan Miller, Bill Munn, Bob Morrell, Larry Myers, Vern Owensby, Lillie Roebuck, Richard Simons, Yvonne Washington, and Jerry Whitton.

Many people provided oral history interviews that are indispensable to any understanding of the issues raised in this book. The following people willingly talked with me, often welcomed me into their homes, agreed that I could use their comments, and helped me immensely: Oatess Archey, Ed Breen, Harley Burden, Jr., Marcus Cannon, James Cameron, Dr. Edmund Casey, Dr. Joe Casey, Dr. Joe Davis, Jack Edwards, Mary Campbell Fuller, Betty Musser, Robert W. Newell, Sarah Weaver Pate, Ann Secttor, Elizabeth Shrock, Roger Smith, James Sutter, Bruce T. Weaver, and Tom Wise. I want to note particularly James Cameron's welcome not only in an interview but in the material he sent me later. We do not tell the exact same story, but my respect for him should be evident to readers.

I am most appreciative of those librarians and archivists across the nation who helped me identify collections. Most important were those professionals at the Library of Congress and the Indiana Historical Society. Wilma Gibbs at the Historical Society provided numerous suggestions; Stephen Fletcher there helped with photographs; Doug Clanin pointed me to an important interview. My favorite librarians in the world are at Indiana University, Bloomington, where they make available to scholars a collection of superb resources: I am especially thankful for the help of librarians Ann Bristow, Nancy Cridland, Lou Malcomb, and Celestina Wroth.

I owe a special debt to several friends and a few strangers who read all or part of the manuscript. Suellen Hoy proved again that old friends are the best friends; her detailed commentary on the manuscript not only saved me from errors but led me to sharpen central arguments. Walter Nugent suggested small and large improvements and provided reassurance at a shaky point. John Gallman helped me focus on readers. Richard Blackett pointed to some places where "cow pooh" needed shoveling and places where there were silences that needed filling. Dominic J. Capeci, Jr., gave me a long and exceedingly thoughtful critique, which I reread many times with great profit. Darlene Clark Hine was a generous and encouraging reader. Cecile Click read the manuscript with a curiosity and intellect that helped me clarify key issues. Bill Munn, Dick Simons, and Ed Breen also read the whole manuscript and made important corrections, which flowed from their local knowledge. Stephen Vincent read the nineteenth-century chapters and made several excellent suggestions. Richard Pierce pushed me to clarify the argument in the last chapter. That Clyde Taylor liked the manuscript made a big difference in many ways. Deborah Gershenowitz gave an enthusiastic and careful editor's eye to small details and the big picture. Bill Berry did a superb job in copyediting, as did Donna Cherry and Sabahat Chaudhary in production.

Colleagues at Indiana University slowed the work during the years that I was history department chair, but they repaid me with the joys of working in an atmosphere of intellectual excitement. Time spent with students was not really lost time either: not only is teaching the only way I can begin to repay debts I owe to my teachers but students have helped me understand and communicate issues such as lynchings and race. Thomas and Kathryn Miller's generosity to Indiana University has substantially assisted my teaching and research; I'm most grateful. I thank also colleagues and students at Hiroshima University during my year there, 1997-98, as a Fulbright Professor. Teaching American history in a Japanese university as I was writing about Marion, Indiana, gave a distance essential to such a subject. I am particularly thankful for the kindnesses of Masaru Okamoto, Reiko Nitta, Koji Murata, Deb Robison, Yuka Tsuchiya, and Tetsuya Fujiwara.

Other friends and strangers answered questions, sent photocopies, and chased down missing facts: James Allen, Jack Blocker, Fitzhugh Brundage, Donald F. Carmony, Louis Ebert, June Felton, Rae Ferguson, Ken Goodall, Hurley Goodall, Todd Gould, Ann Hackett, Tom Hamm, Jerri Libert, Tony Maidenberg, Jim Matthews, Jeff Morehead, Leslie Neher, Bob Reid, Dow

Richardson, Alice Shrock, Randall Shrock, Ken Singleton, John Martin Smith, John Straw, Steve Towne, H. Dixon Trueblood, Nancy Turner, and Karen Bostic Weaver. I am grateful also to Jason Lantzer, who helped with the bibliography, John M. Hollingsworth, who prepared the maps, and Paula Corpuz, who made the index.

Finally, to my family: to the memory of my mother, father, and grand-mother, who so shaped my own choices; to my son, John, who kept reminding me of the dangers of getting old and cranky; to my daughter Julia, who reminded me where sick babies fit in the scheme of things; and to Jeanne, for all things.

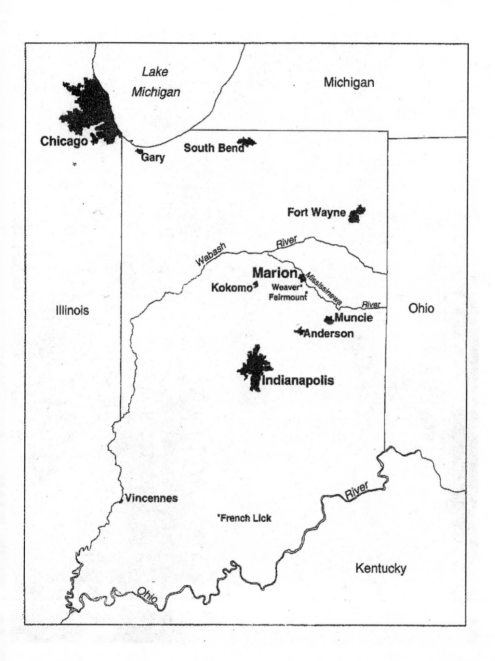

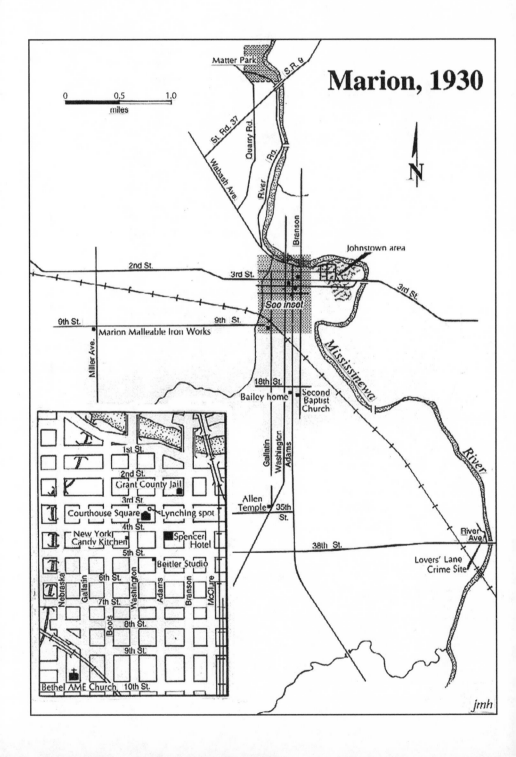

Marion, 1930

Matter Park

St. Rd. 37

Quarry Rd.

Wabash Ave.

River Rd.

S.R. 9

River

Branson

Johnstown area

N

0   0.5   1.0
miles

2nd St.

3rd St.

3rd St.

See inset

Mississinewa

9th St.

9th St.

Miller Ave.

Marion Malleable Iron Works

18th St.

Bailey home

Second Baptist Church

River

Gallatin

Washington

Adams

Allen Temple

35th St.

38th St.

River Ave.

Lovers' Lane Crime Site

1st St.

2nd St.

Grant County Jail

3rd St.

Courthouse Square

Lynching spot

New York Candy Kitchen

4th St.

Spencer Hotel

5th St.

Beitler Studio

Nebraska

Gallatin

6th St.

Washington

Adams

Branson

McClure

7th St.

Boos

8th St.

9th St.

Bethel AME Church

10th St.

jmh

Introduction

This is a book about race. It masquerades as a book about a lynching. The book begins with the murder of Claude Deeter and the alleged rape of Mary Ball, crimes that led a mob to lynch Abe Smith and Tom Shipp in Marion, Indiana, in 1930. Those acts of hatred and violence are important in and of themselves, worthy of telling. They make a good, although frightful, story. But I use the lynching as the proverbial two-by-four to the head, as a way to turn the reader's attention to the lines of color that run through twentieth-century America. This is a book about America's struggles to understand racism, its greatest tragedy and mystery.

Race is both a constant and a changing part of the American story. By focusing a spotlight on one place and one event we can see more clearly the persistence and fluidity of racial matters as whites and blacks struggle with its complexities. I try to keep the spotlight as close as possible to the Courthouse Square of Grant County, Indiana, the community's geographic and symbolic center, the scene not only of the lynching but also of much else important in the history of this particular place. Around this typical midwestern courthouse the reader can see central themes of twentieth-century America played out in terms of ordinary people's lives. One can even detect some progress, some reason to hope that things are getting better. Certainly one can see that ordinary people have choices, that they can decide to work toward equality and justice or toward hatred and even violence.

The lynching of August 7, 1930, was only one expression of lines that divided black and white. Lines of color had been present before that night of terror, but now they were drawn more deeply, not only in the lynching but also in the investigation and trials that followed under the courthouse dome. Because the formal legal process failed to convict any member of the lynch mob, there was no closure and no way to erase the tragedy from the community's history.

The lynching did not go away. Indeed, the stories, the memories, even, some said, the collective guilt, increased as the community slouched toward the end of the twentieth century. This book is about those memories, how they got made, how they changed, how some grew stronger and some faded as times and people changed. Everything is fluid in Marion, Indiana, and in America, including memory.

The first chapter tells the story of the Marion lynching. Chapter 2 presents a general background of lynching's dark history in the nation, in the Midwest, and, with a surprising twist, in Grant County. Chapter 3 provides a sketch of this particular place, of the ordinary but compelling qualities that made it such an attractive home to many black and white residents—a total of 51,066 in 1930 in the county, including 24,496 in the county seat of Marion, of which slightly over a thousand were African American. Chapter 4 focuses on African Americans who lived in Grant County, from the pioneers who arrived before the Civil War to the courageous few who organized the Marion branch of the NAACP.

Chapters 5 and 6 present the immediate aftermath of the lynching. Here the reader will see clearly the differences of race, as most whites drew tighter the boundaries that separated them from their African American neighbors, using the instruments of law as their marking devices. Chapter 7 brings to the story's center two of the main actors: Flossie Bailey, a black woman, perhaps the most courageous citizen in all of Marion's history, and James Cameron, the third black youth accused of murder and rape, who narrowly escaped the lynch noose. Chapter 8 shows why the lynching did not fade from memory, how a powerful photograph taken the night of the event helped keep it alive and how Cameron returned, as if from the dead, to tell his story. Indeed, chapters 8 and 9 show

how Cameron's story came to be the dominant story, used not simply to retell what happened but to draw moral lessons from the tragedy. Cameron, the intended victim of a lynch mob, emerges not only as a survivor but also as a heroic conscience.

The attention given Cameron should not obscure other stories told by ordinary people, black and white, as they struggled with lines of color. Especially because Cameron chronicled his story with a particular point of view and such compelling power, it is all the more important to listen carefully to other voices. For this is also a book about how stories get made, how people create different versions of one event.

I allow the people in this book to tell their stories through their words and deeds and with less of my own analysis and interpretation than some readers might like. I chose this leaner form for two reasons. First, I wanted to move the narrative along quickly and encourage the general reader to keep turning these pages. And second, I wanted to allow space for the reader to think about these events, to see possibilities of various meanings.

This is a book of nonfiction. I have stayed close to the sources. They are particularly rich—a richness that forced me to abandon my 1992 summer project to write a short, simple article about the Marion lynching. But there are still questions the sources do not answer, particularly in fleshing out the lives of people, in fully explaining what they thought and why they did what they did. That is the cost of writing about ordinary people, who so often leave behind incomplete records of their lives.

Marion, Indiana, is an ordinary place, which I try hard to bring to life. I do not provide the massive and fascinating detail that readers can find in Robert and Helen Lynd's classic books on nearby Muncie, Indiana, which they called Middletown. The Lynds deliberately excluded African Americans from their study, however, and thereby missed the biggest story, the one that today we most need to know and understand.

There is no smoking gun that explains exactly why this tragedy happened at this particular place and time. It could have happened in lots of places in America. Indeed, it did. But, again, real individuals made real choices in 1930 and in the decades that followed. This book is about those choices—about humans doing terrible and cowardly things to others and humans doing generous and courageous things, about violence and justice denied, and about memories suppressed and memories revived. Through all these lynching stories run lines of color.

CHAPTER ONE

A Night of Terror

The first sounds the prisoners heard were murmurs and bits of conversation. Beginning around 6:30 P.M. on Thursday, August 7, 1930, the words grew louder as more and more people gathered on the sidewalk, street, and yard in front of the Grant County Jail in Marion, Indiana. "Get 'em," some shouted. "Kill the niggers." Louder and louder, the sounds of vengeance cut between the bars of the three-story jail and into the cells where Tom Shipp, aged 19, Abe Smith, 18, and James Cameron, 16, listened and waited.[1]

The three black teenagers were in separate cells, connected by the crime they had confessed to the night before. On August 6, they had ambushed a young couple parked in the local lovers' lane along the Mississinewa River. Claude Deeter, aged 24, a Marion factory worker, fought the three assailants heroically but could not resist the bullets fired from a revolver by one of the three. His companion, 18-year-old Mary Ball, was pushed down in the weeds and thorns along the riverbank and raped, press stories reported.

Marion police were soon on the case. With Mary Ball's description of the threesome's old Ford touring car, they identified Shipp, Smith, and Cameron as suspects. By 2:00 A.M., August 7, police had the trio in the Grant County Jail. Questioned intensively, they soon confessed.

At Marion General Hospital Claude Deeter lay dying of gunshot wounds. His family rushed to his bedside from their farm near Fairmount, a few miles south of Marion on State Road 9. The doctors advised the Deeter family that there was no hope. Of strong Pentecostal faith, his mother quietly told her son he was dying and urged him to forgive his attackers. He forgave. At 1:30 on Thursday afternoon, August 7, Claude Deeter died, at peace with God, his sister later recalled.

There was no peace in Grant County. The three young men were now liable for murder. The front-page story in the *Marion Chronicle* Thursday evening summarized their plight: "Three Marion youths—all colored—today cringed in the shadow of the electric chair."

The crowd that formed in front of the Grant County Jail the evening of August 7 was not willing to wait for a slow march to the electric chair at the Indiana Penitentiary and not willing to contemplate the possibility of a detour to sentences other than death. Many in the crowd had seen Claude Deeter's bloody shirt, which police hung from a City Hall window that Thursday morning, a red flag over Boots Street. Many had heard Mary Ball's tale of robbery, rape, and murder, a story told and retold that day. The anger grew with each hearing. Some people in Grant County wanted vengeance. Now.

Some in the crowd that Thursday night had gathered earlier in Deeter's hometown of Fairmount to tell the stories of murder and rape and to argue about a course of action. Others had talked in a pool hall near the Courthouse Square. In restaurants, cigar stores, and dress shops people talked about the crimes and the "colored boys" who committed them. Phone lines crackled, often with several talkers vying for time on the party lines. Many said that the criminals would escape the electric chair. There was too much lawlessness in Grant County, they said, too little punishment. Some set their minds to action. They organized, planned, and waited for darkness. At about 8:30 P.M. they arrived in front of the jail.

As rumors circulated that something was about to happen, several worried citizens called Sheriff Jake Campbell and other officials to warn them. Grant County Prosecuting Attorney Harley Hardin also heard the rumors and walked over to the jail to talk with Sheriff Campbell. The sheriff was a proud and stubborn man, even bullheaded, some thought. He assured Hardin there was no need to worry: the prisoners were safe. Everyone knew that there had never been a lynching in Grant County.

Flossie Bailey also telephoned the sheriff and received similar assurances. Bailey remained concerned, however. She was president of the Marion branch of the National Association for the Advancement of Colored People (NAACP). She knew that elsewhere in America angry mobs had lynched black men accused of murder and rape. She knew that racial passions had flamed into violent riots, even in neighboring Illinois, which had witnessed upheavals in Springfield, East St. Louis, and Chicago.

Despite Sheriff Campbell's calm assurances, rumors of violence continued through the summer afternoon. By early evening he was sufficiently worried to consider moving the prisoners out of the city. Entering the jail garage, he discovered that someone had let the air out of the tires of both his Studebakers and drained the gas tanks. Sheriff Campbell called the city police station for additional help.

People continued to gather in front of the jail. Bodies and cars blocked traffic. There was some pushing, more shouting, and lots of perspiration in the hot and humid Indiana night. Details of the alleged murder and rape were repeated, more and more heatedly. Rage against the three youths in jail seeped over to all African Americans. Deputy Sheriff John O. Fryer remembered a deep voice rising above the din: "You can't get law enforcement here: they let the niggers go to school with the white children here and march in the band."

Some observers estimated the crowd at four thousand by 9:00 P.M., when Hoot Ball, Mary Ball's father, entered the jail to talk to Sheriff Campbell: "Give us the keys," the sheriff remembered Ball saying, "and let us get the niggers." To Campbell's pleas for reason, Ball replied, "If this was your daughter, you would do just the same as I am doing . . . the court will give them about two years." The sheriff refused Hoot Ball's demand for the keys. He stood on the jail porch, pleading with the crowd. Sweat dripped from his face. It was his duty to protect the prisoners, he said. He and his deputies stood guard in a jail of solid security, the best in Indiana, he said. City Police Chief Lewis Lindenmuth stood with him. Prosecutor Harley Hardin walked through the excited crowd trying to persuade individuals to go home. *Marion Chronicle* reporter Drysdale Brannon also spoke to lay out the facts of the case to the crowd and reassure them that justice would be served. Theater manager Billy Connors tried to speak, but a woman shouted, "Kill the nigger lovin' son of a bitch!" A fist knocked the dapper Connors aside.

Catcalls and curses echoed louder off the jail's brick walls. Threats to dynamite the jail rang out. Sheriff Campbell worried about the safety of his family, who lived in the residence attached to the jail. He moved his wife (who cooked for the prisoners) and daughter to the nearby Spencer Hotel. "The thing I remember most vividly," the sheriff's daughter later recalled, "was seeing so many people, women, standing out there in the crowd with little, tiny babies in their arms, just hollering 'Get in there and get em, get in there and get em.'"

Not long after Hoot Ball ended his short conference with the sheriff and descended the porch steps, a portion of the crowd became a mob. Somewhere between 30 and 75 people stormed the jail. Many of the several thousand standing behind encouraged the attackers with shouts, chants, and curses. Car horns honked. Shouts and screams filled the night. More and more people kept coming as news spread through the town and into the countryside. Several men left the Elks Club to see what was happening. As moving picture shows ended their audiences exited to the streets and toward the action. Some reporters claimed ten thousand congregated eventually.

The mob attacked the massive jail in the front, on the side, and through the garage. The leaders had prepared for the task by gathering sledgehammers and crowbars from the Marion Machine Foundry, where some of them worked. Nearly all were young men, many in their teens, the same ages as Shipp, Smith, and Cameron. Their muscular arms swung the iron tools hard against the doors of the jail. They beat at hinges and locks and punched through doorframes and walls. Their faces, unmasked, glistened with sweat in the dark night, proud in their physical strength and moral righteousness, their determination lifted by the shouts of encouragement from the crowd.

Sheriff Campbell and his deputies resisted. They refused angry demands for jail door keys, even when threatened with a sledgehammer. They hurled a half dozen tear gas canisters. The mob pushed on. Some were veterans of World War I. They had seen violence and tear gas before. They hurled the canisters back into the jail and turned on a lawn hose to water away the gas. A deputy called the fire department, but when the firemen attempted to attach their hoses to the water mains the crowd angrily pushed them away.

After an hour of hard work the mob was inside the first floor of the jail. Most of the deputies and police officers inside the jail retreated to the sheriff's residence or to the basement. Among those entering the jail were several young women, including two sisters, aged 16 and 13. The mob first seized William (Spuds) Bernaul, held on a charge of raping a black woman. Bernaul was one of several black prisoners in the jail. He had been playing cards with Ed Blotz, a white man charged with murder and then burning the body. Blotz and other prisoners came to Bernaul's defense and pointed to Tom Shipp's cell and then to the top of the cell, where Shipp had climbed in a futile effort to hide. The mob grabbed Shipp and began to club him as they dragged him outside. Mary Ball's sister stood on top of a car and screamed encouragement. A woman closer to Shipp hit him with her bare fist. Another took off her shoe and beat him with it. At about 10:30 P.M. the mob put a rope around his neck and lynched him from the window bars on the east side of the jail. Shipp grabbed the rope to resist strangulation, but several men then held his arms and tied them together. Someone stabbed him before the rope was again pulled tight around his neck and drawn from the jail window bars. Some observers thought he was dead before the lynch noose could effect its purpose. The mob continued to beat the dead body. In a different part of Marion a short while later the dead youth's mother heard the news and screamed into the night.

The mob then made its way to the third floor, where they pulled Abe Smith from his cell. When he bit one man on the right arm, another struck him on the head with a crowbar. Clubbed and beaten, Smith endured a long gauntlet as a half dozen young men dragged him the short block up Third Street to the Courthouse Square. Along the way most of his clothes were torn off. When the men dragging Smith stopped briefly, several women rushed forward to stomp on his head and chest and to scream insults. On the northeast corner of the square, in the shadow of streetlights and the Grant County Courthouse, the mob threw a rope over a maple limb and lynched Smith. No one bothered to record his or Shipp's last words.

Some men returned to the jail and cut down Shipp's body. They carried it to the Courthouse Square, to the center of the town, to hang beside Smith's.

They built a fire under the bodies, but it failed to burn them. Others stabbed and spat at the two dead victims.

Some in the crowd knew they were witnessing a great tragedy. At least two women fainted at the sight of the bloody violence. A 13-year-old boy vomited, down on his knees on the sidewalk. An older woman prayed loudly, beseeching the Lord to stop the violence. Several adults, men and women, cried in anguish, dumbfounded and enraged at what their fellow citizens had done.

The mob was not finished. They returned to the jail for Cameron and dragged him to what was now the lynching tree. But just as the rope fell over Cameron's head, someone stood on top of a car and shouted over the noise. It was Mary Ball's uncle, Sol Ball, according to some. Others claimed it was Rex George, head of the local American Legion. Cameron himself later said it was an angel. Most reports agree that the man's words calmed the mob as he shouted that Cameron was innocent. At the jail Sheriff Campbell had tried the same ploy to protect Cameron. By this time others in the crowd, many of them older people, were also at work quietly calming the mob. It was enough. The spirit of revenge and violence had run its course. Cameron was quietly escorted back to jail to await justice.

The shouts faded as midnight approached. Police from Kokomo, Indianapolis, Muncie, and other nearby towns, summoned by Sheriff Campbell, arrived about 11:00 P.M. They reported a scene of peace and remarkable good humor. One of the mob who had helped with the rope went with his young wife to a nearby restaurant for a late dinner. But the crowds did not disperse. People milled about through the night. A woman nursed her baby. Fathers held up older children to see the two bodies. Many stood on top of cars. Newcomers kept arriving, including the youth group from Antioch Methodist Church that was meeting that evening in a farmhouse six miles east of Marion. Cars—Fords, Hudsons, Chevys—parked at all angles, jammed together like matchsticks around the Courthouse Square and in nearby streets. Gridlock came to the small county seat town.

Souvenir collectors cut pieces of clothing from the two bodies and bark from the lynching tree. One person took a shoe home to display. At one point the penis of one of the bodies was visible, but apparently mutilation did not extend to the genitals. Someone wrapped a towel and feed sack around Smith's body to hide his nakedness. The most prized souvenir was rope, cut in small segments: dozens of spectators took pieces home. Strong young men returned sledgehammers and crowbars to the Marion Machine Foundry, too precious to keep as souvenirs.

Photographers came and their flash powder lit up the night. A young boy turned the bodies so the cameras could get face shots. Local photographer Lawrence Beitler flashed his camera to make what would become one of the most famous lynching photos in all of American history. The bodies hung in the damp night air.

At about 2:00 A.M., August 8, 1930, Grant County Coroner Orlando L. Stout came to take away the victims. His appearance roused the quiet crowd, which still numbered about a thousand people. They turned Stout away. The bodies must hang as warning, they shouted. Not until 5:45 A.M. did Sheriff Campbell cut down the bodies, allowing them to fall with a thump to the ground.

The Marion lynching was over, or so some thought.

CHAPTER TWO

"Strange Fruit" in the American Democracy

The death of Tom Shipp and Abe Smith at the hands of a lynch mob was not a unique event. Such bloody tragedies had frequently played on the American stage. So well rehearsed was the nation's drama of lynching that members of the Grant County mob surely knew they were actors standing in a long tradition. Without studying a script they knew their lines and stage movements: crowds of angry citizens shout their outrage and epithets at the beginning of the spectacle; a knotted rope appears; the mob forcefully removes the victim from the jail; some beat and mutilate him; fire ignites to burn a dead body; the body remains hanging as symbol; souvenir hunters grab pieces of rope and clothing and in some instances even body parts; a photographer captures the scene of victim, mob, and spectators. The play is ended. Civilization is redeemed.[1]

LYNCHING AND CIVILIZATION

From 1880 to 1930 angry mobs lynched 4,697 fellow Americans. Of these victims 3,344 were African Americans.[2] Race was a central factor in this tragedy, as in many of America's tragedies.

Some suggest that lynching was a southern, not American, drama. Certainly most took place in the South, over 95 percent of the nation's total during the 1920s. The peculiar nature of race relations in the former Confederate states left a sad legacy of white restriction and violence against blacks, the most vicious of which was lynching. In recent years historians have begun to explore the complexity of southern lynching. Most scholars emphasize that whites felt threatened by blacks, that whites were fearful that blacks might challenge the subordinate economic, social, and political status forced on them by whites. A lynching of a black man was a clear statement of white solidarity against any black threat to the status quo. Witnessed by large crowds and accompanied by great publicity, with all the gruesome details reported in the press, the ritual proved even more powerful if it happened on a public stage such as a busy street corner or courthouse square. Sometimes the mob moved the dead victim to such a place even if death had occurred in a less visible spot. A lynching was a performance that sent a message of white supremacy, warning all blacks to stay in their place. It was a weapon of terror that could strike anywhere, anytime, against any African American.

Scholars have argued that lynchings often related not only to race but also to gender. White myths of black male sexuality created images of a savage beast consumed by lust for white women. In this fantasy whites were civilized, blacks were uncivilized. White women were the "purest" form of civilization, black men the most savage and "unclean." Sex between a black man and a white woman was a defilement of the ultimate sort. Sexual attraction opened up the possibility of a genuine human relationship, with the potential even of equality between a black man and a white woman expressed in sex and even love. Part of this story included the fear of some white men that white women were sexually attracted to black men. Moreover, such a relationship was liable to produce "mixed" and therefore "unclean" offspring. White women, so white men wanted to believe, would never willingly engage in sexual relations with a black man. Only rape provided lustful black men with sexual access to white women.

In such tangled webs of race and gender, white men were obliged to protect white women. Men who protected white female purity were also protectors of community values and of civilization itself. White men understood that a black rapist represented the ultimate threat to their own place in that community and that civilization. A white woman who feared black rapists would need to seek a white man's protection and thereby accept the subservient status such protection implied. White men who engaged in lynching claimed they were protecting their women. And they proclaimed to all their place at the top of the social, economic, and political ladder, above white women and above all African Americans.

When during the 1920s some smart young women began to dress in shorter skirts, bob their hair, smoke cigarettes, and talk openly about sex, some men feared loss of their traditional power. The new women of the Jazz Age even showed enthusiasm for African American music of the blues and jazz, for wild "African" styles of dancing, even for enjoying the company of black men. How could lynching be justified if the victim of black male lust was such a brazen new woman? Rather, she had to be weak and vulnerable, virginal and innocent if the contest between civilization and savagery was to be valid and if white men were to fulfill their destiny as protectors of dependent white women.

Myth and deliberate lies ran through these strands of thought about race and gender. Although whites often claimed rape was the cause and justification of lynching, in the great majority of actual lynchings the victim was not in fact accused of being a rapist. Indeed, the largest number of victims of rape were black women, a fact hardly ever acknowledged by white men, whose own sexual attraction to black women was widely known and widely covered up.

It was a crusading black woman, Ida B. Wells, who began to make these arguments in the 1890s. Wells asserted that the cry of rape was often false and often a "shield" and "screen" to "excuse some of the most heinous crimes that ever stained the history of a country." But as late as 1930 few whites were prepared to listen to the facts and truths of lynching.[3]

All cultures fashion myths that help create communities of like-minded people, folks who can stick together and nourish and sustain each other. All people create versions of "us" and "them," whether of male and female, of black and white, of upper class and lower class, of our town and your town, of my family and your family. Such creations can be benign, even necessary. But in no place in America did this mythmaking become more malevolent and tragic than where it created the foundation for lynching. White men lynched black men, thousands of black men. White women tolerated and even encouraged such savagery to protect civilization, to maintain their community boundaries, to cement bonds of us and them, of black and white.

The tragedy of lynching played on America's central stage in the years between the Civil War and World War II. D. W. Griffith's film *Birth of a Nation* (1915) explained its justice and necessity to white Americans as they watched the black brute "Gus" pursue the innocent white heroine across the screen. The great jazz singer Billie Holiday gave sad voice to its evil in her version of "Strange Fruit," which she first sang in 1939:

> Southern trees bear a strange fruit,
> Blood on the leaves and blood at the root:
> Black body swinging in the Southern breeze,
> Strange fruit hanging from the poplar trees.[4]

One critic has claimed recently that "no song in American history has ever been so guaranteed to silence an audience or to generate such discomfort."[5]

Billie Holiday captured the grotesque and melancholy strangeness of black bodies hanging, but the bodies she mourned were hanging in the South, as were the lynchings portrayed in most other forms of American expression. Lynching was a southern tragedy, most Americans believed, a part of the South's peculiar history and special form of race relations. The numbers show clearly that most lynchings occurred in the South, but lynching was an American, not southern, tragedy, as much as some pious Yankees wanted to think otherwise.

BLOOD IN THE HEARTLAND

From 1880 to 1930, 123 black Americans died at the hands of northern lynch mobs, 79 of them in the Midwest.[6] White mobs lynched Zachariah Walker in Coatesville, Pennsylvania, in 1911; 3 black circus workers in Duluth, Minnesota, in 1920; and Cleo Wright in Sikeston, Missouri, in 1942. These and other northern lynchings featured brutalities that forced some Americans with Yankee sensibilities to admit that there existed among them the cruelties and hatreds they associated only with the most godforsaken places in the South.[7]

There is considerable evidence of the capacity for violence against "others" among northerners in general and midwesterners in particular. The conquest and removal of Native Americans left bloody ground in the American heartland. After his men captured four Indians at Vincennes, Indiana, in 1779, George Rogers Clark, the great hero of the Revolutionary War in the West, ordered his frontiersmen to tomahawk the warrior prisoners as they sat defenseless on the ground. Before throwing the bodies in the Wabash River, Clark's men took their scalps. As another of the frontier's most famous Indian fighters and politicians, William Henry Harrison (later the American president), observed in 1801, most frontiersmen "consider the murdering of Indians in the highest degree meritorious."[8]

But the record of frontier violence and legal justice is mixed. In 1824 a small group of white men set upon several peaceful Seneca Indian families camped along Deer Lick Creek in central Indiana (only a few dozen miles from the future site of Marion). Claiming the Indians had stolen their horses, the men savagely murdered all the Indian men, women, and children, mutilated their bodies, and plundered their valuable goods. What makes the Deer Lick Creek Massacre (sometimes called the Fall Creek Massacre) notable is that the four white men were tried and convicted of murdering Indians, at great expense and travail for authorities and citizens. Three white men died by the hangman's rope, all in formal legal proceedings in a time and place so close to the frontier that the ability of one of the associate judges to read the printed word was in serious doubt. And this most interesting of frontier trials produced the recorded words of Judge William W. Wick. As he handed down the death sentences, Wick heaped eloquent indignation on the murderers and even on the community traditions of "them" and "us":

> By what authority do we hauntingly boast of our being white? What principle of philosophy or of religion established the doctrine that a white skin is preferable in nature or in the sight of God to a red or black one? Who has ordained that men of the white skin shall be at liberty to shoot and hunt down men of the red skin, or exercise rule and dominion over those of the black?

The Deer Lick Creek Massacre suggests the wide extremes of violence and of justice that were the contradictory heritage of the midwestern frontier.[9]

The struggle between violence and legal justice heightened in the late nineteenth century. As industrialization challenged old ways and as rapid change seemed to bring lawlessness and crime, some took refuge in vigilante justice. Indiana, like other midwestern states, struggled mightily with issues of law and order in the several decades after the Civil War.

Vigilantism boomed in the late nineteenth century, as bands of men attempted to impose their will on those they judged in violation of community norms, from adultery or abuse of children to theft, rape, and murder. Sometimes the mobs gave the violators a good beating. Sometimes they lynched them. The exact numbers are not known, but there were at least 61 persons lynched in Indiana between 1865 and 1903, 41 whites and 20 blacks. More whites than blacks; but blacks were only 2 percent of the state's total population, while black victims accounted for a third of those lynched.[10]

Most of the black victims of Indiana lynch mobs were accused of murder or rape. All died without benefit of trial; they were usually taken from a local jail with little or no resistance from the sheriff. Most died as large crowds watched in approval. In 1886, for example, a mob of masked men took a black farm laborer accused of murder and rape from the jail in Vincennes and lynched him on the Knox County Courthouse Square, not far from where George Rogers Clark's men had tomahawked and scalped Indian prisoners.

Such Hoosier lynchings increased in frequency in the late 1880s and 1890s, as they did elsewhere in the Midwest and in the South. In 1899 the Indiana legislature finally passed a law that required a sheriff to call on the governor for militia protection if a lynching was threatened. The law also gave the governor authority to remove from office a sheriff who surrendered prisoners to a mob. The new law was only weakly enforced, however. In 1900, in the Ohio River town of Rockport, a crowd estimated at over a thousand watched a mob lynch three black men accused of murdering a local barber. A few weeks later a mob in Terre Haute lynched a black man accused of assaulting a white schoolteacher. After hanging him from the Wabash River Bridge, they threw the body on a huge bonfire as thousands again watched.

A new Indiana governor in 1901 finally showed the will to enforce the antilynching law. Following a lynching in 1902 in Sullivan County, Governor Winfield Durbin initiated a fact-finding hearing to consider removal of the sheriff. The attorney for the Sullivan County sheriff stated at Governor Durbin's hearing that in dealing with the lynch mob, "The sheriff had to face his best friends, men with whom he had lived and worked all his life." He could not shoot into the mob, especially after some of the men told him they would rather die than live with the horror of white women assaulted by black fiends. Governor Durbin stood firm and removed the Sullivan County sheriff from office. When on July 4, 1903, holiday racial tensions in Evansville flamed into rioting after a black man shot a white policeman, Governor Durbin sent a company of state militia to the city on the banks of the Ohio River. Before the riot ended 12 people died in gunfire, including a young girl observing the action, and 30 were wounded.[11]

Durbin was the first Indiana governor to show real courage in the face of lynch mobs. He stated his position eloquently in an essay that appeared in the national magazine *Independent* soon after the Evansville riots. Durbin quoted Benjamin Franklin that a lynch mob is "a monster with many hands and no brains." He dismissed the justification of using "mob law in vindication of the virtue of woman" and condemned the assertion that "mob law is essential to the proper regulation of the relations between the negro and the white man." Although Durbin condemned "the stupid passion of race hatred," his primary appeal was not to racial justice but to the maintenance of law and order.[12]

Durbin's opposition to lynching was shared by many who feared vigilante justice and its rejection of law and court, of judge and jury. The long tradition of vigilantism in America was based on assertions that the people were the source of all law and that direct action by the people was a democratic right. Durbin and others rejected that vigilante tradition as one that would lead from mob rule to dictatorship, not democracy.[13]

Governor Durbin's combination of words and forceful action succeeded. After 1903 there were no more lynchings in twentieth-century Indiana, with the exception of those in Marion on August 7, 1930. State and local authorities did their jobs. In Indianapolis in 1920, for example, a mob of some six hundred men marched to the Marion County Jail seeking a black prisoner accused of murdering a 14-year-old girl. They met the city's police force, which had surrounded the jail and equipped itself with riot clubs and guns. Even though the crowd swelled to about two thousand angry citizens and even though shots were fired, the police stood their ground, made 15 arrests, and eventually convinced the beast of many hands and no brains to disperse. That same year in New Albany a mob threatened a black man accused of attacking a woman. Local officials removed the prisoner to safety in the state reformatory at nearby Jeffersonville.[14]

But even before Governor Durbin's tougher policy there had been such instances of averted lynchings. Indeed, in Marion, Indiana, in 1885 there was one such event, a story of many meanings.

A THWARTED LYNCHING, 1885

On Saturday evening, July 11, 1885, at about 10:00 P.M., Mollie Linston, aged 20, Retta Leach, 15, and Ella Leach, 13, decided to walk downtown. The three girls later told their story many times to newspaper reporters, justice officers, and ordinary Marion citizens. On their way home, long after dark, they passed Frank Wallace leaning against a lamppost. "Good evening, girls," Wallace said. "Who's that?" Retta Leach asked. "It is nobody but a nigger," Mollie Linston replied. Wallace heard her remark and sprang toward the girls with his arms outstretched. In great fright they ran the five blocks home, Wallace following behind, they said. He never touched them, but as they arrived at the gate to the Leach home, Wallace threw a stone. Although in their stories the girls never said that the stone hit any one of them, Mollie Linston nonetheless collapsed at the gate, apparently unconscious. A doctor rushed to her bedside, and not until Sunday afternoon did she leave her sickbed. During the night, some said, Wallace was prowling around the neighborhood. At 9:00 A.M. Sunday morning, police found him and put him in jail.[15]

In an interview with the *Marion Chronicle* reporter, Frank Wallace gave a detailed account of his whereabouts that Saturday evening. He said he was with "some of the boys." The local reporter transcribed Wallace's words thusly, adding his own identifying labels in parentheses:

> I came to town by the Grand View hotel and found the boys over near
> McClure's corner, where I found John Robinson, Charley Hardman (colored),

and Andy Slagle and Charley Patterson (white). Afterwards we found Marion Willis (white). We all went out to McClure's sheep pen and stayed all night. We had a half pint of whisky.

Perhaps Wallace spent the night with his five friends—three white and three black men, drinking together on a Saturday evening. Rumors about Wallace were soon flying through Marion. Some said that the 65-year-old black man had several times approached women on the street at night and frightened them. The *Chronicle*'s industrious reporter "followed up several of these rumors, but none of them proved reliable." People also claimed that Wallace had abducted "a little white girl" a year earlier and kept her locked in his room on Third Street. The reporter found that Wallace indeed had had a girl in his room for some time, but she was "a hard case"—aged about 16 and willingly living with Wallace. No charges were ever brought in this "abduction" case. Wallace, the *Chronicle* reporter concluded, "has never been known as a loafer, but is a quiet, hard-working man."

Two rumors the reporter verified: 10 years earlier Wallace had been convicted of raping a black girl, aged 14, and had served 3 years in the state penitentiary for his crime; and Wallace had been married to a white woman who had divorced him while he was serving his time. He seemed 20 years older after returning from the penitentiary, the reporter noted, no longer the "fine looking darky with splendid physique" he had been when he had moved to Grant County during the Civil War.

On Sunday afternoon, as Mollie Linston was getting out of bed, several hundred men and boys gathered near the jail, convinced that they had to protect young white women from this old black man. Calls to lynch Wallace rang out through the hot summer air, yet the crowd of many hands and no brains remained disorganized and uncertain. Two events, at least, contributed to their confusion. The *Chronicle* reporter asserted that had Mollie Linston "died on Sunday Wallace would have been lynched that night. Or had it been a night during the week when the saloons were open a crowd would soon have worked themselves into a proper condition of mind to have attacked the jail."

Even after Mollie Linston recovered from whatever had ailed her the need for justice remained. On Monday, July 13, whispered conversations occurred in knots of men gathered around the Courthouse Square. Some formed a "vigilance committee," and at 11:30 P.M. 21 masked men came marching toward the jail. Two in the front carried sledgehammers, a third a rope. With growing numbers of onlookers behind them, the masked men knocked on the jail door and demanded that Sheriff Orange Holman open up. He refused and the men with the sledges broke it down with two swings. Sheriff Holman and City Marshal L. A. Von Behren were inside. They were not armed, but each grabbed a chair and raised it to hold off the masked attackers. As the sheriff and marshal struggled, shots rang out from inside the jail and from outside. Most of the revolvers fired into the ceiling and the air, but one bullet pierced Sheriff Holman's coat. More tragically, a couple of minutes after the gunfire began James Kiley, aged 21, fell to the jail floor, a bullet in his right temple. All noise and struggle ceased. The masked men quickly left the jail. Kiley was carried to a nearby restaurant, where he died at 1:00 A.M. People milled about the streets for the rest of the night but no attack on the jail resumed.

The next day, Tuesday, the county coroner held an inquest. The sheriff and marshal testified, as did the doctor who attended to Kiley. The coroner concluded that Kiley died from a gunshot wound made by an unknown person. Funeral services were held the following day at St. Paul's Catholic Church, a wooden frame building on Branson Street. In his sermon Father John Grogan dwelt on the wickedness of mob law and placed responsibility for Kiley's death on the heads of the mob that stormed the jail. Some shared Father Grogan's views. In a sidewalk gathering, J. P. Nicol, a workman at Keller & Mead's chair factory, loudly condemned mob violence. Jim Havens disagreed and said that Wallace should be lynched. Nicol replied, "Then you are no better than the nigger," which prompted Havens to knock Nicol to the ground and kick him. Bystanders cheered.

Tuesday afternoon brought a "holiday appearance" to Marion as people from all over Grant County flocked to the downtown. Newspaper reporters from other towns arrived, "all expecting a high old time about midnight." As the sun set several thousand people waited, attracted by rumors that the "vigilance committee" would appear at half past eleven. In a grove near Third Street a crowd of men and boys attempted to organize themselves. Someone produced a rope and plaited a hangman's noose, which stirred greater excitement. Only about a dozen volunteered to act, however. One of them addressed the crowd, as an Indianapolis reporter recorded his words: "Men," he said, "we are about to fight for the protection of our wives and daughters."[16] They formed a line and marched off, determined, they said, "to take the nigger and hang him" from the portico of the county courthouse. A large number of spectators followed at a distance as the brave dozen marched from the grove. Sheriff Holman greeted the vigilance committee at the jail door and told them he was determined to protect his prisoner. It was his duty, he said. Two other men also spoke in support of the sheriff. Even before they had finished speaking the mob began to disperse into the crowd. The crowd melted. Frank Wallace would live.

A week and a half later, the *Marion Chronicle* reporter wrote about the problem of women on the streets of Marion at night. Some were prostitutes, he had to admit, women "whose vocation makes it necessary for them to have the freedom of the town." And while a man seeking their services is "usually very careful of his approaches, he will undoubtedly make mistakes. . . . Many good and pure women have been accosted on the streets by libertines." This risk was especially large for young women "wandering aimlessly about without escorts, having no apparent object beyond seeing and being seen." Such girls "are usually two or three together and in many instances are impudent and noisy."

In this context, the *Chronicle* writer turned to the "three girls who testify that Wallace assaulted them." They were on "a frivolous errand," he wrote. "One of them at least had been on the street before and attracted attention by her conduct." Indeed, "if they had not been approached by any one else than Wallace they missed their object, and had they been allowed to go home without being stopped by some one they perhaps would have been disappointed." The reporter did not charge the three with prostitution; and he admitted the principle that "a woman has as much right on the streets at night as a man." But he clearly believed that Marion's streets were "not the place for young girls to be found at night alone."

Thus, readers of the *Marion Chronicle* might well have concluded that Frank Wallace was no more guilty than the many other men and boys who often called out to young women walking the streets on a Saturday night. Readers might even have doubted that this old black man assaulted, pursued, or threw a stone at three innocent girls. He was "guilty," however, of once having been married to a white woman. Wallace told the Indianapolis reporter that this marriage was a "curse," the real source of prejudice against him in Marion, and that he was leaving town, never to return.[17]

The thwarting of the mob in 1885 became a part of Grant County's recorded past. The very next year the first published local history appeared. The massive and handsomely prepared volume mostly celebrated the pioneers of the county, but the writers included a few paragraphs about the attempt at mob law a year earlier. The local historians offered two conclusions about the events of July 1885: "it is only when the voice of passion is hushed that justice can be meted out"; and "much credit is due to the Sheriff, Orange Holman, and L. A. Von Behren for the fearless manner in which they performed their duty." They noted in passing that Frank Wallace was later tried and acquitted by a local court. There was no mention of Kiley and the other vigilantes who thought they were protecting white women and the boundaries of their community.[18]

In some ways Grant County was out of step and not so ordinary. In 1885, when other communities tolerated lynchings, Grant County did not. At a later time, in 1930, when lynching seemed to be a part of a past long dead, or present only in the wicked South, Grant County became the scene of a lynching.

The history of Grant County, Indiana, in the next 45 years contains no hard evidence that explains why Sheriff Holman resisted a mob in 1885 and Sheriff Campbell did not in 1930; why Frank Wallace lived and Tom Shipp and Abe Smith died; why justice reigned in one instance and passion in another. The two events are sufficiently different to make comparisons tenuous. Certainly Sheriff Holman acted with more determination to do his duty than did Campbell, who was perhaps lulled into complacency by the absence of lynchings in the community's past. The mob of 1885 was less organized and clear in its purpose, especially after one of their own died in the accidental shooting. In the community at large in 1885, one reporter concluded, there was "no popular sentiment justifying the attempted lynching."[19] And certainly Frank Wallace's "crimes" were lesser by far than the charges of rape and murder that so stirred the mob and the community in 1930.

In the end, why a lynching happened or did not happen may be beyond explanation or may even be nothing but chance circumstances.[20] Still, the history of Grant County, this ordinary place in America's heartland, suggests patterns of everyday life that may help illuminate not only the 1930 lynching but also its aftermath.

CHAPTER THREE

An Ordinary Place in Time

It is tempting to think of the mob that lynched Abram Smith and Tom Shipp as ignorant "rednecks," fanatical racists, or unwashed Ku Klux Klanners. Such simple labels help separate "bad" Americans from "good" Americans and comfort those who rush to abhor a vicious evil such as a lynching. As reassuring as such labels are, the evidence suggests a more complicated story for Grant County and for America.

CELEBRATING PIONEERS

Grant County was an ordinary place, a place that celebrated as its heroes its ordinary people, the pioneers who built farms and homes on the flatlands of the Midwest in the early nineteenth century. To early-twentieth-century citizens dependent on streetcars, telephones, and electricity, those hardy pioneers were the embodiments of hard work, individualism, fair play, and American democracy. In commemorating their pioneer founders, modern-day inhabitants of Grant County asserted their claim to an American distinctiveness from, and even superiority over, other nations and peoples.

Like much of America generally and the Midwest particularly, Grant County's popular understanding of its history centered on the pioneer era.[1] That history sat squarely in the middle of the westward movement of the frontier. The county was authorized by the Indiana General Assembly in 1831, a heavily wooded and generally flat plain dotted with swampy areas and broken by the Mississinewa River and several smaller streams. The last of the glaciers had left behind not only flat land but also a deep, rich soil, nearly as good as any on the face of the earth, a part of the American Corn Belt that stretched its fertile reach across the Midwest. To this land of promise came the pioneers, almost all of them native-born Americans, most white, but some black, who moved from more settled places in the East and South. Martin Boots and David Branson purchased the first land from the federal government in 1825-26 and built their log cabins near what would soon be the Courthouse Square. Citizens built the first of three courthouses in 1834 of simple logs. Next to it was the log jail built two years earlier. The county grew steadily during the next decades, following patterns of agriculture and community life set on earlier frontiers and repeated in later midwestern pioneer settlements. Growing corn and wheat and raising livestock; moving toward commercial agriculture by the time of the Civil War; developing a village economy of general stores and necessary services mixed with small-scale manufacturing; building community institutions such as churches and schools—all this was ordinary life in Grant County in the first three-quarters of the nineteenth century.

By the early twentieth century, Grant County citizens had lifted their ordinary pioneer forebears to near godlike status. In 1921 the enterprising students at Marion High School who gathered oral history interviews of local citizens dedicated their published volume to "the fearless men and heroic women who battled the wilderness, who made self-sacrifice a joy." A few years earlier the Octogenarian Club of old settlers built a log cabin as a civic shrine, which they later moved inside a new Memorial Hall Museum in the city's Matter Park. Each August, along with family reunions, Grant County folks made a pilgrimage to the log cabin to look at pioneer relics and imagine what those days had been.

During various centennial celebrations in 1912, 1916, 1925, and 1931, folks dressed up in pioneer clothing, rode in ox-drawn wagons, and staged historical pageants. The Grant County Centennial celebrated in October 1925, for example, included a parade of more than a thousand people, with a procession of covered wagons driven by descendants of the first pioneers. They camped on the Courthouse Square and reenacted the entering of land claims. An airplane stunt flyer provided a modern touch. In the evening Indiana Governor Ed Jackson and United States Senator James Watson spoke, followed by square dancing.

The citizens of Grant County knew, of course, that the pioneers were not the first people to occupy the land. The organizing framework in which they understood Native Americans was captured in the *Centennial History of Grant County,* published in 1914: the book's first chapter was titled "From Savagery to Civilization." There was an easy common awareness of a people before Europeans, because dotting the county were alterations of the landscape commonly known as Indian mounds. Pioneers partially leveled one such mound, 10 feet high and 60 feet in diameter, to build the first courthouse. When that log structure was replaced a few years later by a new structure, men dug open the Indian mound and removed a human skeleton before proceeding to build the second courthouse on top. These and other remnants of previous occupation were interesting curiosities. Early writers assumed their purpose was for religious ceremony, including human sacrifice.

A more significant mark of Native American life for many Grant County citizens centered on the pointed conflict between the Miami Indians and pioneer settlers, which ended in the latter vanquishing the former. A central piece in Grant County memory and commemoration was the Battle of the Mississinewa, fought along the river northwest of Marion in December 1812. Although a small step in the defeat and removal of Native Americans from the Midwest, the Battle of the Mississinewa assumed heroic proportions by the time of its centennial in 1912. Public accounts of the county's past devoted large attention to the battle, an event still commemorated in annual reenactments.

Far less attention was devoted to the removal of the Miami people in 1846. Against their will, the federal government forced the majority of them west to Kansas Territory. Those who remained in Indiana soon lost their lands and their

Miami language. By the turn of the century many had moved to Marion and nearby towns to find city jobs and to face the "100% American" pressure for assimilation into the white culture. Some Miami made efforts to preserve their culture and kin networks: by the 1920s they enjoyed a reunion and the Maconaquah Pageant, created to educate whites and younger Miami about the old ways. The Miami tribal council frequently met in Marion to work for Indian claims, including federal recognition as a tribe. Their weak power and status were symbolized when Grant County officials in 1944 forced a sheriff's sale for back taxes of the acre of land on which the Miami school and Baptist Church had stood. This sacred ground contained the largest Indian cemetery in the state, including the grave of Meshingomesia, a well-known nineteenth-century chief. Meshingomesia had been remembered earlier, in 1919, when the Marion Country Club changed its name to the Meshingomesia Country Club.[2]

Grant County's shared memories also included substantial room for Civil War stories. Local accounts focused on the first volunteers who rushed to the courthouse soon after Fort Sumter. Fife and drums played and the crowd cheered as each man signed his name to the roster. Before it was over, 2,405 men from the county fought in the war, supported patriotically by families at home. Even Grant County's pacifist Quakers contributed 124 soldiers, more than the 119 local Quakers who chose conscientious objection.[3] The Civil War brought internal conflict to much of Indiana and the Midwest. Some in Grant County did not share the Lincoln administration's goals. Local histories mention a skirmish between so-called Copperhead resisters and Unionists at Jonesboro and a brawl near Fairmount. But such conflict was generally submerged in the community's Civil War memories, in the warm celebration of the reunified nation and its progress in the decades after 1865.

THE GAS BELT BOOMS

Grant County changed after the Civil War. Railroads and factories came as they did elsewhere in the Midwest, but more quickly and more forcefully than in most places. Grant County citizens expressed great pride in their industrial achievements, but the confusions and tensions of economic change contributed to the tendency to view their pioneer past through rose-colored glasses, to remember ordinary people of extraordinary achievement and an imagined past of less strife and anxiety.

The spark of change was the discovery of natural gas in 1887. Attracted by the promise of low-cost fuel in seemingly unlimited quantities, industrialists, entrepreneurs, promoters, and ordinary workers of all types flocked to the area, more than doubling the town's population in the 1890s. Newcomers, black and white, arrived from the South, from Kentucky and Tennessee, joined by job seekers from rural Indiana, all attracted to the higher-paying work in the booming factories. Workers came also from Europe, mostly from Great Britain, Ireland, and Germany. Poles and Italians and other eastern and southern Europeans were less attracted to smaller industrial midwestern cities like Marion.[4] Companies making glass products, such as fruit jars, found the cheap natural gas especially appealing, but all manner of factories popped up, including paper mills and large foundries, the most notable of which was the Marion Malleable Iron Works. Connected to national markets by a web of railroads, Marion boosted itself as the "Queen City" of the gas belt. And even though the once abundant natural gas sputtered out around 1905 and some factories abandoned the region, the city and the county continued to prosper on the new industrial base.

Industrial prosperity brought new challenges. One was child labor. Progressive reformers were appalled by conditions in the glass factories of the Midwest. Visiting Marion in 1904, reformer Harriet M. Van Der Vaart was outraged at the numbers of children under the age of 16 working in local glass factories. At Marion Flint Glass Company she thought "the conditions worse than any factory visited." Renowned photographer Lewis Hine came to Marion in October 1908 and documented with his camera the appalling scenes of young children in factories.[5]

More evident too with industrialization was strife between labor and capital. With the factories came workers who insisted on belonging to labor unions, who were willing to strike, willing to engage in violence against strikebreakers, and even willing to vote for Socialist Party candidates. In 1913 Socialists won three of the seven seats on the Marion City Council and the Socialist candidate for mayor received 23 percent of the vote. Marion glassworkers and molders gave strongest support to this left-wing party, favoring such reforms as public ownership of utilities, eight-hour workdays, and municipally owned coal yards—reforms others in Marion and Grant County saw as rejections of the democracy and individual freedom the pioneers had built.[6]

World War I brought an intensification of labor militancy and sparked a counteroffensive from the newly formed Grant County Manufacturers Association. Although the Socialist mayoral candidate won 31 percent of the vote in 1921, the tide soon turned. Political and civic leaders, joined by the local police force, made clear by the early 1920s that labor militancy had no place in Grant County. And the return of prosperity after 1922 dampened citizen and worker discontent.

ROARINGS IN THE 1920S

By the mid-1920s Marion presented a picture of comfort, prosperity, and progress, an image of all that was good in America. At the center of the town stood the Grant County Courthouse. Built in 1880 of Indiana limestone, it was the third courthouse on that location. Its Greek Revival style, with massive Corinthian columns, proclaimed the new courthouse as Grant County's civic temple. On top of the dome stood an eight-foot statue of Justice; everyone called her "Lady Justice." She held a balance in her left hand and looked down on a tree-filled yard that surrounded the courthouse and was dotted with monuments and markers—one inscribed to the "Marion boys who gave their lives during the World War," others to first pioneers Martin Boots and David Branson and to local Civil War veterans. Shops near the square sold souvenir cream and sugar servers with pictures of the courthouse and Lady Justice painted on the sides.

Lining the Courthouse Square in the 1920s were banks, clothing stores, drug stores, ice cream parlors, cigar stores, and theaters, some spreading a block or so off the square. On Saturdays these downtown streets were packed with people doing their shopping, seeing a motion picture show, enjoying an ice cream soda, conducting business in the courthouse and the nearby law offices, visiting the handsome Andrew Carnegie–funded public library built in 1902 just south of the square. Often people stopped to talk as they walked from store to store, for this was a community that expected warm face-to-face conversation, where people called each other by first name, often a nickname, as they discussed the weather, the baseball scores or the Marion High School Giants basketball team, the birth of a baby, a funeral, a visitor from Indianapolis or Chicago. On patriotic and ceremonial occasions the square was the gathering place and site of community ritual, the center of the town and of Grant County.

Mary Campbell, daughter of Grant County Sheriff Jake Campbell, grew up in Marion in the 1920s. Seven decades later she had fond memories of the community, of walking around the downtown square, where you knew "practically everybody you met," of sitting with friends in the New York Candy Kitchen, "run by the Greeks," who made the best ice cream sundaes and banana splits. Often Mary and her friends would gather at her family's home, the sheriff's residence attached to the Grant County Jail. They made popcorn, wound up the phonograph player, rolled up the rug, and danced to the popular music of the day. They knew all the dances. But her parents were strict Methodists and would not allow her to go to the public dances at the Civic Hall. They did allow her to go to the Indiana and Paramount movie theaters, however, where her dad had free passes. And there were Methodist youth gatherings and streetcar rides to Matter Park for picnics and band concerts.[7]

Out in the county, families lived in smaller towns or villages, the largest of which were Fairmount, Gas City, and Jonesboro to the south, and on farms scattered through the county. The farm family of William and Grace Deeter was typical. The Deeters operated a 320-acre farm two miles west of Fairmount, where they lived in a house with a telephone but no electricity. A windmill and gasoline engine pumped water to the house. Their eight children attended school in Fairmount, but not before sitting down for prayer and breakfast together each morning. The Deeters stopped farm work early on Saturday to go visiting and shopping in Fairmount or Marion. The boys played basketball in the barn in winter. On Sundays the family attended the Pentecostal Church in Marion, where the parents' admonishments against such sins as smoking and drinking were reinforced. The oldest son, Claude, born in 1905, worked for his father and other farmers in the area, but in 1927, like many other farm boys, got a factory job at Superior Body in Marion. In 1929 he bought a new Chevrolet, which he proudly drove through the county and perhaps more than once stopped on the lovers' lane next to the Mississinewa River. Claude Deeter was a good worker, physically strong, and well liked.[8]

There were many sources of pride for Grant Countians regularly featured and sometimes boasted of in the two Marion daily newspapers, the *Chronicle* and the *Leader-Tribune,* and in the weekly *Fairmount News.* The papers described fancy downtown theaters, with air conditioning in summer; the beautiful churches of the major denominations, their steeples rising near the Courthouse Square; the Industrial Baseball League; the large swimming pool in Matter Park; the Meshingomesia Country Club for bridge luncheons and golf matches; and the dozens of family and church reunions held each August, most at picnic tables in Matter Park. And there was the Marion High School basketball team's victory over Martinsville in the Indiana state basketball tournament in 1926. The two nights following that victory brought thousands of fans to the bonfires and cheers on the Courthouse Square. This state championship was the highest achievement imaginable for a Hoosier town, though many also expressed pride over the state band championship three years later.

But there was trouble in Grant County in the 1920s and reason to fear that the modern era of growth and industrialization had brought a loss of direction along with its material prosperity. There was, some feared, too much immorality, too much crime, too much corruption. Fast automobiles gave a new freedom for drives to county roadhouses, for back-seat sex, even for robbery. The old ways of the beloved pioneers had been forgotten and pushed aside by the Jazz Age of Fords, flappers, and bootleggers.[9]

The front pages of the Marion newspapers in the 1920s rang out with headlines and photographs of murders, bank robberies, Al Capone's latest venture, Hollywood adulterers, and the other sins of the world. Advertisements for films that played at Marion's Indiana Theater did nothing to reassure anxieties. Viewers of *Wild Company* would see on screen "wild ways and jazz days" where "parents are indifferent and children in search of thrills pick their own paths for play."[10]

Magazines brought the same fears. In the *Ladies Home Journal* Grant Countians could read about "Our Jazz-Spotted Middle West," where writer John R. McMahon lamented the spread of roadhouses, illegitimacy, and drunkenness, not only in the big cities of the East but in the small towns of the Midwest. McMahon was especially critical of the "moral smallpox known as jazz," which created "a physical stimulus of a degrading kind," and "the invention of the Afro-American dance, that unholy mingling of the civilized with the savage." Surely not everyone was happy when Bix Beiderbecke and his Wolverines came to Marion in April 1924 to play their fast-paced new music. Doubtless some Marion youth even traveled to Indianapolis, where on Indiana Avenue, the heart of the African American neighborhood, they could go to places like the Cotton Club to listen to black musicians and experience the thrill of bootleg liquor and the sophisticated company of black and tan audiences. Such music and dance were only the symbolic indicators that across Indiana and across America change was bringing decline, a falling away from the old ways to immorality and even crime. An Indiana government conference on Law Observance and Enforcement in October 1929 pointed to alarming deficiencies in controlling crime even though the state's prisons were filled to the bursting point.[11]

There was certainly crime and immorality in Marion. Child labor reformer Harriet Van Der Vaart reported in 1904 that Marion was "a very rough town." There were "saloons in every direction," she wrote, and those "saloons and gambling houses are open all day Sunday."[12] Prohibition after 1919 did not close the saloons. During the 1920s on East 38th Street near the Mississinewa River a disreputable section known as "Dark Secret" featured saloons offering gambling, bootleg liquor, and prostitution. Speakeasies and blind pigs selling alcohol were scattered through the city. And in the countryside enterprising folks built home stills for their own needs and for sales to thirsty customers. Everyone knew such activities were common. The divisions were over what to do about them.

There was general agreement that local law officers were not a promising part of any solution to Marion's crime and immorality. The cops "were not the smartest bunch of individuals and they had absolutely no training," Grant County Deputy Prosecutor Thurman Biddinger later recalled. "They were pretty lucky if they caught somebody," and, Biddinger added, they sometimes tipped off bootleggers and others prior to a raid. Deputy Sheriff Orville Wells was memorable because he always had tobacco juice running down his chin and could never hit the spittoon. Grant County Sheriff Jake Campbell was more fastidious with his Mail Pouch chew. He weighed 240 pounds and had a large belly that hung over his trousers. Sheriff Campbell had served on the city police force from 1914 to 1927, when he was elected sheriff. He often wore a white shirt, but no tie. He and his handful of deputies had no uniforms and no cars beyond their personal vehicles, for which they had to buy gas from their meager salaries. The city police boasted uniforms, but their law enforcement capacities were not much better. The Indiana state police, still in an embryonic stage, were of little help. Their few officers patrolled highways on motorcycles and mailed in their daily reports of crime and misdemeanors because they did not have radios. All state and local law enforcement officials were subject to popular election, directly or indirectly, so that partisan politics was part of their job. Sheriff Jake Campbell was also chairman of the Grant County Republican Party.[13]

The most impressive hope of criminal containment was the Grant County Jail. Built in 1904, it contained 60 cells and had seven iron doors between the cells and the outer door. Sheriff Campbell made good use of it. In his four years in office, from 1927 through 1931, he, his deputies, and his wife (who was the jail matron) saw 5,472 prisoners pass into their cells, compared to 3,026 incarcerated by his predecessor in his four years. It was hardly sufficient, many thought.[14]

Mayor Jack Edwards, elected in 1929 at the age of only 27, best represented Marion's tradition of relaxed and selective law enforcement. A semipro bantamweight boxer, insurance agent, grocer, and Democratic precinct committeeman before he was elected mayor, Edwards loved the high life of the Jazz Age. Of course there were lots of places in Marion selling bootleg liquor and allowing gambling, he admitted later, but "we never took it seriously." Mayor Edwards did turn away syndicate gambling and rackets from Chicago. Only locally owned blind tigers, blind pigs, speakeasies, and roadhouses were allowed; the mayor estimated there were 15 to 20 in the city, some of which he patronized.[15]

While many condoned and even welcomed Mayor Edwards's approach to law enforcement in matters of gambling, Prohibition, and prostitution, nearly every citizen drew the line at murder. And when murders went unsolved or unpunished, discontent with law enforcement festered.

Such was the case on October 3, 1929, when a bomb exploded in the local labor headquarters, killing three men. Three weeks later a car bomb killed a union official when he started his car. On February 3, 1930, another car bomb was set but discovered before it did its damage. At the end of the month still another man died in a car bombing. All five victims were members of Mould Makers Union Local No. 36, yet strangely there were no publicly stated grievances related to the union. As fears spread and local police scratched their heads, Mayor Edwards hired a detective from Terre Haute, but the bombers were never identified. The murder cases of the five men remained unsolved, evidence to many citizens of an incompetent or untrustworthy system of law and order.[16]

Not only were criminals, even bombers and murderers, at large in Grant County, but the punishments inflicted on criminals who were caught and jailed seemed to many absurdly lenient. When a black garage worker shot a white youth and received only a light sentence there was lots of angry talk around the Courthouse Square. People talked too about the couple accused of poisoning a young foster child. The woman was acquitted, the man released after a short jail sentence. The people of Grant County were not satisfied with their criminal justice system. There were some attempts to improve things, as when County Prosecutor Harley Hardin hired a law student, Thurman Biddinger, in summer 1930 to help with the large volume of work. Few thought it was enough.[17]

THE KNIGHTS OF THE KU KLUX KLAN

The clearest indication of unhappiness about law enforcement, corruption, and immorality in Grant County was the strength of the Ku Klux Klan. This volatile organization of white Protestants attracted as many as five million Americans in the early 1920s, from Pennsylvania to Oregon, by promising to unite the good people of the community against the forces of moral, spiritual, and civic decline. The glue that bound Klan members most tightly was Prohibition. They were convinced that alcohol and saloons were the real and symbolic source of immorality and corruption, of turning away from the traditional values of family, hard work, and God, of tearing down what the heroic pioneers had created. The Klan demanded enforcement of the Prohibition laws. In their condemnation of saloons and dance halls and of adultery, premarital sex, and drunkenness, Klan members expressed their fervent patriotism, often in bold red, white, and blue colors. And they displayed always their Protestantism, symbolized by the burning cross and realized by the close ties between the Klan and mainstream Protestant churches, especially Methodists, Baptists, and Disciples of Christ. The Klan preached vigorously the traditional values of family, work, and community. Klansmen asserted their obligation to protect white Protestant women from all that degraded their purity. Some Klanswomen modestly championed their rights as women, but always within the context of fighting vice and immorality that threatened family values. The Klan's moral crusade was particularly attractive to Hoosiers, whose traditional Protestant and patriotic values ran deep. Between a quarter and a third of all native-born, white Indiana males belonged to the Klan in 1925. An unknown but sizeable number of females also joined the Women of the Ku Klux Klan.[18]

The Ku Klux Klan had enemies other than saloonkeepers and dance hall proprietors. Catholics, Jews, and blacks seemed alien and threatening to many Klansmen. Such people were not 100 percent American, not like the pioneers, and they did not respect traditional white Protestant versions of decency and order. Klan propaganda spewed hatred and ignorance toward "them," those who were not "us." Drawing on decades of American racial, religious, and ethnic bigotry and intolerance, the Klan packaged and marketed these old, old stories with a new passion that spread the venom of white Protestant supremacy across the fertile Hoosier landscape.

But the Klan in Indiana and in Marion did not engage in significant violence against blacks, Catholics, Jews, or other groups or individuals. Despite contrary images today, the Indiana Klan of the 1920s was a mostly nonviolent organization. It did not lynch anyone in Marion or anywhere else in Indiana. While there were surely acts of intimidation in the state, there is no record to suggest any focused attention on blacks, Catholics, or Jews in Grant County. The Klan in Indiana and Grant County had more important issues in the political arena.

The first signs of Klan activity in Indiana appeared in 1920. The organization's power in the Hoosier state reached its high point in 1924 when Ed Jackson, the Republican candidate for governor and widely believed to be a Klansman, was elected, along with a majority in the General Assembly who supported the Klan. At the federal level most of the Indiana congressional delegation elected in 1924 were members of or friendly to the Klan. More important than federal or state-level politics was the moral crusade at the local level. Across Indiana and the Midwest local Klans set about providing political leadership that would forcefully cleanse their communities of alcohol and sin.

The Klan made its first big splash in Grant County with a massive parade and initiation ceremony on November 26, 1922. Seven mounted trumpeters, all masked, led the Saturday evening parade, followed by an electrically lighted cross mounted on an automobile. Next were Klan marching bands from Marion and from nearby Muncie, followed by five hundred Klansmen on foot who had traveled by auto and interurban train from Indianapolis, Muncie, Kokomo, Tipton, Elwood, Wabash, and elsewhere. American flags and crosses were sprinkled among the marchers. Thousands of spectators lined the downtown streets. It was one of the largest crowds in recent memory.[19]

After the parade people moved to the baseball field at Marion's Goldthwaite Park. The initiation ceremony began at 10:00 P.M. with the singing of "Onward Christian Soldiers." Muncie photographer W. A. Swift was there. His three surviving pictures show a temporary stage of wooden planks with a large American flag as backdrop. Behind the stage a wooden cross rises high above the crowd. Klan officers stand shoulder to shoulder on the stage with arms folded in haughty style, ceremonial swords at their sides. The officer known as the Masked Knight arrives on a black horse to give the main address. To the left are Klan musicians, including a couple of tuba players. Klansmen make a large circle surrounding the stage and the initiates. They wear white robes with pointed hoods, their faces covered by masks. Several American flags wave among them.

The initiates draw closer to the stage. The photographer Swift estimated the new members at two thousand, a local newspaper reporter guessed seventeen hundred. In Swift's first two photographs the men stand in overcoats, their collars turned up, their hands in their pockets. All wear hats, a wide diversity of hats, from workmen's cloth caps to businessmen's fedoras. Many are well dressed. As the night cold seeps in, a slight breeze appears to move the flags. Swift flashed his third photograph after the men had heard the speeches and taken their oaths. Now kneeling on the cold ground, they remove their hats and bow their heads. Some are balding, some gray haired, but many are more youthful. They are united by the oath they have all taken to their Christian God, their American nation, and their belief in white Protestant supremacy. Behind the stage someone has lit the large cross, the fiery cross burning to symbolize the intensity of their belief. By midnight it is all over. The shivering Klansmen and throngs of spectators head home. A special shift of Marion police is on duty to direct the orderly crowd.[20]

From its new headquarters above the Woolworth Five and Dime near the Courthouse Square the Mississinewa Klan No. 14 set out to clean up Marion and Grant County. At a Young Men's Christian Association fund-raising dinner in February 1923 the area Kleagle (recruiter) stood to announce a cash gift of $400 to the Y and to outline the principles of his organization. But the Knights were also more direct participants in doing good. Klan informants eagerly pointed out to police the location of liquor stills. The organization's weekly statewide newspaper, the *Fiery Cross,* carried Grant County names too, including an old woman who had "run a blind tiger and house of assignation for years" and several men "claiming to be taxi drivers, [but who] are in reality nothing but booze peddlers and pimps for prostitutes." The Klan boasted it was cleaning up the city despite the sad fact that some officials were in cahoots with bootleggers and other criminals. Captain Jake Campbell of the city police cooperated. In November 1923 he staked out the house of a bootlegger on South Boots Street, observed him selling 35 quarts of Canadian whiskey, and then led the raid that put him out of business.[21]

Grant County's 1925 membership lists numbered 2,329 Klansmen, just over 15 percent of native-born white men in the county. Grant County's Mississinewa Klan was not as large as neighboring Delaware County's (Muncie) or Howard County's (Kokomo), where the percentages were almost twice that of Grant County. Included among Grant County members were not only blue-collar factory workers but also middle-class businessmen and professionals. The local Klan head, or Exalted Cyclops, was Alfred Hogston, a Marion attorney. Another officer was Albert Hall, the Marion school superintendent, who won a seat in the U.S. Congress in 1924 with strong Klan backing. Many believed that a man had to be a Klan member to get elected in Grant County in the mid-1920s. As elsewhere, the Republican Party was most closely tied to the Hooded Order. It was widely assumed that Jake Campbell was a member. So too Harley

Hardin, later county prosecutor. Marion shoeshine boy James Cameron later remembered standing near a drinking fountain to watch a Klan parade and recognizing many of the town's citizens—including Jake Campbell, the man Cameron would later struggle hard to forgive for the Marion lynching—when they lifted their hoods to take a drink. Some Klan members took the organization's professed goals seriously, some doubtless saw it as no more than a necessary vehicle to ensure their standing in the community, to attract customers for their businesses or law practices, or to win votes at election time. For some it was simply another social organization, a club of friendly, like-minded neighbors, little different from Rotary or Elks.[22]

To the great shock of many, the Indiana Klan quickly withered away after 1925. In November that year its leader, a bombastic charlatan named D. C. Stephenson, was convicted of rape and second-degree murder. Once the Indiana Klan's great hope, Grand Dragon Stephenson was now its most embarrassing liability. His conviction opened doors to other investigations, which in 1927 extended to the Grand Dragon's former ally Governor Jackson, who was indicted on bribery charges. By this time all Indiana politicians and most former Klan members were running away fast from a very smelly organization. The 1929 local elections in Indiana saw a massive rejection of the Republican Party, now tainted by its recent Klan connections. In Marion, Democratic newcomer Jack Edwards won election as mayor. Five of seven city councilmen elected were Democrats, reversing earlier Republican majorities.

Understanding the timing of the Ku Klux Klan's rise and fall in the 1920s alters widely held assumptions that connect men in white sheets and hoods to the Marion lynchings.[23] Doubtless in that vicious mob the night of August 7, 1930, were former Klan members, as there were in the large crowd that watched the mob and as there were among those charged with defending the prisoners inside the jail. It's even possible that Lawrence Beitler's 1930 lynching photograph shows some of the same men Swift's camera captured in 1922. The Klan itself was dead by 1930, however. It was not the Klan that lynched Abe Smith and Tom Shipp. And it is therefore not possible to place blame on "others," on evil or silly men in robes and hoods or on conspiracies that involved an organized "outside" force. The Indiana Klan was guilty of much evil and much foolishness, but it was innocent in the Marion lynchings, or rather no more guilty than many others in this ordinary place in America's heartland who continued to believe in "us" and "them."

CHAPTER FOUR

Lines of Color, Lines of Community

Part of Grant County's ordinariness was the obvious presence of people who were not white Americans, people whose appearance and lives were in some ways different from the white majority. The history of African American people in Grant County is much like the history of African Americans elsewhere, a history woven with lines of color and marked by struggles to deal with the changing boundaries those lines created. In challenging the color line, blacks in this one place created a community of their own and also a civil rights organization that connected them to African Americans across the nation.

WHAT IS AN "EATING HOUSE"?

As the leaves were beginning to turn color in late September 1917, Vennie Burden and Marsha Burden entered Marion's New York Candy Kitchen. This combination ice cream parlor and candy store was located on the Courthouse Square at 408 South Washington Street, between the Marion National Bank and the Davis Drug Store. Established in 1899 and known to everyone, the New York Candy Kitchen was "the Sweetest Place in Grant County," its ads claimed.[1]

The Burden sisters had walked downtown to shop, and even though the day was cool they were thirsty and wanted to sit down and rest. Vennie Burden ordered a chocolate soda, Marsha Burden a dish of ice cream. One of the two proprietors, a Greek American named Louie Chochos, took their order and walked away. Described as "a large, chunky fellow" with a black mustache, Chochos soon returned and said, "We can't serve you." "Why?," Vennie Burden asked, "we have been served here before." "Because you are colored," Chochos replied.[2]

The Burden women, aged 28 and 38, were sisters married to two members of the Burden family, a pioneer black family of Grant County. Many times before they had sat and eaten in the New York Candy Kitchen; about two dozen times, Marsha Burden testified. They were shocked to be denied service. But their surprise turned to anger when, Marsha Burden claimed, Chochos "even laughed at us when we left out of the room."[3]

Vennie and Marsha Burden were not amused. And they did not turn the other cheek. The proud sisters retained two lawyers, who filed suit in Grant County Circuit Court. They demanded a jury trial and public airing of their grievance. They knew that the law was on their side, that Indiana, like most northern states, had a public accommodation act. The Indiana Civil Rights Act of 1885 promised all Hoosiers, regardless of color or race, the right to use restaurants, public transportation, hotels, theaters, and other public places. In fact, however, the law was largely ineffectual. Black Hoosiers seldom had the financial means and courage to challenge Indiana's many hotels and restaurants that served only white customers. Legal suits were costly and included the risk of being labeled a troublemaker. Most important, on the few occasions courageous blacks did bring suit, Indiana's courts usually ruled against them.[4]

Doubtless knowing the odds against them, the Burden sisters nonetheless went to trial. Their lawyers were Julius Caesar Judkins and William M. Amsden. These two black men knew the local culture well enough to understand that one of the first necessities in the trial was to establish their clients' respectability. Vennie and Marsha Burden each testified that they were "clean" and that they never went "out on the street looking dis-respectful." And their lawyers brought forth a white neighbor, Eliza Philips, who had been sitting in the ice cream parlor that fall day. She confirmed that the Burden sisters were "ladylike" in their appearance and behavior. Thus, Judkins and Amsden told the jury, the sole cause for the refusal of service to each woman was "because of, and for no other reason except that, she was a person of African descent and a Negro."

The next step for Judkins and Amsden was to establish the meaning of Indiana's 1885 civil rights law. The few court cases brought under the law usually turned on narrow interpretations. In the New York Candy Kitchen case the key question came to be the definition of the words "eating place." Page after page of the court transcript focuses on this single issue.

Amsden and Judkins called Marsha Burden's husband, Jasper Burden, a successful, hard-working carpenter and contractor who was well known and respected as a lifetime resident of Grant County. Jasper Burden testified that he had eaten ice cream in the New York Candy Kitchen about 50 times. With the eye of a skilled craftsman he described for the jury in great detail the physical arrangement of the ice cream parlor. On the right side as one entered was a large candy case. To the left was the soda fountain. And back of it were a dozen tables, each with chairs to seat four people. Here the people of Grant County came to eat ice cream or drink a soda, to rest and talk.

The lawyers for Chochos and his partner, Peter Carelas, were Henry J. Paulus, Gus S. Condo, and John R. Browne, all from Marion. Their questioning of witnesses was slight, their evidence meager. Perhaps they counted on Indiana traditions in denying challenges to patterns of discrimination by troublemakers like the Burden sisters. But, in fact, the jury of twelve white Grant county men sided instead with the Burden sisters and in May 1918 awarded a verdict for $25 to each woman. There was justice, it seemed, in Grant County.

But now the attorneys for Chochos and Carelas began to fight. They asked for a new trial, which the Grant County Court denied, and then requested an appeal to the Appellate Court of Indiana. In February and March 1919, both sides filed their briefs with the appeals court.

Attorneys for the New York Candy Kitchen argued that the Grant County jury verdict was contrary to law. The establishment was "not an eating-house" as specified in the 1885 legislation because "nothing was sold in said candy kitchen by the appellants except candy, ice cream and sodas." *Webster's New International Dictionary* (1917) specified "cooked provisions" as definition of eating. "From time immemorial, an eating house or a restaurant has been recognized as being a place where food and the substantial necessaries of life are cooked and prepared to be eaten thereat. Candy stores where ice cream and sodas are served are not eating-houses and restaurants." And, the lawyers asserted, the Indiana legislature in 1885 did not have such places in mind. The lawyers also cited public accommodation cases in Illinois, Iowa, New York, and Connecticut in which courts upheld narrow and restrictive definitions of restaurants.

Lawyers Amsden and Judkins responded in their brief that the "New York Candy Kitchen was in fact an EATING PLACE." They wrote in large capital letters the words "EAT" and "EATING" every time they quoted them in testimony, which they did often. Entering the dictionary duel, the Burden sisters' lawyers cited definitions of these words from *Webster's Unabridged Dictionary, Webster's New International Dictionary,* and *Funk and Wagnalls New Standard Dictionary* to assert that "the evidence is conclusive and indisputable that it is equipped as a restaurant with tables, chairs, and accommodations for the public generally." The lawyers refrained from arguing that the New York Candy Kitchen came under the general phrase of the 1885 law to include "and all other places of public accommodation," because they acknowledged that the breadth and vagueness of those words allowed room for challenge. Instead, they staked their case tightly to the meaning of eating house, which they argued this ice cream parlor with tables, chairs, and waiters clearly was. There may not have been ice cream parlors in Indiana back in 1885, the lawyers admitted, but the legislature then "was not intending to split hairs as to technicalities in definition of words, but certainly intended to insure to all the inhabitants of this State the enjoyment of all privileges in a truly humane and democratic commonwealth."

The Appellate Court of Indiana was quite willing to split hairs. In November 1920 it reversed the Grant County Circuit Court and upheld the right of the New York Candy Kitchen to deny service to African Americans. The higher court added another dictionary to the duel, the *Century Dictionary,* and a new hair to split. The key word now was "meals." "The Legislature," the court held, "when it used the expression 'eating house' referred to a place where the public might go and be served with meals." Ice cream, soda, and candy were not meals. The laws of Indiana provided the Burden sisters no legal right to demand service at the New York Candy Kitchen.[5]

This one small civil rights case stretched across more than three years of time and across the wide and tangled terrain of race in America. It turned on narrow definitions of law: What was an eating house? What was a meal? The appeals court ignored other questions: What is equality? What is justice? What does it mean to be black in America? Nor did the court respect the sense of justice expressed by the 12-member jury in the original case. State judicial interpretation of law overrode local sentiment. Ensuring that African Americans could sit and eat with white Americans was not part of the way things worked in the early twentieth century.

The Burden sisters—the women Louis Chochos laughed at—were ordinary women who thought they knew their place and thought it included eating ice cream in "the Sweetest Place in Grant County." That anytime and anywhere Vennie Burden, Marsha Burden, or any African American, even in the North, might be thrown out, embarrassed, laughed at—that final reality might be the largest meaning of this small case. Lines of color ran like spiders' webs through daily lives, separating blacks from the white community, making them "others" in ordinary places like Marion, Indiana.

THE FLUID COLOR LINE

Vennie and Marsha Burden saw the American color line drawn in an Indiana ice cream parlor. It was not a unique event. "The problem of the Twentieth Century is the problem of the color-line," prophesized the great black historian and activist W. E. B. Du Bois in his *Souls of Black Folk*, published in 1903.[6] The century proved Du Bois right: the line that separated black and white Americans clearly was *the* problem of the century. Those omnipresent lines of division, slippery and wobbly lines that varied in form and intensity across time and space, are beyond easy understanding. Sometimes hard and clear, more often amorphous and shifting, the color lines were America's great mystery and great tragedy, as small as Louie Chochos's laugh, as large as the death of two Marion teenagers.

Early-twentieth-century Americans, northerners especially, tended to see the color line as a southern problem. Five years after Du Bois published *The*

Souls of Black Folk, investigative journalist and progressive reformer Ray Stannard Baker offered his description in a book he titled *Following the Color Line*. Baker focused mostly on the American South, where lines of color were clearly drawn in restaurants, parks, and railroad cars. Simple signs proclaimed "Whites only" and "Colored only." Baker found the color line drawn in blood too, by the southern mobs that lynched blacks accused of crimes or those merely thought guilty of forgetting their place in a society so clearly dominated by whites.[7]

But Baker's investigative nose led him to follow the color line north of the Mason-Dixon line too. He found the lines different from those in the South but not erased, especially not in the lower Midwest. "In certain towns in Ohio, Indiana, and Illinois . . . ," for example, "no Negro is permitted to stop over night." In Greensburg, Indiana, where a small black population lived, Baker described a riot in which a white mob attacked their innocent black neighbors because of an alleged crime committed by a mentally limited black laborer.[8] In this Midwest, where ordinary heartlanders claimed that pioneer democracy and equality had taken firmest root, color lines separated black and white Americans.

The Midwest was created by free labor, by pioneers—mostly white, but some black—who built log cabins, planted corn, dug canals, taught Sunday School, and made babies. White midwesterners drew the line against slavery from the beginning and sent their sons to a war in 1861 that destroyed slavery. And for a short time after the Civil War midwesterners moved toward possibilities of equality, represented in Indiana's Civil Rights Act of 1885. But Indiana and the Midwest never created a place of equality for black Americans. In the first decades of the twentieth century it was impossible to find a spot north of the Ohio River where lines of color were not drawn.

From time to time lines of color were written in law. In 1840 the Indiana legislature passed a bill "to prohibit the amalgamation of whites and blacks," a bill that fined not only an interracial couple who dared to marry but the minister or magistrate who performed the ceremony. This "anti-miscegenation" law remained on the books until 1965. Indiana's constitution of 1851, commonly considered the culmination of pioneer democracy, prohibited blacks from serving in the state militia. A proposal to remove the restriction by amending the constitution was soundly defeated by voters in a special election in 1921.[9]

More important and pervasive color lines were drawn by custom and enforced by white local opinion. Such was the case of the so-called sunset laws—not laws but customs that made clear any black person should be out of town before dark. As black children began to attend public schools in larger numbers in the late nineteenth century many Indiana communities created separate public elementary schools for black and white students. The patterns of school segregation in Indiana and other midwestern states were mixed; in some communities there was always integration; in others segregation was the norm. The color line varied across space.[10]

There was variation too across time. The decade of the 1920s, which brought a loosening of some traditions—more syncopated music, more back-seat sex, and more bathtub gin—also brought a general tightening of the color line. The pioneer historian of race in Indiana, Emma Lou Thornbrough, has documented how in the 1920s white Hoosiers mounted "a movement for segregation on a scale previously unknown."[11] As black kids sought high school educations, larger cities in the 1920s began to build new all-black high schools. This Hoosier version of Jim Crow extended from Gary to Indianapolis and south to Evansville. In the state's new parks, blacks were excluded from swimming pools. In Muncie, an industrial town in the center of the state, the sociologists Robert and Helen Lynd reported in *Middletown*, published in 1929, that blacks were not allowed "in the larger motion picture houses or in the Y.M.C.A. or Y.W.C.A.; they are not to be found in 'white' churches; Negro children must play in their own restricted corner of the Park." Returning to Muncie a decade later, the Lynds concluded that "the cleft between the white and the Negro people of Middletown is the deepest and most blindly followed line of division in the community."[12]

Across the Midwest, African Americans could never be certain exactly where the line of color ran. There were always anxious questions: which restaurant might serve me, which hotel might provide a bed for the night, which movie theater would admit me, and would it be the balcony or the main floor? Could I, should I, say hello to a white woman passing on the sidewalk? Should I look her in the eye if I said hello? Of necessity, African Americans developed antennae that alerted them to the openings and porous places in the color line and to places where the line was drawn deep and hard, a line in shifting sand and a line in hardened concrete.

Black Americans learned their place in order to survive in white America—in Grant County, Indiana, as well as in the South's Black Belt. They learned, as Dr. Martin Luther King wrote in his letter from the Birmingham jail, to endure "living constantly at tiptoe stance, never quite knowing what to expect next."[13] But black Americans pushed, sometimes subtly, sometimes hard, to lighten, to move, to erase lines of color. At the same time as they pushed, black people created their own institutions, all-black havens on the other side of the white color line, places of safety and of community, places where Louie Chochos could not enter and could not laugh.

The color line in Marion, Indiana, was as amorphous, as wobbly, as changing as elsewhere in the Midwest. One indication of its character comes from the early-twentieth-century Grant County histories. Everyone knew that there had been blacks in Grant County for a long time. Referred to in polite circles as "colored people," they were always identified and marked by this label. In a local history project, students at Marion High School included five African American oral histories among the dozens they gathered and printed in a 1921 collection titled *"Lest We Forget": Reminiscences of the Pioneers of Grant County.* The students did not ignore black history, as was often the case in those days, but after the names of each of the five they added the word "(Colored)." This constant noting of race doubtless prompted one of the five black interviewees, "Junius Pettiford (Colored)," to tell the student interviewer, as she transcribed his words, "In Hebe'n theah will be no 'colah.' All will be white with God." In Grant County, however, there was color, always. The color white was the norm, even for Junius Pettiford. The color white was so ordinary that it was not really perceived as a color; only black was a color, the one that always was marked, seen, noted.[14]

On the Courthouse Square soon after World War I grateful citizens placed a plaque in memory of the 28 "Marion Boys Who Gave Their Lives in the World War." Twenty-six of the names had no description; two names were followed by "(col.)." In death William Cromwell and Rollins Wade were still colored.[15]

A COMMUNITY OF THEIR OWN

Early-twentieth-century white local historians did not always exclude African American residents but, like the Marion High School students, usually gave them a separate chapter or section, structured so that there was "Grant County history" and "colored history," the latter a separate story from the main one.[16] This mixture of inclusion and separation made some sense, for it reflected the daily lives of black Grant Countians.

The story of black pioneers was and still is told in parallel terms, as heroic as that of white pioneers. The story centers on the community of Weaver, one of dozens of all-black communities that once dotted the midwestern landscape. The first black pioneers settled in Grant County in the 1840s, free people and former slaves from the South, especially North Carolina. The large Quaker population of Grant County assisted some black families and provided a more welcoming environment than in many other parts of the Midwest. The largest numbers of black pioneers settled in Liberty Township, in the southwestern portion of the county. Within that symbolically named township they clustered around an area known first as the Crossroads and later as Weaver, after one of the most prominent early families. By 1860 there were 285 residents. Most of these pioneers, like their white neighbors, were farmers. Most were able to purchase land. They worked hard and prospered well enough on the rich land of the Midwest Corn Belt to create a thriving community. They built an African Methodist Episcopal Church, called Hills Chapel, in 1849, a Baptist Church in the 1850s, and a Wesleyan Methodist Church in the 1870s. They opened a school, known as Number 2 School, about 1869, a post office in 1880, a blacksmith shop, a livery stable, and a general store operated for a long time by John Henry Weaver. In the 1840s and 1850s the people of Weaver played a significant role in the underground railroad. Joined by antislavery Quakers, they helped escaped slaves follow the North Star to freedom. In the early 1860s young men wearing Union blue left Weaver to fight more directly against slavery.[17]

Weaver included numerous people whose lighter skin color made visible their family links to white fathers in the South and in some cases to Native Americans. Some time around 1858 a boy named James T. Pettiford journeyed with his mother from North Carolina to a new home in Grant County. Fifty years later Pettiford testified that "every body" in his North Carolina birthplace knew that his father was a "full-blooded Cherokee Indian" and that his mother's mother was also "recognized as an Indian." Nonetheless, Pettiford stated, now he was "recognized in the community in which I live as a colored man."[18]

Some Weaver people and their descendants were light enough to be "recognized" as white. They could choose to pass, to cross the color line. A few opted for that course in hopes of better job opportunities and greater equality. Some Weaver people, because of their lighter skin color and because of their pioneer settlement, seemed to view themselves (and were viewed by many whites) as more socially elevated than other African Americans who arrived later, in the twentieth century. But nearly all Weaver people were in their hearts and minds people of color and so "recognized" by others.[19]

The people of Weaver lived in a certain harmony with the white neighbors who surrounded them. "We had nice times," recalled Georgia Weaver Jones, born in Weaver in 1899. "There wasn't any prejudice." Jones and other Weaver residents fondly remembered the July Fourth celebrations, which attracted huge crowds of white as well as black people enjoying together a carnival-like atmosphere in the hot summer sun. The national holiday provided horse racing, baseball, concerts by the Knox Military Band, and a large number of out-of-town visitors, including members of Weaver families who had moved elsewhere. Older residents also would later remember white folks joining them at the revival meetings held in the woods near Hills Chapel to savor the combination of religious gathering and social visiting. And they remembered the threshing rings of sweaty men in overalls who joined together to bring in the wheat harvest and to separate and stack it, threshing rings of black and white Grant Countians working together and ending the long day with a picnic dinner and tired, happy laughter and talk.[20]

Local accounts of Weaver portray a community of harmony and peace. Many African American families in Grant County today proudly trace their origins to the early Liberty Township families, including the Weavers, Burdens, Pettifords, Becks, Gullifords, Wards, and Caseys. But Weaver was a black community, a place where lines of color were always drawn, even if sometimes forgotten in later memories. Only black Hoosiers attended Weaver's churches and school, which had black ministers and teachers. There were all-black baseball teams, including the Weaver Farmboys and the Weaver Hot Dogs. The Knox Military Band that gave such wonderful summer concerts was composed only of black musicians. August celebrations of Emancipation Day attracted hundreds of black visitors from surrounding communities, who joined in cake walk contests, dancing, fireworks, and sporting events—blacks having a good time together and commemorating the end of America's slavery. Only black marriages won social acceptance, which often meant seeking a mate in another of the Midwest's all-black rural settlements or in nearby cities such as Indianapolis or Chicago. And in the end there was a black cemetery for the dead of Weaver. In *Biographical Memoirs of Grant County, Indiana,* published in 1901, some 580 families paid the fee to be memorialized in print: there were no members of the Weaver, Burden, Pettiford, or other leading families of Liberty Township in this mug book. The color line circumnavigated the community of Weaver, Indiana.

Charlotte Fenstermaker was born in 1910 and grew up only a half mile south of Weaver. In a 1994 interview this elderly white woman captured the complex reality of her childhood. She played with Weaver kids, she remembered, because "there was no prejudice at that time." But the Weaver school and Hills Chapel were "just for blacks only," she recalled: "See, at that time blacks and whites didn't mix. . . . We were friends, but we didn't mix."[21]

Weaver reached its peak at the turn of the century. By the 1920s, as in many farm communities across America, Weaver residents were moving to jobs in factories and cities.[22] Many moved the short distance to Marion, where the color lines were more complex, but where there were reasonable expectations of living peacefully among white neighbors. After all, Marion was the place where in 1885 a courageous sheriff had turned back a white mob intent on lynching a black man.

There were only occasional signs of racial violence as in a Marion baseball game in late summer 1900 between the Clippers and the Orioles. Black and white players and fans enjoyed the Sunday afternoon at the Fourteenth Street Park until a disputed call by a white umpire led to a racist slur, then heated arguments, and finally the umpire swinging a bat at the head of the black catcher. At the sight of blood, according to the *Marion Leader*, "The ebony-hued contingent in the crowd of rooters, who were in the majority, got their ire up" and chased the umpire into a nearby house. But what the newspaper labeled "a small race war" ended quickly when one policeman arrived to protect the umpire and readily calmed "the mob of colored men."[23]

In contrast to such episodes was the peaceful glow of Marion's tribute to Booker T. Washington on his death in 1915. A local newspaper estimated that an audience of over fifteen hundred turned out—with "both races about equally represented"—to hear eulogies and music honoring the nation's most celebrated African American leader. Black and white speakers and musicians shared the platform in the town's Civic Hall. The program claimed that Washington was "the most powerful medium in bringing about a better understanding between the two races in this country."[24]

Doubtless more important than such grand tributes was the fact that in this industrial town many fortunate black men could find work in the factories, especially at the Malleable Iron Works. The young Weaver kid Tom Shipp was surely pleased when he got on at "the Malleable" in the late 1920s. It was hot, hard work, not always steady, but the pay was good. Other black men found jobs as janitors, chauffeurs, and laborers, jobs like Abe Smith and James Cameron had as "shoeshine boys." Women employed outside the home did housekeeping, laundry, and other domestic work.[25]

African American migrants came from beyond Weaver, searching for jobs and schools, for relatively safe communities in which to raise families, for places where there were other black Americans. From rural Indiana and from south of the Ohio River they came. By 1920 there were over a thousand blacks in Marion, just under 5 percent of the total population of 23,747, and three times the number in the town in 1890. Most worked in the kind of low-paying, tenuous, less desirable jobs that were everywhere the lot of black Americans. Marion was certainly not the brightest midwestern star attracting black newcomers, certainly not a Chicago or Cleveland or Indianapolis, where black populations increased rapidly in the 1920s. Indeed, after growing through the first two decades of the century, Marion's African American population remained stagnant during the 1920s as these big cities attracted a larger and larger share of the great migration to the Midwest. But there was modest hope for a good life in Marion.[26]

By the 1920s Marion had a small black professional community, with offices mostly in the downtown Wigger Block. Julius Caesar Judkins and John Will Burden were black lawyers. Burden was perhaps the best-known African American in town. A graduate of Purdue University, he taught school in Weaver for many years; a hard taskmaster who was widely respected, he later entered law practice and became a prominent voice in the community. John Will Burden may well have been a helping hand in Vennie and Marsha Burden's challenge to Louis Chochos. Another widely known resident was Dr. Walter T. Bailey, the physician. There was also a black dentist, Dr. John A. Welch. One of Marion's most unusual black professionals was Samuel Plato, a talented architect who left behind several notable churches and homes, many built in partnership with the black building contractor Jasper Burden. There were several black ministers. Black-owned businesses included a funeral home, a street contractor, and a grocery store. Clients and customers of these black professionals and businessmen often included whites as well as blacks.[27]

There were also black civic employees, sufficient in their visibility to suggest hope for ambitious young black men (but not women). As early as 1894 there was a black policemen, William Pettiford. Through the first half of the twentieth century there was a community understanding that permitted two black city policemen and two black firemen, never just one, never three. Whites set a quota, refusing to open up jobs beyond the two; some blacks doubtless thought this concession of two better than none, since two jobs were unusual for mid-sized midwestern towns, many of which had not a single black cop or fireman. In larger northern cities there sometimes were black policemen, but they were often assigned to black neighborhoods. Marion was too small for such specialization. Its black policemen patrolled throughout the city, and unlike some blacks cops could and did arrest white people.[28]

One of Marion's best-known black cops was Harley Burden, Sr. Born in Weaver and part of the large Burden clan, he moved to town about 1910 and in 1916 joined the police force, a job he held for 26 years. He made enough money even in the depths of the Great Depression to send a son to Indiana University. There was some jealousy in the black community by that time; people would sometimes say, "Harley, why don't you retire and give someone else a chance?" It was hard to be angry with Harley Burden, however. Everyone in town knew this friendly, outgoing man, who waved to all and knew most of the town's gossip. Often he was assigned to patrol in Bucktown, a tough, working-class white neighborhood near the Malleable, where saloons had plenty of business during Prohibition and where men found reasons to fight. There Harley Burden was known and respected. The occasional racial slur from a drunken brawler caused white folks to come to the black cop's side. Perhaps Harley Burden was less objectionable in Bucktown too because, as a black Marion barber recalled, Harley "looked like he was white." Some downtown druggists and cigar shop owners hated to see him come into their stores, whatever his looks, because he would often say, in the long tradition of small-town cops, "I'm looking after your place" as he reached into a cigar box to pick up a few stogies.

It is doubtful that Harley Burden ever forgot he was a black man, however. Even as he patrolled across the lines of color, he was often specially summoned in serious cases involving black residents. The city police captain called him back to work the night Claude Deeter was shot and sent him out to talk to the mothers of Shipp, Smith, and Cameron. He and his wife, Addie Burden, had joined the Marion branch of the National Association for the Advancement of Colored People (NAACP) six weeks before the lynching. Eleven years earlier Harley Burden had sung in the black men's quartet at the civil rights group's organizing meeting. And Harley Burden surely knew that Louis Chochos had laughed at his sister-in-law, Marsha Burden, about a year after he joined the police force.[29]

Harley Burden and his family lived in a neighborhood of nearly all white families. Most black families tended to concentrate in a few parts of the city: in an area near the Mississinewa River known as Johnstown, because of its tendency to flood; a neighborhood around 10th and Nebraska; and an area around 35th and Washington Streets, the South Marion neighborhood in which Cameron, Shipp, and Smith lived. Many owned their own homes, almost as many, by percentage, as did whites in Marion. Although there was some concentration of black residences, neighborhoods were not tightly segregated. White families lived mixed among black families, and some black families also lived in other parts of town, in mostly white neighborhoods. "We all lived everywhere," Joseph Casey recalled, though as late as the 1950s black families could not purchase homes in some of the town's best neighborhoods. Older black residents also remembered young black and white kids playing together and as teenagers hanging out and even dating occasionally.[30]

But black residents in Marion had no illusions of equality. They knew about color lines, and they knew too how to create institutions of their own. Most black kids attended the Payne Elementary School, a segregated school. James Cameron and Tom Shipp went there. In the Indiana Theater downtown they could watch Hollywood films only from the balcony. The public swimming pool near the pioneer log cabin shrine in Matter Park was closed to them. Several of the more prosperous black families spent summer vacations at Fox Lake in northeastern Indiana, an all-black family resort that drew people from around the Midwest. Young men played baseball on an all-black team against other "colored" teams, including the Indianapolis ABCs. These black baseball teams had uniforms when the Grant County sheriff deputies didn't. There were several black basketball teams, including church teams and the Marion Flyers.[31]

In Marion's two newspapers a separate section titled "Colored News" reported funerals, receptions, visits, and travels. The "Colored News" announced worship, missionary society, and choir meetings for Marion's all-black churches. These institutions were key anchors of the community, places of extensive social contact. Bethel A.M.E., the oldest, established in the 1880s, at 10th and Nebraska Streets, attracted the most prominent members of the community. There was also Allen Temple A.M.E., built in 1901, at Washington and 35th Streets and Second Baptist on South Branson between 18th and 19th Streets.

"Colored News" also announced lodge and club meetings. Women's clubs were particularly numerous. In Weaver there had been the Ten Si Foy Club, in Marion the Sorosis Club, Eurydice Club, Domestic Art Club, and many others. Marion's black clubwomen were particularly pleased to host the State Federation of Colored Women's Clubs of Indiana in 1915. With their motto "Lifting as We Climb," the women heard Madam C. J. Walker, the Indianapolis manufacturer of hair care and beauty products, and others speak of race pride and achievement.[32]

African Americans in Grant County, as elsewhere, created a community of their own, one adjacent to, and outside of, the white community. They knew each other, knew who to trust, knew who had particular skills and knowledge, whether to fix a flat tire, to raise money for the church, or to fight the battles of race. Black people in Grant County were not victims. Individually and collectively they pushed again and again against the color line. Their pushes were often subtle, sometimes not even noticed by white folk, and often not recorded in a manner that left clear traces for the historian. But from time to time the ongoing struggle to lighten and erase the lines of color became public. That was the achievement of the Burden sisters when they challenged Louie Chochos's laugh. And at their best such public challenges to the color line brought together large numbers of Grant County African Americans. The Burden case was a family case, yet it had the support of not only two black lawyers but also a large number of black citizens. Indeed, the Burden sisters doubtless took strength from a wider and more formal movement of challenge within the black community in Marion and in America.

THE NAACP AND FLOSSIE BAILEY
CHALLENGE THE COLOR LINE

The organizational meeting of the Marion branch of the National Association for the Advancement of Colored People occurred on November 28, 1918, at the very time the Burden case was moving to the appellate court. There could have been no greater show of support and solidarity than the effort to form this new organization in this small black community.

Marion blacks were not alone. Formed in 1909, the NAACP soon became the leading civil rights organization in America. Although white Americans initially played a large role in it, blacks led at local and state levels. In Indiana by 1915, African Americans had formed branches in Indianapolis, Terre Haute, Evansville, Gary, and Vincennes.[33]

Fifty-five black Grant Countians signed the application for a branch NAACP charter in late 1918. Each paid the dollar membership fee. The 55 names encompassed most of the professional and better-paid members of the black community, including 3 ministers, 2 physicians, a chiropractor, a teacher, a mail carrier, an insurance agent, and the architect Samuel Plato. Also on the membership application list were 7 laborers and 7 janitors. There were 18 women, 15 of whom listed their occupation as housekeeper, 2 as domestic, 1 as matron.[34]

The New York office approved the branch charter application in January 1919, by which time the new organization was in the midst of plans for a grand public meeting to announce its birth. Held in Stinson Memorial Hall at the Soldiers Home on Sunday afternoon, February 9, 1919, the meeting honored Abraham Lincoln and Theodore Roosevelt. The Soldiers Home Band played the "Star-Spangled Banner" and the Reverend J. D. Ponds of the Weaver A.M.E. Church gave the invocation. The Ladies Quartette sang "Steal Away to Jesus." Flossie Bailey, wife of Dr. Walter T. Bailey, presented a paper on Abraham Lincoln, and W. W. Hyde, from Indianapolis, gave the keynote address on

Theodore Roosevelt—two African American orators celebrating white heroes. The Weaver Civic League Quartette, composed of policeman Harley Burden and three Gulliford brothers, sang "Swing Low, Sweet Chariot." The Reverend F. M. Story of the Second Baptist Church gave the benediction.[35]

The momentum continued, for a while, even as bloody racial conflict marked the experience of Americans elsewhere. A Marion newspaper ran an article announcing an NAACP membership meeting at Bethel A.M.E. Church in December 1920 and reassured white readers that the organization was for them and all Marion citizens. And in spring 1921, NAACP field secretary William Pickens gave a "highly interesting and instructive" plea "for better understanding between the white and colored people of the country." The newspaper reported his audience in Civic Hall at over a thousand citizens, white and black.[36] But this grand beginning soon sputtered. The records of the Marion branch in the Library of Congress show no further activity until 1927.

During the 1920s there were other signs of dashed hopes and worsening conditions. Voters in Grant County rejected an amendment to the Indiana constitution that would have allowed blacks to join the state militia, though the percentage voting against the amendment was smaller than in the state as a whole. And there was the rise of the Ku Klux Klan, the hate organization that took over the Republican Party of Abraham Lincoln and Theodore Roosevelt.

And yet, after a half-dozen years of apparent inactivity Marion blacks resumed their effort to build a local branch of the NAACP. In early 1927 an organizing committee formed and scheduled a mass meeting for March 14. The effort failed. Not until two years later, in March 1929, did another push finally produce a formal organization, one that would survive and in 1930 flourish.[37]

The key to the eventual success of the NAACP branch was Katherine Bailey, known to everyone as Flossie, though in more formal settings she was sometimes addressed as "Mrs. Dr. Bailey." Wife of the leading black doctor in town, Walter T. Bailey, she was energetic, sophisticated, and committed, an impressive public speaker and an efficient organizer. Everyone knew her. Decades after her death people still vividly remembered her. "She held her head high and set an example for everyone," Edmund Casey recalled. "She was a hot rod," James Cameron remembered, involved in everything. Cameron knew her at the Bethel A.M.E. church they both attended, where she led the Missionary Society and eventually became head of the state A.M.E. Missionary Society. Born in nearby Kokomo in 1895, she married Walter Bailey in 1917. He was a graduate of Meharry Medical College who came to Marion in 1914. The Baileys had a son a year after their marriage, their only child. Flossie Bailey's many responsibilities and large organizational talents did not smother a warm heart that extended simple kindness to dozens. When she learned of two rural black children who had no means to travel to Marion for high school, Bailey arranged to pay for their transportation.[38]

Sadie Weaver Pate's eyes lit up when she warmly remembered Flossie Bailey many decades after she had worked for the Baileys in the 1920s, helping the doctor in his office and Mrs. Bailey in the house. There was lots of housework because the Baileys often had guests staying with them at 1907 South Adams Street. Black families in the Midwest visited frequently and generally stayed in each other's homes rather than hotels. NAACP leaders from around Indiana met at the Baileys' home and sometimes stayed overnight. Robert L. Bailey (no relation), a leading black Indianapolis lawyer, visited frequently on NAACP business and often brought along his family, sometimes coming for Thanksgiving to the two-story house with the big front porch on South Adams.[39]

Flossie Bailey expertly led the new Marion branch. One of her first successes was to bring Oscar DePriest to Marion in September 1929. The only African American member of Congress, DePriest addressed a crowd that packed Allen Temple A.M.E. Church. He urged blacks to vote and "to stand together." Lawyer John W. Burden spoke also, as did Flossie Bailey. And the 35-voice NAACP Choral Club sang. The rally was a great showcase for the new branch. A local newspaper gave front-page coverage and printed an editorial urging "a spirit of tolerance and fair play for all races and all classes."[40]

In her report of March 1930, Flossie Bailey showed 34 members who paid their one-dollar NAACP dues. In June 62 new members joined. On August 27 (after the August 7 lynching) another 45 added their names and one-dollar memberships, and in late October 1930, 14 more, for a total of 155 members. At least 9 of the members were white, including Drysdale Brannon, a reporter for the *Marion Chronicle*, and Jack Edwards, the city's mayor, but nearly all others were black. On the lists were the names of Grant County's leading families: Weaver, Jones, Pettiford, Burden, Casey, and others. Often entire families joined, each paying a dollar.[41]

At the moment in Marion's history when a mob lynched two African Americans there was a growing and active civil rights organization in existence; an organization strongly based in the local community and also connected outside it; an organization, led by a "hot rod" woman, that was prepared to challenge vigorously the effort of a white mob to redraw in blood the line of color. The NAACP could not save the lives of Shipp and Smith, but perhaps it could shape what happened next.

The Stories Begin

The battered bodies of Abram Smith and Thomas Shipp hung from the maple tree on the Courthouse Square from late Thursday evening, August 7, until dawn on Friday, August 8, 1930. During those dark hours the stories began, stories told by all kinds of people, told in varieties of format and meaning, told with facts and with lies, with anger and sadness, with pride and shame. All manner of influences shaped these accounts of the Marion lynching but none so strongly as the lines of color.

PROTECTING THE PEOPLE

The first concern of Marion's African American residents that tragic night was their own safety. Sheriff Jake Campbell later testified that after the lynching, "I heard some fellow holler in the crowd 'let's get a torch and go in Johnstown,' and some fellow hollered 'let's go and get some more niggers.'"[1] That long night, Flossie Bailey wrote, "was one of horrors, thousands milling around down town and running wild in the streets uttering threats." Not trusting Sheriff Campbell or the city police, Flossie Bailey called the Indiana governor's office within an hour of the lynching. Learning that Governor Harry Leslie was away on a

Canadian fishing trip, she eventually reached his assistant, L. O. Chasey, and appealed to him to send state protection. Chasey not only refused but "was very nasty and hung his receiver up on me," Bailey claimed. She and other members of the Marion branch of the NAACP then went to see Mayor Jack Edwards, himself an NAACP branch member. The mayor also called Chasey, who told him that only if Sheriff Campbell requested help could he respond.[2]

During that night of terror Flossie Bailey also set phone and telegraph lines humming to rouse from their sleep state NAACP leaders. Following her alarms state officials prepared a telegram to Governor Leslie, sent at 3:05 A.M., August 8: "Two Negroes lynched in Marion Ind and Negro section threatened with destruction by mob. Please use fullest extent of law to protect them." Even before that telegram, at 2:29 A.M., Robert L. Bailey, Indianapolis lawyer and Flossie Bailey's state NAACP partner, sent a telegram to the NAACP national office in New York City: "Three [sic] Negro boys lynched tonight in courthouse yard Marion Indiana. Negro Section threatened with fire. Wire instructions to state president." The New York NAACP office on early Friday morning dispatched a strongly worded telegram to the Indiana governor urging action and another telegram offering support to the state president of the Indiana NAACP, which completed the circle of messages of alarm: the state president was Flossie Bailey.[3]

As Flossie Bailey worked the telephone and telegraph lines on that hot August night many black residents of Marion fled in fear of white retribution. Some went to Weaver to stay with relatives. Marsha Burden went to Chicago, where her sister Vennie now lived. Fear mixed with rage among those who stayed in the lynching town. Whites cruised up and down South Adams Street in front of the Baileys' house and deliberately backfired their motors as they shouted warnings. Inside, Flossie Bailey worried that Friday evening would bring mobs to attack the jail for other black prisoners and that "a race riot" threatened.[4]

Tensions certainly persisted throughout the following day. Lawrence Beitler made copies of his dramatic photograph of the two bodies hanging from the tree and by Friday afternoon was doing a brisk business selling them for 50 cents apiece. Eager souvenir hunters stripped the bark from the lynching tree. A *New York Times* reporter offered what he claimed were three representative comments from whites: a Sunday school teacher who said it was a good thing "such animals were removed from society"; a barber who remarked that the lynching "had served its purpose if it prevented a recurrence of such crimes"; and Mary Ball, the young woman who claimed she was raped, who "only wished that she 'could have pulled the rope and would do the same for the other one [James Cameron].'"[5]

Fears spread among white people too. Newspapers reported that as many as four hundred blacks had gathered Friday evening in Johnstown for an "indignation meeting" before police dispersed them. Stories circulated that Marion blacks had armed themselves and that "gangs of Negroes were coming in from other cities to aid in reprisals." One of their targets, people said, was Sheriff Campbell, who was under heavy protection in his jail residence. In nearby Fairmount, town leaders put eight special policemen on duty in case angry blacks came after the friends of Claude Deeter, who some thought had been ringleaders of the mob.[6]

A summer Friday evening brought crowds moving restlessly but peacefully through downtown Marion, consumed with curiosity. There was great relief, nonetheless, when the Indiana National Guard finally arrived in Marion just before dawn on Saturday, August 9. In full uniforms, heavily armed with machine guns and rifles, bayonets fixed, the 130 white guardsmen patrolled the downtown streets and especially the neighborhoods of Johnstown and South Marion, protecting African Americans and discouraging retribution. Claude Deeter's funeral services in Fairmount Saturday afternoon brought more anxiety, but Saturday night was quiet. Whenever two or three people gathered on a sidewalk Indiana guardsmen ordered them to disperse. At Sunday church services, ministers called for order, as Mayor Edwards had requested them to do. Black families who had fled in fear began quietly to return home.[7]

There remained considerable anxiety about funeral services for Shipp and Smith. Their bodies had been taken to the J. E. Johnson Mortuary in Muncie. When a white crowd gathered there in anger many Muncie blacks armed themselves. The Delaware County sheriff joined blacks to keep whites away from the mortuary. Sunday the two grieving families brought the bodies to their homes in Marion; national guardsmen stood out front in response to threats that a mob was preparing to burn the bodies and the houses. In an act of some bravery, Mayor Edwards called on Shipp's and Smith's families to offer condolences. With armed guardsmen in attendance, Shipp was buried

Monday morning in a Marion cemetery. Guardsmen then escorted Smith's body to the cemetery in Weaver. As the sun set Monday evening the Indiana Guard left Marion—prematurely, thought some blacks, who still feared for their safety and their property.[8]

SEEKING JUSTICE

The return of peace brought louder calls for justice, for arresting the members of the lynching mob, for trials, for punishment. Flossie Bailey began such calls before dawn on August 8, even as her first concern was ending the violence. As fears of more mob action receded, Bailey turned the full force of her immense energies to seeking allies among African Americans and sympathetic whites. Doubtless Bailey could push harder because she was female; whites may well have silenced a black man displaying such visible challenge.

Much of Mrs. Bailey's initial hope rested on Walter White, acting head of the NAACP. "Please send us a National representative to help in our investigation," she wrote White on August 9, and repeated her request the next day. Walter White knew as much about lynching as any American. His book *Rope and Faggot,* published in 1929, was based on dozens of personal investigations he conducted in the 1920s. As a boy in Atlanta he had seen a mob beat a black man to death. Thirty-seven years old, he was of middle-class origins, with hair and skin so light that he could—and sometimes in lynching investigations did—pass for white. On August 11 White presented Bailey's appeal to his NAACP colleagues. They agreed that he should go to Marion and should also hire a private investigator.[9]

White set about arranging details of the trip. Should he stay "at one of the hotels or with colored people," he asked Flossie Bailey. She advised him to stay at the Spencer Hotel, but "it will be best to keep your racial identity a secret as the hotels do not keep colored people." She included a list of people he should interview, including the sheriff, mayor, and several sympathetic white witnesses. By this time Bailey was certain her telegrams and phone calls were being monitored and could communicate with White only by letter or by going to nearby Kokomo, her hometown, to phone him.[10]

White arrived in Marion on August 15 and spent two nights at the Spencer Hotel, a black man crossing the lines of color. He rented a car and drove around the city and out into the county and talked to dozens of people. Returning to New York City, he prepared his report and sent it to state government officials on August 22. White charged "gross if not criminal negligence" among Grant County law officers. From his interviews with Mayor Edwards, City Police Chief Lewis Lindenmuth, other policemen, and witnesses, White concluded that it was "beyond question that Sheriff Campbell is guilty of gross failure to perform his duty as sheriff," and that he should be removed from office. White considered it even more important that the murderers be tried and punished to remove the stain on Indiana and Grant County. But local officials would not do that, he predicted. Grant County Prosecutor Harley Hardin told White that he was "reluctant to proceed vigorously with the arrest and prosecution of the lynchers, basing this reluctance upon the fact that he feared such action would infuriate the mob and stir it to new activity." Many in Grant County told White that "there is little hope of conviction if the matter is left to local officials." Consequently, White urged the Indiana governor and attorney general to "take the initiative in seeing that prosecution of the Marion lynchers be carried through with efficiency and dispatch." To assist in that action, White enclosed, from his investigations in Grant County, a "list of persons reported to have participated in the lynchings of August 7." The list was not hard to compile, for "the lynchers are well known," White wrote.[11]

RAPE STORIES

Walter White's investigation also focused on Mary Ball's claim of rape. Ball was 18 years old, a good-looking woman with bobbed, wavy hair, of working-class origins. Her story was "chiefly the cause for the lynchings," White concluded. Moreover, the image of a black male raping a young white woman would surely stand in the way of convicting lynch mob leaders. Most newspapers featured Mary Ball as an innocent victim. She and Claude Deeter were to be married on September 22, the *New York Times* reported, her nineteenth birthday. A correspondent wrote Governor Leslie that "those two black rapists that were hung got just what they deserved." Nearly every day the newspapers "publish an article where some black fiend has attacked a white girl or woman," he claimed. "White women and girls need some protection from these black devils." Doubtless many in the mob on August 7 and many whites forever after believed that protecting women was at the center of the Marion lynching.[12]

Walter White did not believe Mary Ball's story. He found no evidence to support her claim and lots of evidence to throw doubt on her "character" as a pure and innocent victim. White reported that Deeter's parents denied that the couple were engaged. They were parked in an area notorious for "petting parties" and "jazz parties." An article in the NAACP magazine *The Crisis* highlighted the spots on Mary Ball's character and claimed that "For generations, we black folks have been the sexual scapegoats for white American filth in literature and lynching." The lies that make black men into "wild beasts" of "filthy lust" are "deliberately nailed to every possible Negro crime and broadcast." Why was it, White asked, that there were two white rapists in the Grant County jail on August 7, but they were not sought by the mob?[13]

White was too much the Victorian gentleman to repeat in public the full details of the stories that began to circulate in Grant County about Mary Ball. Such stories were told especially among blacks. Mary Ball was in fact the girlfriend of Abe Smith, people said. She often wore his jewelry, they claimed. Ball, Smith, Cameron, Shipp, and perhaps even Deeter hung out together, a "black and tan" group that enjoyed good times together—and sometimes became a holdup gang. Some said Mary Ball was the decoy to attract young men to the lovers' lane, where her companions then robbed them. The gang quarreled among themselves that night along the Mississinewa River, a fight broke out, and Deeter was shot. African Americans in Grant County would tell versions of this story down to the end of the twentieth century. Harley Burden's son was certain Ball was not raped: Smith "was going with her; why would he have raped her," Harley Burden, Jr., said in 1998. The cops found Mary Ball wearing Abe's watch, he added. Almost always in stories told by blacks there is the detail of Smith's jewelry on Mary Ball's body. There is also the crossing of color lines. Some believed she lived with a black man; one black man even claimed, in 1977, that she later married a black man.[14]

And there is the "character" issue. Many blacks and even, privately, a few whites later agreed that Mary Ball represented the hot side of the 1920s, that she was sexually promiscuous, that she was far from the innocent white virgin portrayed at the time. Claude Deeter's sister later admitted that "her character wasn't what it should be." The Deeter family knew nothing of her prior to Claude's murder, even though newspapers claimed that they were to be engaged, a claim the family very much doubted. Roy Cox, a white policeman in 1930, later recalled that all Marion cops knew Ball "because she was no good." In fact, "we had her listed as a prostitute," Cox said in 1977. In 1954 a Marion NAACP leader reminded the New York office that "Two Negro men were lynched for, supposedly, raping a white prostitute." Evelyn Thompson, a black woman, bluntly told an interviewer in 1977 that Mary Ball "was nothing but a prostitute"; Thompson remembered seeing her near the Courthouse Square wearing a thin dress without underwear, deliberately provocative.[15]

Whether Abe Smith raped Mary Ball or instead gave her his watch will likely never be known. White folks tended to believe in the young woman's purity, or at least pretended to, and therefore to argue Ball's need for white male protection. Blacks saw Mary Ball's story as part of the fabric of lies that degraded black men. The several versions of the incident are only one more set of stories that fall along the color line. The white telling of the story was surely the dominant version in 1930, the version told by people who had the power, the version that made it so hard for Walter White and Flossie Bailey to get whites to hear their calls for justice.

OFFICIAL RESPONSES

Walter White was correct in doubting action from local officials. A special Court of Inquiry opened on August 13, but County Prosecutor Hardin told the press that "the public has evidenced no desire to press prosecution" and that efforts to do so would be futile and even dangerous because arrests of reputed mob members would produce a race riot. Several white folks told Hardin that if any accused lynchers were put in jail a mob would release them by force. On the other side of the color line, Hardin added, black residents had threatened to kill any accused lynchers. Hardin was not one to push the issue; he was a candidate for reelection that fall and, in the words of one detractor, he "didn't have any more backbone than a jellyfish." Witnesses before the Court of Inquiry refused to name names, and even after a list of six names finally was drawn up, Grant County Judge O. D. Clawson, a close friend of Sheriff Campbell, refused to approve an affidavit.[16]

The day Judge Clawson refused to act, Flossie Bailey wrote Walter White. Talk of race riots was "intended to intimidate the colored people so they will be afraid to proceed and to keep the germ of lawlessness alive in the minds of whites," she charged; but "instead of being intimidated I am determined to do everything possible to assist in bringing these men to trial." Bailey and her Hoosier NAACP colleagues were meeting that night to organize a delegation to call directly on the Indiana governor.[17]

On August 20 ten NAACP leaders from Marion and Indianapolis went to see Governor Leslie. They presented a petition that asked Leslie to remove Sheriff Campbell from office, to urge the prosecutor and judge "to bring to justice the lynchers," and to promise "to the citizens of Grant County who are afraid to testify and point out members of the mob known to them" that if they come forward "their lives and their property will be protected to the limit if it takes the State Militia so to do." It was not a satisfying meeting. The governor was too busy, he said, to give the NAACP delegation more than a few minutes. And, Flossie Bailey reported, "He was reserved almost to the point of indifference. He said he would make no statement at this time . . . neither did he feel justified in interfering with the local authorities." He mentioned that he had received Walter White's appeal for action but that he would not answer it. Nor did the governor respond to a request for information from the Atlanta-based Commission on Interracial Cooperation, which had just initiated a massive study of lynchings. Leslie had his secretary, L. O. Chasey, send a note to the commission, but it was among the "the least responsive" from the nation's governors.[18]

The chilly air in the governor's office should not have surprised anyone. When Leslie's right-hand man, L. O. Chasey, had hung up on Flossie Bailey the night of the lynching, it was only the first snub from the statehouse. Chasey knew the local situation well. Marion was his hometown. He was a good friend of Sheriff Campbell, and he was in town the weekend after the lynching. In a personal and confidential letter to a Marion friend who was the Washington correspondent for the *Indianapolis Star,* Chasey explained that the lynching was caused by "delay in the administration of justice in the courts." "Shyster lawyers and incompetent judges are largely responsible. . . . Technicalities have been allowed to stand in the way of justice too long." No jury would ever convict in this case, he predicted. And, referring to Claude Deeter and Mary Ball, Chasey added his final defense: "You know as a father the question comes to me with unusual force—what if it had been my son or daughter." To another correspondent Chasey wrote that the lynching was "not in any way a race question." In fact, he insisted, "it could just as well happened to two white boys should they have perpetrated a similar outrage." One of the governor's Republican friends wisely advised him not to trust Chasey, who "has too many Grant County connections and political friendships in the mob."[19]

Chasey continued to exercise his position to prevent any action against Sheriff Campbell, his friend and fellow Republican. He visited his hometown again on August 14 to gather more information for Governor Leslie. Two days later he and the governor agreed to embrace the official local position and advised the sheriff and local authorities to use caution in seeking out lynchers so as not to incite a riot. Prosecutor Hardin was so delighted he took a public swipe at the NAACP delegation that had visited the governor: "Agitators seeking speedy punishment for leaders of the mob will keep on till they cause a race riot."[20]

NEWSPAPER STORIES

White folks in Grant County and elsewhere joined the defense that Chasey and Hardin made. The cause of the lynching, people said, was the heinous nature of the crimes of murder and of rape mixed with a justifiable mistrust of the criminal justice system, particularly since the five earlier deaths caused by bombings had gone unsolved. On August 8 the *Marion Chronicle* ran an editorial that claimed that the "lynching was done not by men of violent and lawless dispositions." Rather, "These men are ordinarily good citizens, but they were stung to the quick by an atrocious crime and spurred on to their violent act by a want of confidence in the processes of the courts." The local newspaper commented on the recent

bombings in Marion and the "spirit of lawlessness" that was sweeping across the
nation. The weekly paper in Fairmount, Claude Deeter's hometown, told the
same story of how the murder and rape caused the "breaking point of public
patience."[21]

The Marion lynching was a national story. Staff members in offices of the
Tuskegee Institute and the Southern Commission on the Study of Lynching
clipped from the nation's press scores of stories on this Indiana lynching.
Headlines and editorials, from the *Topeka Capital* and the *Akron Times-Press* to
the *New York Herald,* condemned the lynching, usually in much stronger
language than that in the Marion newspapers. In many southern newspapers
there was regret expressed over mob violence but often a pointed reference to a
northern lynching, which proved, as the *Concord (N.C.) Times* editorialized, that
"the mob spirit is not sectional." Indeed, the *Rome (Ga.) News-Tribune* claimed,
the Indiana lynching proved that "human nature is pretty much the same, North,
South, East and West," and asserted that the "only reason there are more
lynchings in the South than in the balance of the country is because there are
more negroes in the South."[22]

One of the factors in the wide newspaper coverage of this Indiana lynching
was Walter White's own reporting. A week after returning to New York City
from his investigative visit to Grant County, he sent out a press release with a
detailed account of his findings and also prepared a long article for the *New York
World.* The latter was well written and reported with precise and extensive detail
the tragic events along lovers' lane, the mob's behavior at the jail, the horror of
the lynchings, the failure of the sheriff, and the "general consensus of opinion
in Marion that if the matter of apprehending and punishing the lynchers is left
in the hands of the prosecutor it is highly improbable, if not certain, that no
convictions will be obtained." White's powerful piece was widely circulated and
quoted not only because it was so well crafted but also because he energetically
pushed its wide distribution. He even sent copies to Indiana's governor and
attorney general, to NAACP leaders in the state, and to Marion officials,
including Sheriff Campbell and Prosecutor Hardin.[23]

In newspapers that served primarily African American readers, from the
Amsterdam News of New York to the *Washington World* to the *Pittsburgh Courier,*
the Marion story was even bigger news. For these black newspapers the issue was

race, an issue other papers played down and sometimes explicitly denied. Few were more thorough or more outraged than the *Chicago Defender,* one of the nation's premier black newspapers. In its August 16 pages the *Defender* ran, in addition to news stories, an editorial cartoon titled "The Wabash Runs Crimson to the Sea"; a copy of Lawrence Beitler's photograph of the two bodies hanging from the tree, the crowd below, under the title "American Christianity"; and an editorial titled "What of Indiana?" which lambasted the state for crime and corruption, for welcoming Grand Dragon D. C. Stephenson and the Ku Klux Klan, and for denying Smith and Shipp the trial that the criminal Stephenson had had because they were black and he was white. The *Defender* continued in subsequent issues extensive coverage of efforts to seek justice, including an editorial cartoon titled "The Crucifixion," depicting Justice on a cross set deep in Marion's soil.[24]

Closest to Grant County geographically was the *Indianapolis Recorder,* in many ways the Hoosier black paper. It regularly carried reports of African American reunions, marriages, social visits, and church services from towns and cities across the state. Every week for months the *Recorder* ran a story on Marion, usually on the front page, along with editorials pushing for justice. Sheriff Campbell had to be removed from office and mob members "smoked out of their holes and punished to the full extent of the law," not just for Marion but for all of Indiana. The entire state had been "robbed of its good name," the *Recorder* insisted.[25]

Many mainstream Indiana papers also saw the lynching as a state issue and as a terrible blot on the state. They too called for justice, but in tones different from the *Recorder* and the *Defender.* The *Indianapolis Star* and the *Indianapolis News* were typical in emphasizing the cause of the lynchings as fears that criminals would not be punished. The *Indianapolis News* ran a front-page cartoon two days after the lynching that depicted a law enforcement official whose automobile was stopped by a flat tire caused by "technicalities." The *News* mentioned race only to deny vehemently that it was an issue. The two young men were lynched "not because they were members of one particular race but because they had been guilty of two atrocious crimes." In its violence the mob assaulted all Hoosiers, not just "a certain class of our people."[26]

There were a few general-circulation Hoosier papers that took more critical stands. The *Kokomo Tribune,* published only a few miles from Marion, not only deplored the lynching but also faced the race issue squarely: "Race prejudice doubtless had much to do with the mob impulse and with the shocking cruelty with which it carried its vengeful purpose into effect." Would the sheriff have offered so little resistance if the culprits had been white?, the Kokomo editor asked. "It is only natural that Marion's colored colony harbors such a suspicion."[27]

The *Indianapolis Times* made perhaps the most vigorous and sustained appeal for justice among the state's general-circulation papers. A day after the lynching, in its lead editorial, titled "They Must Be Punished," the paper asserted that "the disgrace that is Grant county's is Indiana's disgrace," and that "Indiana must act now to wipe out this stain." Again and again in the weeks that followed the *Indianapolis Times* repeated this call for state action. This challenge was not one for Grant County alone nor for African Americans alone. Indeed, after Flossie Bailey and her NAACP colleagues made their unhappy call on Governor Leslie, the *Times* castigated white Hoosiers, who, it argued, should have rushed to the statehouse even sooner to demand action.[28]

The *Indianapolis Times* was unusually progressive among Indiana newspapers. It had won a Pulitzer Prize in 1928 for its campaign against Ku Klux Klan corruption in state politics. Walter White was well aware of this liberal reputation; as he prepared to travel to Marion he wrote ahead to arrange a meeting with Boyd Gurley, the editor of the *Times,* because, he said, Clarence Darrow, the crusading lawyer best known for his defense of teaching evolution in the public schools in the Scopes trial in Tennessee, had told him that Gurley "is absolutely all right." The two did not meet then—Gurley was out of town— but they began a correspondence. White sent the Hoosier editor his *New York World* article and followed closely the *Indianapolis Times* stories and editorials. In early September he wrote Gurley to offer encouragement and praise for "the magnificent drum-fire you have kept up."[29]

There was one curious silence in the stories told in newspapers and elsewhere, especially those told for white audiences. The victims of the mob quickly disappeared. Abe Smith and Tom Shipp ceased to exist as characters in the drama. From the moment the mob broke through the jail doors Smith and Shipp became symbols of an evil that had to be destroyed, wiped away, purified by the ritual of lynching. They had been murderers and rapists, nothing more.

Because they were no longer human beings there were few stories to tell about the two teenagers, few details of their short lives to give texture or humanity to them as criminals or as victims. Often their names appeared in the newspaper stories, always marked by the word "negro" or "colored." Nothing else. In the tales told in the days and years to come these two central actors, the initiators of Marion's great tragedy, became bit players.

WHITE ALLIES

In moving closer to the tenor of reporting in the African American press, the *Indianapolis Times* and the *Kokomo Tribune* showed that the color line was not the only determinant of reactions to the lynching and succeeding events. Not all whites closed their eyes to the issue of justice. Even in Grant County there were differences among white residents, though no public opinion polls or other evidence exists to determine exactly those differences. One range of local response is represented by Mary Ball's mother; the "colored men got what they deserved," she told the press. On the other end, Claude Deeter's parents, even as they were making funeral arrangements for their murdered son, spoke differently. His father told reporters that "God should have been the judge." His mother said that "the mob had no right to do it." Both indicated that their deep Christian faith caused their opposition not only to mob law but to violence and capital punishment.[30]

The most visible white advocate for justice in Marion was the city's mayor, Jack Edwards. Youthful and energetic, he had a special relationship with the black community. Absent from town the night of the lynching—an absence some blacks bitterly remembered decades later—Mayor Edwards tried hard to restore order. He worked closely with Flossie Bailey and other NAACP members. He visited the homes of both the Smith and Shipp families and bowed his head to offer sympathy. The *Indianapolis Recorder* claimed that Edwards was "the only official friend of colored Marion." Walter White publicly called the mayor "the only bright spot in official Marion" after Edwards offered full cooperation when White visited the city to investigate the lynching.[31]

Some other whites in Grant County made gestures of support to Flossie Bailey and other blacks. Bailey reported to Walter White the names of several lynchers, as "handed to me by some white people, who of course, do not wish their names revealed." An investigator from the Commission on Interracial Cooperation after studying the Marion lynching noted that "there were many white persons in Marion who looked upon the mob outbreak as an evidence of lawlessness and barbarity, and as absolutely inexcusable," although he also reported that "no group of white people made an organized effort to prevent the lynchings or to secure conviction of the lynchers." But feelings of shame and even gestures of goodwill by sympathetic individual whites were overshadowed by the more visible taunts, threats, and warnings Flossie Bailey and her husband continued to receive. Dr. Bailey was warned not to make house calls at night. He armed himself and continued his work.[32]

Although there was some white support, the burden to push for justice fell heaviest on African Americans and especially on Flossie Bailey and her NAACP friends. It was doubtless true, as a black Indianapolis lawyer wrote Walter White, that "if the Negroes did nothing white people certainly would not." Not all blacks were willing or able to do something, however. As Walter White bitterly wrote a friend, "Unhappily, the brother is still asleep, and the vast majority of them don't care how many lynchings take place as long as they themselves are not incinerated." The National Medical Association met in Indianapolis two weeks after the lynching. This gathering of African American physicians discussed the Marion tragedy but decided, much to Flossie Bailey's regret, not to pass a resolution or take other action. On the other side, few whites would cross the color line to assist unless called, prodded, and pushed by blacks. Usually it fell to a handful of black leaders to do the pushing, to petition the governor, cajole friendly newspapers, and organize meetings. In Marion and in Indiana these were the NAACP leaders above all.[33]

Flossie Bailey continued to build the Marion branch of the NAACP. A meeting on August 26 produced 45 new members. Her major efforts now were statewide, however, as she and Walter White planned the second annual meeting of the Indiana NAACP. Bailey and White sought as keynote speaker for the 1930 meeting Meredith Nicholson, a widely revered Hoosier writer, who in the mid-1920s had condemned the Indiana Klan. ("We are governed by swine," he wrote in 1926.) Nicholson's appearance would "focus attention in some spectacular way upon the inaction at Marion," White hoped. The Hoosier author accepted their invitation, but then, for unknown reasons, reneged. The gathering proceeded in the southern Indiana resort town of French Lick in late October. Held in the Hotel Waddy, a blacks-only hotel (boxer Joe Louis would honeymoon there five years later), there was only one white speaker, Donald F. Carmony, whose remarks were titled "If I Were a Negro." Carmony was a young history professor from Indiana Central College (later renamed the University of Indianapolis). Crossing the color line at the French Lick NAACP convention got him into some warm water with the school's president, who was fearful for the institution's reputation. Walter White came to French Lick to denounce the failure of justice that had followed the lynchings. Indianapolis attorney Robert L. Bailey reported on the work of the legal redress committee, and the assembly passed a resolution of commendation for the efforts Robert L. Bailey and Flossie Bailey had made to push for punishment of the Marion lynchers. The *Indianapolis Recorder* carried full reports of the gathering. The *Marion Chronicle* did not mention the meeting. Indeed, the *Chronicle* generally failed even to notice the existence of the NAACP except to announce in "Colored Notes" a concert by the NAACP chorus at a local church service.[34]

Among potential supporters for racial justice none was more powerful than the Republican Party. It dominated Indiana in the 1920s. Since the days of Abraham Lincoln black Americans had voted Republican. From time to time the party responded with a gesture of support, but not in the Marion lynching. At the national level, President Herbert Hoover refused Walter White's plea to condemn the Marion lynching; at the state level, white Republicans echoed the snub. The close Ku Klux Klan ties to Indiana Republicans had earlier caused a weakening affection for the party among black Hoosiers, which grew weaker still after the Marion tragedy. Some African Americans argued that blacks should abandon the party that refused to push for justice in Marion. They noted that at a Republican barbecue in Linton, Indiana, the state's two U.S. senators and other party leaders spoke, but none mentioned the lynchings. Blacks sympathetic to the Democratic Party reminded their colleagues that it was a Republican governor who snubbed the NAACP delegation and that it was the Grant County Republican chairman, Jake Campbell, who was the cowardly sheriff. Flossie Bailey became increasingly furious with Republican inaction, though she did not fully switch to the Democratic Party for another ten years or so.[35]

There was one major Republican officeholder who broke with his party's ranks. Indiana Attorney General James Ogden was a native-born Hoosier, an 1899 graduate of Harvard Law School, a staunch Presbyterian, and an ambitious Republican. He was also among the many people Flossie Bailey called the night of the lynching. By Saturday morning Ogden had two of his men, Deputy Attorneys General Merle Wall and Earl Stroup, in Marion interviewing witnesses. They also met secretly with Flossie Bailey and other leaders of the Marion NAACP and promised they would do all they could to identify members of the mob. Within a week Bailey was convinced that Attorney General Odgen was the only hope remaining for official justice. Thus began a three-way line of communication, from Bailey to White to Ogden, from local to national to state levels. When Grant County Prosecutor Hardin told Walter Bailey in a sidewalk conversation that it was proving impossible to get witnesses to testify, Flossie Bailey wrote White in New York urging him to act, which then led to a strongly worded letter from White to Ogden. Law enforcement in Marion "has completely broken down," White wrote. "The entire country is watching to see if Indiana has courage and honesty enough to effect the punishment."[36]

There was hope, for Odgen soon stated publicly his differences with Hardin and with Governor Leslie. Ogden told the press that statements by local and state officials that attempts at prosecution would lead to further violence were groundless. The *Indianapolis Times* reported these differences in such a manner as to leave little doubt that Ogden was talking frequently with that liberal paper's reporters. Ogden stayed in contact also with Walter White. Without identifying the NAACP leader, Ogden reported to the press the findings of an undercover investigator that contradicted Sheriff Campbell's version of the events of August 7. Grant County officials were soon furious with Ogden, even getting into a petty dispute over fees owed to a court reporter. Mayor Edwards later called him "a son of a bitch" and "a crusader" who "was trying to make a name for himself."[37]

The many stories that began within hours after the lynching of August 7 came from people as different as Flossie Bailey and Mary Ball, as far apart as Walter White and Harley Hardin. These and other storytellers sought audiences to accept their particular versions and consequently to act or not act, to seek justice or to let pass the events of August 7. There were some whites who sought justice, just as there were blacks who sought to forget and move on with their lives. For most whites, however, it seemed more important to maintain the implicit compact of white solidarity that the lynching had tightened and made more precious. In defending the mob's action or in remaining silent, most whites conformed to the dominant story and thereby agreed to draw deeper the line of color that placed them apart from and above their African American neighbors. The lines of color caused the fundamental differences in the tales told, in the audiences sought, and in what the listeners heard. Color colored everything.

The stories told in newspapers, sidewalk conversations, phone calls, letters, and telegrams were soon to be told in courts of law. Perhaps Lady Justice, standing above the Grant County Courthouse, would be blind to stories colored by color.

CHAPTER SIX

"A Fair Mob"

The stories told in Grant County and around Indiana and the nation about the events of August 7 were eventually told in courts of law. Lady Justice, scale in hand, perched atop the dome of the courthouse, but she lacked sufficient strength or wisdom to punish a single person for the deaths of Tom Shipp and Abe Smith. Inside her courthouse the white community of Grant County used the machinery of justice to state their solidarity, to draw boundaries of separation, and to demonstrate their power over their black neighbors.

"I DIDN'T RECOGNIZE NOBODY"

The first major encounter of law and lynching came when the Court of Inquiry opened before Center Township Justice of the Peace Sturgeon Watson. Held in the Superior Court Room of the Grant County Courthouse, the Court of Inquiry called 30 witnesses in three days of proceedings that began on August 13, 1930. The transcribed record of those days of questions and answers is 317 pages in length and constitutes one of the most fascinating documents resulting from the crimes of August 6 and 7.[1]

Three men asked the questions. Harley Hardin, the county prosecutor, offered only a small number of the hundreds of questions asked of witnesses, and many of his questions related to the crimes along the Mississinewa River on August 6 rather than to the lynching. Hardin took Sheriff Campbell through the details, including the two stickups the gang had allegedly committed the week before, Abe Smith's previous arrest for auto theft, Smith's admission that he assaulted Mary Ball while Cameron held her, and confessions by Smith and Cameron that Shipp shot Deeter. Hardin paid particular attention to details of Mary Ball's alleged rape and to the scratches on her arms and face. The county prosecutor often addressed witnesses by first name, a small-town familiarity that those who testified reciprocated when answering "Harley's" questions.[2]

Merle Wall and Earl Stroup, the outsiders, carried the burden of the inquiry, although a local newspaper claimed they were only assisting Hardin.[3] The two deputy attorneys general had arrived in Marion the day after the lynching and began immediately to gather evidence, assisted by their investigator, Arthur Bruner. Grant County bubbled with rumors of what had happened and who had been involved; even outsiders from Indianapolis had heard some of them. Within a few days Bruner had a list of names and two reports.[4] From the outset Wall and Stroup's style was far more aggressive, more probing, more focused on punishment for the lynching than was Hardin's. Wall and Stroup's questions suggest that even before the proceedings began they had gathered enough evidence to form certain hypotheses and even some conclusions. It is clear also that the two men from the state capital grew increasingly frustrated as Grant County citizens responded to their questions.

Wall and Stroup focused on evidence related to two issues: identity of members of the lynch mob, especially its leaders; and the conduct of law enforcement officials at the Grant County Jail in protecting Shipp and Smith. To gather evidence, they called the eight county and city lawmen who defended the jail when the mob dragged Shipp and Smith out, as well as other citizens who were present that night.

Roy Collins was the first witness. Sworn to tell the truth, like all who followed, Marion's assistant chief of police had stood on the jail steps with Sheriff Jake Campbell and other lawmen to keep the mob from entering. In a conclusion that many other witnesses would repeat, Collins said, "I couldn't tell you a soul that was there." Asked for physical descriptions, Collins responded, "I couldn't describe nobody, it looked to me like a whirling mass of humanity, that is all I can tell you."[5] Charles Bellville, a 16-year veteran of the city police force, was at the jail too, but testified, "I didn't recognize nobody." Pushed harder by Wall and Stroup, Bellville said, "They looked like strangers to me."[6] Many witnesses testified that streetlights were on, that the porch light at the jail was burning, but still it was hard to identify mob members. John O. Fryer, a deputy sheriff who had lived in Marion for 48 years, said, "I never saw so many strange people around here in my life."[7] "They were all strangers to me," testified Frank Neely, a Marion policeman for 17 years.[8] Bert White, deputy sheriff and formerly police chief for a dozen years, had this exchange with Stroup:

Q. You have no doubt talked to a number of people who were spectators there and saw a lot of this.

A. Yes sir.

Q. Who?

A. I couldn't say.

Q. Acquaintances of yours were they?

A. Well, people—business people that were there in the crowds that night and was there on the street: I expect the whole town was down there.

Q. Can you name any particular person?

A. No sir I couldn't name any particular person.[9]

Rumors abounded that many in the mob were from Fairmount, where Claude Deeter and his family lived. Mrs. George Laughlin, who operated the 30th Street Cafe in Marion, told the Court of Inquiry that "all I heard, it was outside people; people around Fairmount was the ones in the mob."[10] But R. F. Parrill, who was in the crowd at the jail, testified otherwise. Parrill worked in his family's Fairmount business, a combination furniture and undertaking establishment that had charge of Claude Deeter's funeral. "I didn't see a single person from Fairmount that I knew," he said.[11] There were rumors too that many in the mob were workers from the Malleable Iron Works, but when investigators asked policeman Chester Marley and others if they recognized anyone from "the Malleable," they said, "no sir."[12] Police Chief Lewis Lindenmuth testified that the mob "was young fellows; they looked like working men," but he could not connect them to the Malleable.[13] Other rumors had a group of 20 or 25 men gathering in a poolroom on the square to plan the lynching, but Charles F. Schick, a poolroom proprietor, absolutely denied that, as did the owner of a cigar store and restaurant where people hung out. That Wall and Stroup had to follow up on such rumors without good evidence indicates how desperate they were for reliable information.

A few witnesses did name names, however, most commonly those of Charles Lennon, Robert Beshire, and Asa Davis. Wall and Stroup had gathered many other names in their own investigations, including their meeting with Flossie Bailey and others from the Marion NAACP. They were particularly interested in identifying a barber named Bailey who, it was rumored, Smith had bitten on the arm as Bailey helped drag him from the jail. Witness after witness claimed not to know this Marion barber.

Part of the challenge of identification was ongoing confusion over the meaning of the word "mob." The word was used frequently and without precise meaning, but in several instances there were efforts to make distinctions among the several thousand people gathered at the Grant County Jail on August 7. Deputy Sheriff John Fryer distinguished between "members of the mob" and "sight seeing people,"[14] as did several other witnesses. But testimony sometimes suggested a blurred line between the mob and the crowd of sightseers.

Stroup demonstrated the problem when he asked policeman Frank Parker, "If the correct definition of mob is anybody who is in the crowd, who does not resist any members of the mob, then did you recognize any members of the mob?" Determined to keep the mob small and usually unidentified, no witness approached Stroup's broad definition which cast blame on all in front of the jail. Mrs. Laughlin denied that two men she knew were members of the mob because "they were in the crowd around the street. . . . I wouldn't say they were any nearer to the colored fellows than we were."[15] City Police Captain Charles Truex suggested there were 25 or 50 people in the mob, but that if he and other officers had resisted with guns and clubs others from the crowd would have joined the mob. Truex's testimony shows the confusion of terms and the fluidity of the word "mob":

Q. There were only twenty-five or fifty on the front porch doing all this clamoring?

A. Yes sir, how many supporters were back of them, you never know.

Q. How many good citizens would have joined with the men on the determined attack on the officers?

A. Good citizens wouldn't be there.

Q. There must have been some good citizens in that mob estimated at a thousand?

A. I don't mean that; I mean those that took an active part.

Q. Do you suppose that if the officers had taken any active steps, that this great massive mob would have actively intervened against the officers?

A. I will answer that this way, here was fifty taking an active part in this lynching, there might have been a hundred and fifty more that wasn't the very best of citizens that would have been willing to back them up.[16]

"IF WE HAD WENT TO SHOOTING"

Wall and Stroup were at least as interested in the issue of protecting the prisoners as identifying mob members. They received from the 30 Grant County witnesses little satisfaction. Sheriff Jake Campbell testified that no one in the mob was armed and that no one struck or injured any of his officers. The sheriff and his men had side arms, but none pointed a revolver at the mob or even drew them from holsters. Nor did they attempt to use their billy clubs. The sheriff said that at one point he told his men to get out several shotguns that were stored in the jail vault, but that he soon ordered them put away; there were women and children in the crowd. (He did not say, as he had told Bruner the day after the lynching, that there were more women than men in front of the jail.)[17] He did not fire also because he had received reports that the mob had dynamite, though no one saw it. To resist with shotguns, Sheriff Campbell concluded, would have raised the "possibility of a race riot."[18] The sheriff did order tear gas but it failed to disperse the crowd.

The eight lawmen at the jail stood shoulder to shoulder to keep the mob off the porch and away from the entrance. But the mob shoved and pushed hard and forced them back. Many officers retreated to the sheriff's residence, which was attached to the jail, leading Stroup to ask several of them: "Why did you all congregate in the sheriff's residence? Why weren't you in the jail proper where the attack was being made?"[19] None had an answer to Stroup's question, other than that there were women in the residence. Women needed protection.

At least two officers were inside the jail. Wall and Stroup elicited from them detailed testimony about the configuration of steel doors, locks, and hallways. The men testified that they refused the mob's demand for keys, but claimed that they had no orders for more forceful resistance. They watched first as the sledgehammers pounded away at locks and doors and then as the mob ran by them to find the three prisoners.

Wall and Stroup repeatedly pushed on what they clearly had concluded was a weak defense of the prisoners. Wall asked Deputy Sheriff John Fryer, "Did it seem strange to you that an unarmed mob should try to face an armed sheriff in a fortified building, unless they had some idea that their task was going to be pretty easy?"[20] Harley Hardin was more accommodating to his Grant County neighbors. In questioning Police Captain Truex, Hardin asked whether he thought the sheriff used good judgement in not drawing weapons. Yes, Truex said, to do that would be to "kill a multitude of good citizens." Hardin extended his concern for loss of life to include African Americans by offering his own statement of the race riot hypothesis: "Would there have been a probability of mob violence, shooting, burning buildings in the colored section, if the aims of the mob had been thwarted here at the jail?"[21] It was an argument Truex and many other whites endorsed, doubtless having in mind such tragedies as the Tulsa race riot of 1921, in which nearly 300 people died.

The lines of color ran through the proceedings of the Court of Inquiry. Nearly every one of the dozens of references to Shipp, Smith, and Cameron included some label of color. Sometimes referred to as "negroes" (uncapitalized by the court stenographer), more often as "colored men," and occasionally as "niggers," the three teenagers were always far in the background of testimony, never humanized by a detail. Other than this persistent label of racial identification, prosecutors and witnesses explicitly raised issues of race on only a few occasions.

On the last day of testimony, as his frustrations mounted, Wall finally asked W. O. Miller, the jailer who watched the sledgehammers smash the steel locks, "Would it have made any difference in your attitude if the men who committed the crime had been white instead of negroes?" "No sir," Miller replied.[22] Captain Truex agreed, but was unusually forthcoming on the subject of race. "This isn't a race question," he said. "If it had been then . . . every nigger in that jail would have been taken out and hanged," which, Truex claimed, was what lynch mobs did in the South. Moreover, "If it hadn't been a fair mob, they would never have brought the fellow Cameron down there with the doubt in their minds as to whether he was or was not guilty." Truex was one of the few witnesses who went beyond short and direct responses. He elaborated further: "they were only asking for two lives and both of them confessed to two of the worst crimes in the history of the county and they were only asking for two lives. If we had went to shooting we would have filled the morgues in Marion before it was through with."[23]

Every witness concluded that the sheriff did the right thing in not using more force to defend the prisoners. As Wall and Stroup pounded away on this issue, the witnesses held firmer than the steel doors on the Grant County jail.[24] The only crack came when theater manager Billy Connors said that the crowd should have been dispersed when it first began to gather. Connors defended Sheriff Campbell, saying that "a lot of innocent people would have been killed" if he had opened fire. But Connors pointed his finger at the city police: "why they even allowed them to gather I can't understand. I have seen time after time in this community here when we had strikes more or less of some serious nature, three or four men were not even allowed to stop in the vicinity of the plant where they were striking at: why they didn't move them when they had a chance to move them, when there wasn't over fifty is more than I can understand."[25]

Wall and Stroup pointed also at two lesser shortcomings of law enforcement. One had to do with Claude Deeter's bloody shirt. The deputy attorneys general wrung from several witnesses testimony that the shirt was clearly visible in a window of City Hall as people passed on Boots Street the morning and afternoon before the lynching. But Police Chief Lindenmuth stated that hanging Deeter's shirt was not a provocative act but rather that it "had a lot of blood on it" and "one of the boys hung it there to dry."[26] No one knew who put the shirt in the window. Billy Connors saw it still hanging the morning after the lynching, by then doubtless fully dry.

The other secondary issue was the prosecutors' interest in why the bodies of Shipp and Smith had been left hanging through the night. Emery Applegate, a reporter for the *Marion Chronicle,* told the Court of Inquiry that when he visited the scene of the lynching he saw several men "who appeared to be guarding the bodies." County Coroner Orlando L. Stout said he walked to the courthouse yard to take the bodies down but that "the temperament of the crowd was such I thought we might as well not make any effort."[27] Several law officers told Wall and Stroup that they went to the courthouse yard to see the bodies but that they had not attempted to cut them down. Nor did they recognize anyone in the crowd there. Chief Lindenmuth admitted that after police from nearby cities arrived there was sufficient force to cut the bodies down but that it was not done.

On the last day of the Court of Inquiry Harley Hardin told the local press that "it was proving difficult to obtain evidence."[28] Grant County Judge O. D. Clawson agreed and refused to issue warrants for mob members: the evidence gathered should be presented first to a grand jury. As Flossie Bailey looked ahead to the grand jury, she was more hopeful. Leaders of the lynch mob were apprehensive, she wrote Walter White, and "it would take only a small amount of grilling to make them confess, if they cared to make the effort." To increase the effort, she had White again pressure Attorney General Ogden: "Feeling among both white and colored citizens of repute of Marion is still one of great doubt as to whether anything will be done by the local authorities and the conviction is even more strongly expressed that real results will come only through your office," White wrote Ogden.[29]

The Grant County Grand Jury convened on September 3 and met 15 times before adjourning October 9. Many of the witnesses who had testified at the Court of Inquiry were summoned, but many additional names were added, including "Mrs. Dr. Bailey" and Mary Ball.[30] There were early indications of the direction of the proceedings. In a speech to the Kiwanis Club in nearby Peru, Attorney General Ogden criticized the selection of the six-member grand jury by stating that three of them were from Fairmount, Deeter's hometown, which was "not a mere coincidence." The *Indianapolis Times* predicted that Ogden "will proceed by affidavit if the present Grant County grand jury fails to act."[31] The six men listened to the evidence and found no reason to present indictments. They praised Sheriff Campbell in familiar words: "had he acted differently it is more than probable that a race riot would have ensued and several innocent people would have been injured or killed."[32]

A week after the grand jury report, Attorney General Odgen brought indictments on his own against seven Marion residents he had reason to believe were mob leaders. Ogden invited Hardin to join in signing the affidavits but the county prosecutor refused. Ogden also filed impeachment charges against Sheriff Campbell, seeking his removal from office and a fine of $1,000. Procedure required the sheriff to deliver the warrant for his own arrest to County Coroner Stout to serve. Following the arrest Judge Clawson released the sheriff on his own recognizance. Asked if his arrest would hurt the Republican Party in the November elections, since he was the party's county chairman, Campbell responded, "Not a bit; it will help, if anything."[33]

Anticipating negative local response to outside pressure, Ogden carefully explained to the press that "It is not a matter of the state meddling or not meddling with local affairs in communities." Odgen claimed he had no choice: Indiana law required that he prosecute. Ogden's aggressive move, whether required or not, did not have the support of Indiana Governor Harry G. Leslie and met with open hostility from L. O. Chasey, the governor's secretary. The rift within the Republican state leadership was now wide open.[34]

"12 GOOD AND LAWFUL MEN"

The first trial began on December 29 with charges brought against Robert Beshire. Beshire owned a restaurant at Fourth and Branson Streets and had recently been arrested for liquor violations and for keeping a gambling house. A native of Turkey, he had not yet become a United States citizen, a fact his lawyer repeatedly told potential jurors should not be held against him. Jury selection lasted nearly three days and required examination of nearly 100 citizens, because most Grant County men did not want to serve. Women were not invited to serve.[35] The twelve white jurors eventually gathered included nine farmers, one clerk, one church pastor, and one real estate dealer. In a crowded courtroom, with people—including several African American observers—standing against the walls, Beshire claimed that he was a sightseer in the crowd and not a member of the mob on August 7. Beshire testified that his hand was cut when he was attacked by some of the mob who believed he was an African American, a story a defense witness supported. Ogden's deputies, Wall and Stroup, prosecuted. They called 17 witnesses, including Sheriff Campbell and others at the jail that night. Two policemen identified Beshire as a member of the mob, but none of the other state witnesses did so.

The jury deliberated 30 minutes. When foreman J. W. Westfall read the verdict of acquittal the jammed courtroom erupted in strong sympathy. Many rushed to congratulate Beshire. Flossie Bailey had kept Walter White informed as the trial proceeded. Even on the first day she told White that there was little chance of conviction but that there was "something gained that we are having a trial."[36]

A second trial followed Beshire's acquittal. Charles Lennon was a 30-year-old taxi driver with a record of several arrests and a reputation for having a hot temper and a big mouth. Proceedings began before Judge O. D. Clawson on February 23, 1931. Obtaining a jury was an even larger challenge; 127 men who were called sought and found reasons to disqualify themselves. The court desperately considered extending its jury pool outside Grant County but eventually found "12 good and lawful men"—ten farmers, a bridge contractor, and a blacksmith. Witnesses in the Beshire trial had named Lennon as an active leader of the mob. Now Wall brought seven witnesses who testified to that effect, some who saw Lennon leading the mob on the steps, others who saw him inside the jail. Among those pointing the finger at Lennon were Drysdale Brannon, well-known Marion reporter, and City Police Chief Lewis Lindenmuth. Lennon's lawyers did not have him testify, but his brother-in-law, his wife, and his mother-in-law walked to the stand to swear that he was indeed in the crowd at the jail but he left before the actual lynching.

In his closing argument Wall made a forceful case for conviction but asked the jury for 2 to 21 years in prison rather than life or the electric chair. The jury deliberated through a long afternoon and evening and once told Judge Clawson that they were split 11-1. As they debated more than a dozen lawmen guarded the courthouse because rumors had circulated that Lennon's friends would take violent action if he were found guilty. After 18 hours of deliberation the jury reported its verdict. The one unidentified holdout changed his vote to acquittal.

Lennon was free. That night, a Saturday night, there were celebrations "all over town," Flossie Bailey reported, celebrations of "the terrible mockery of calling him not guilty."[37]

Bailey always knew the odds of conviction were slim. She wrote on March 3 that "we should not lay down under the injustices without a big fight, and even if we cannot win, we at least have our own self-respect." Before Lennon's trial she had invited William Pickens of the NAACP to Marion to help give courage to Marion's blacks and to keep the pressure on local whites. Pickens reported on his visit in an article published in the *Nation*. "It was astonishing," he wrote, "to see and feel the mob atmosphere that still prevailed nearly seven months after the murder." Formerly cordial relationships between blacks and whites in Grant County were now marked by suspicion on both sides. Threats circulated that blacks would suffer recriminations if Lennon were convicted, even though no African American was called as a witness, a member of the jury, or in any other capacity in either of the trials. Flossie and Walter Bailey continued to receive threatening telephone calls. Pickens stayed at their house on his Marion visit, and he too received harassing calls. Whites drove through streets where blacks lived and deliberately caused their automobiles to backfire.[38]

There was considerable discouragement among Grant County African Americans. "The majority of them," Flossie Bailey wrote, thought "what is the use of trying to get something done when we know that it is useless." Few bothered to attend the opening of Lennon's trial. Refusing to give up, Pickens and Bailey organized a meeting of the Marion NAACP branch to encourage members to attend Lennon's trial rather than leave "the whole spiritual domination of the courtroom to the mob." For the last three days of Lennon's trial black faces looked quietly and solemnly toward the judge and jury. On the last day, 20 Grant County blacks, including the regal Flossie Bailey, sat in the courtroom among hundreds of whites. They stayed to the end. It was, Pickens thought, an act of great courage. It was doubtless part of the reason the Southern Commission on the Study of Lynching reported that in all the nation's lynchings in 1930, "only in Marion did Negroes voice a protest."[39]

In mid-March, just over seven months after the deaths of Claude Deeter, Tom Shipp, and Abe Smith, Attorney General Ogden announced that he was dropping the indictments against the other men charged with being part of the mob and also against Sheriff Campbell. The acquittal of Beshire and Lennon left little likelihood of conviction in the other cases, Ogden concluded. The two were not among the most stalwart or upstanding of Marion's citizens but rather were closer to the margins of the local community, doubtless one reason Ogden and his deputies selected them for prosecution. If Beshire and Lennon could not be convicted it was unlikely anyone else would be.

This surrender brought "to a close the final chapter in the case," the *Indianapolis Recorder* stated. The African American newspaper congratulated Ogden, Wall, and Stroup "for having tried their level best to perform their official duty." However, "the lack of cooperation of Grant County citizens with the State authorities in prosecuting the case was disgracefully miserable." Grant County, the *Recorder* charged, was still "saturated with the poisonous spirit of the chivalrous Knights of the Kerosene Kan." Newspaper articles from across Indiana and across the nation, clipped for the Tuskegee Institute files, showed African American and many general-circulation papers offering negative portrayals of the community in which no one in the lynch mob was ever brought to justice.[40]

The Grant County Courthouse was the stage on which whites expressed their solidarity as a community, a white community different from blacks. Even those white citizens who might have thought it an "unfair mob" kept largely silent as the color lines were drawn, lines that created boundaries that had to be maintained, lines more important to them than the rule of law. Implicit in the majority voice was the assumption that the mob of August 7 had carried out the will of the people, that the lynching represented the traditions of pioneer democracy, of popular will, of higher law. It was a fair mob.[41]

Local juries, prosecutors, and judges spoke for this popular will and higher law. And they spoke for the powerful community of color, or, as they saw it, of no color. Lady Justice continued through the 1930s to grace the courthouse dome. It fell to another woman, a real woman, to try to balance the scales.

CHAPTER SEVEN

"All Over Now"

A 1931 report titled *Lynchings and What They Mean* concluded that "after a time, the 'best citizens' usually come to feel that 'it is all over now, and the sooner it is forgotten, the better for the community.'"[1] Neither for Flossie Bailey nor for James Cameron was the Marion lynching over.

"WHAT A WOMAN!"

Her spirit and energy burst off the pages in the dozens of letters Flossie Bailey wrote to NAACP leaders in Indiana and the organization's national office in New York City. Often ill during the 1930s, she continued her correspondence. From her sickbed she wrote William Pickens, NAACP national field secretary, to outline upcoming branch meetings in Marion, French Lick, and Evansville, and to ask, almost demand, that he appear at each as guest speaker. She was "trying to keep as quiet as possible," she wrote Pickens, so she could attend the annual meeting in St. Louis. Pickens had seen many such letters from Mrs. Bailey, but he couldn't resist scribbling on the top of this one, "What a woman! If only we had 1 in every town!"[2]

Flossie Bailey began her long and hard struggle to organize the fight against racism as early as 1918, when she led the effort to form a Marion branch of the NAACP. That first effort failed. Over the next two decades she experienced many failures, including her determined struggle to punish members of the mob that lynched Tom Shipp and Abe Smith. In the months between the lynching of August 1930 and the last trial in February 1931 Bailey's primary energies focused on obtaining legal justice. That work won her the Madam C. J. Walker Medal, a national honor given "to the person who has done the best work in the NAACP during the year."[3] At the same time, however, Bailey broadened her efforts far beyond the lynching and far beyond Grant County.

Flossie Bailey was an organization builder, using telephone, telegraph, letters, and face-to-face meetings to create and invigorate NAACP branches across Indiana in the early 1930s. She was a "born leader," "very cultured," "a good-looking woman," Harley Burden, Jr., later recalled. Poised and articulate, she always dressed in fine clothing and stylish hats. Her heroic role in the lynching story gave her credibility and visibility, and her elevation to state president of the NAACP in 1930 gave her a pulpit, but her main source of success was a constant attention to the hundreds of details necessary to build civil rights organizations across the state. In December 1930 she began working closely with Pickens and Robert Bagnall, national director of NAACP branches, to plan a spring organizing campaign in Indiana. Bailey identified the communities with the best potential for action and made the initial contacts so that the New York organizers could follow up. In late February 1931 Bagnall spoke in Indianapolis, Anderson, Muncie, Kokomo, Marion, Terre Haute, and Evansville, while Bailey continued to report to New York of mass meetings, baby contests, fundraisers, and dues paid in Crawfordsville, French Lick, Greencastle, South Bend, and Gary.[4]

Bailey's net broadened to include young people as well as adults. She created a youth division of the Marion branch, which functioned through the 1930s. In 1934, for example, the local branch organized a program for Negro History Week at Marion High School. Three students conducted the school's morning assembly: Joe Casey spoke about Booker T. Washington, Walter Charles Bailey, Flossie's son, spoke on the history of the NAACP, and Harley Burden, Jr., presented a vocal solo.[5]

Another initiative from Flossie Bailey was "to try to associate with the state conference some prominent white people of the state, just as the National Office has the prominent people of the country."[6] One result was her invitation to Attorney General James M. Ogden to speak at the NAACP state convention in October 1931. Ogden praised the civil rights organization and its leaders and then spoke mostly about the Marion lynching. He strongly condemned Grant County Sheriff Jake Campbell, whom he called "spineless," and Prosecuting Attorney Harley Hardin, who Ogden told the audience was "weaker even than had been anticipated." The lynching, he concluded, was "a sorry tale of defeated justice; it is in fact a travesty of justice."[7]

The major purpose of Bailey's early organizing efforts was to force the state of Indiana to pass a serious antilynching bill. Indiana had enacted antilynching legislation as early as 1899; that, along with a more committed political leadership, had seemed to put an end to lynching in the state after 1903. The campaign for stronger laws continued nonetheless in the state and across the nation, especially in the years immediately after World War I, when racial tensions and violence flared. The NAACP was the primary leader, assisted by black churches, newspapers, and clubs. NAACP strategy was to investigate and publicize each lynching and to urge state governments to pass legislation that held the sheriff responsible for stopping a lynch mob. To the NAACP national leadership the Marion lynching was just another chapter in a long book of tragedy; not unique, but more notable because it happened in the North rather than Mississippi, Georgia, or Alabama.[8]

For Flossie Bailey and other Hoosiers the campaign to pass an Indiana antilynching law was a way of responding to a local tragedy within the framework of law and justice. After Indiana Democrats introduced a strong antilynching bill in the House in February 1931, Bailey organized and chaired a mass meeting in Indianapolis of state NAACP members. When opponents stripped the bill of its teeth, claiming that such laws were unenforceable if the people were determined to have vengeance, Bailey wrote to every branch in the state and to leaders of black lodges, clubs, and churches urging them to badger their state senators. Bagnall traveled the state and combined branch organizing with pushing for the bill's passage. The NAACP official spoke not only to local branches on the subject but also to white organizations such as Optimist Clubs,

Exchange Clubs, and Democratic Party organizations and to committees and individual members of the state legislature. This political maneuvering and grass-roots pressure caused the effective provisions of the bill to be reinserted, and a bill with teeth was passed and signed by the governor in March 1931. The new law provided for the immediate dismissal of any sheriff from whose jail a prisoner was lynched. The fact of a lynching was alone sufficient evidence for firing. In addition, the 1931 law provided that the family of any person lynched could sue for damages up to $10,000. By passage of this law, the *Indianapolis Recorder* exulted, "Indiana has automatically retrieved its high status as a safe place in which to live."[9]

The antilynching law passed just after officials admitted defeat in their effort to convict members of the Grant County mob and after they dropped charges against Sheriff Jake Campbell. To see mob members and the sheriff go unpunished broke Flossie Bailey's heart. In reporting her unhappiness to Pickens she ended her sad letter confident that the new antilynching law would have an effect on Sheriff Campbell's successors, making them at least "a little more careful." Among Bailey's many strengths was an ability to find some positive note in the midst of defeat. And always she looked ahead to more battles, trying in the next legislative session to amend the state constitution so that the prosecution could seek a change of venue and thereby form a jury less influenced by local passions and community ties.[10]

Bailey and her NAACP colleagues worked hard also for a federal antilynching law. This was an old struggle that always foundered on the rocks of lack of interest and fear of overweening national government power. The Marion lynching gave proponents of national legislation new ammunition. Several Indiana newspapers joined NAACP leaders to claim that because local and state officials had not done their jobs in Marion the federal government must step in. Moreover, as the *Indianapolis Times* editorialized, "The problem is not alone southern or sectional; it is national. Indiana recently made its contribution to the list." Federal legislation was necessary.[11]

Flossie Bailey threw herself into the fight for the federal antilynching bill. In spring 1934, for example, she reported to Walter White that the Marion NAACP youth division had organized and sent to Indiana's congressional delegation a "petition signed by most of the young people's organizations both white and colored in the city, including [youth from the] YWCA, high school, [and] Marion College." She also called the local newspaper editor, who published an editorial favoring the federal bill, wired President Franklin Roosevelt, and sent materials to the Marion Lions and Kiwanis Clubs, which promised to wire the president.[12]

Tougher laws might deter mob violence, but also important were more courageous responses by white and black Hoosiers when mob rule threatened. A good demonstration of such in Marion came in early August 1937, almost seven years to the day of the anniversary of the lynching. Flossie Bailey reported the events to Walter White: "rumors and threats were made to take 3 colored young men out last night, from the jail, where they were serving a 30 day sentence on a statutory charge in which two white women were also arrested." The sheriff wanted to "fight it out once and for all" with the gathering mob, but "several of the leading white and colored citizens insisted on him taking" the prisoners to the state reformatory at Pendleton for safekeeping. Indiana Governor M. Clifford Townsend stayed in close touch ready to send aid if necessary.

Most impressive, Bailey reported, "about 100 colored men, serious, sober and armed, gathered in the down-town district, ready for whatever might occur." Here, she concluded, "was one of the finest demonstrations of determination to protect themselves I have ever seen and served as a complete dampener to the mob spirit."[13] It was a very different course of events from that of seven years earlier. History did not repeat itself in Marion.

Flossie Bailey's fight for racial equality went far beyond lynching, to dozens of cases of injustice. She took up the cause of racial discrimination in Indiana hospitals, particularly at Indiana University's Robert W. Long Hospital in Indianapolis, which did not admit black patients or allow black medical students to train on its floors. She attacked the "increasing tendency to have separate schools," a drift in "alarming proportions" toward more school segregation. She and her husband brought suit against a Marion movie theater after they were denied admission because they were black. The couple insisted on a jury trial, which ruled against Flossie Bailey. They then drove Dr. Bailey's case all the way to the Indiana Supreme Court, which ruled that "We can not agree with the appellant [Dr. Bailey] that the exclusion of a person from a theater because of his race or color gives such person a right of action under the common law of this state." In fighting her battles, Mrs. Bailey pushed the national NAACP office to provide financial support for lawyers taking on civil rights cases in Indiana. And she never forgot about her nemesis, Jake Campbell, now former sheriff. When Campbell attempted to secure appointment as postmaster of Marion, Bailey fired off letters to Indiana's two senators, to Walter White, and others to stop the appointment. Jake Campbell found other work. It was largely though not entirely due to her efforts that the report to the national NCAAP board in November 1931 singled out Indiana as "developing an able and militant leadership in the Association."[14]

All this activity Flossie Bailey conducted from her home on South Adams Street, the official address of the Indiana state NAACP office as long as she was president. Her husband and son clearly supported her, but the family was often concerned about the consequences of her immense NAACP commitments. Her health was precarious; she had serious heart problems. In 1934 she was in bed for six months and finally entered the local hospital. The day before her surgery, she was strong enough to hand write a long letter to Walter White reporting on Indiana activities and promising him that "if I live, as soon as I am well, I will surely bring our branch up in all [financial] obligations." Her son, Walter Charles, was also not well and had an operation in late 1930 from which he recovered slowly. And her husband, a busy medical doctor who clearly supported his wife's goals, doubtless did not always receive the care and attention middle-class married men were accustomed to in the 1930s. Perhaps he grumbled a bit. Pickens wrote him after Flossie received the Walker Medal to ensure the doctor's continued support of both the cause and his wife's ambition. "Not only Mrs. Bailey and you, but also Walter Charles deserved a medal for the courage of your life in Marion," Pickens wrote. The NAACP official acknowledged that "you and Walter Charles have had to sacrifice much because of her pre-occupation or absences from home. I hope, however, that we will be fortunate enough to have her continue as State President for at least another year."[15]

In addition to these personal challenges, Flossie Bailey's ongoing work for racial justice struggled against three major burdens of American life in the 1930s. One was the Great Depression, the worst long-term economic suffering the American people had ever known. As always, African Americans suffered the most, which caused serious hardship in collecting dues and raising money for civil rights activities. The struggle to put food on the table left most Grant County blacks little time or energy for NAACP meetings and civil rights causes, a source of constant regret for Flossie Bailey, who again and again shouldered the burdens nearly alone. Always, it seemed, there were distractions, some as terrible as the 1937 flood, which Bailey reported, "is a terrible, terrible situation, and as usual those things hurt our people worse."[16]

The second obstacle facing Bailey was gender, male and female. Nearly all her colleagues in leadership positions in the state and national NAACP were men, black men who might have been reluctant to have a strong woman join the fight. Yet the NAACP correspondence and records show consistent high regard and respect for this Marion woman. Doubtless Bailey benefited from her marriage to a professional man who shared her goals, and, of course, from the obvious high quality of her talents and commitments. It would have been a foolish man, white or black, who took her lightly.

Perhaps being a woman was even an asset at times. Bailey could be a bit more outspoken than a black man. She could take a few more risks in the assumption that although many whites might approve of Jim Crow segregation and might even condone mob terror, the codes of American civilization generally protected women from violence, even black women. Still, Flossie Bailey was an uppity woman. She endured both subtle and direct threats. She had reason to fear for her safety on numerous occasions.

The final challenge facing Bailey was race. The lines of color were always there, always limiting her choices, always skewing the outcome. There is evidence of some modest progress in blurring the lines of color in antilynching legislation, in the dramatic increase in NAACP branches across the state, in white involvement in some NAACP activities, and particularly in helping to prevent another lynching in Marion in 1937. Bailey knew more defeats than successes, however. Yet she "held her head high and set an example for everyone," one old friend remembered decades later.[17] She soldiered on, seeking change, pushing herself and others, always with her eye on the prize, on the possibility that Lady Justice would indeed balance the scales for Grant County and for America.

The long years of the Great Depression took their toll on all Americans, including the Baileys. By the late 1930s Dr. Walter Bailey was in bad health. Around 1940 he suffered a stroke and closed his medical practice. The couple fell on such hard times that friends had to help them financially. The Baileys moved to Indianapolis, where Dr. Bailey died in 1950. Two years later Flossie Bailey died. The couple's remains were interred in a Marion cemetery.[18]

Flossie Bailey's last letter in the NAACP Papers at the Library of Congress is an apology to Walter White written in early 1941, a regret that she could not do more and a hope that other capable leaders would take over the local and state organizations. That simple letter is one of her many legacies. Walter White never forgot her. At her death he wrote, "never did I see greater courage and integrity than was displayed by herself and her late husband as they demonstrated in the Marion riot." She was, White concluded, "a courageous and gallant lady."[19]

JAMES CAMERON AND CLASS JUSTICE

While Flossie Bailey attempted to seek convictions of members of the lynch mob, others in Grant County wanted James Cameron punished.[20] The 16-year-old Cameron was the third person (with Shipp and Smith) arrested for the murder of Claude Deeter and the rape of Mary Ball. According to Sheriff Campbell, Cameron confessed. "We didn't have to question him very much," Campbell had testified at the Court of Inquiry. "He held the girl, tried to hold her mouth shut to keep her from hollering," Campbell said. Cameron told the sheriff he feared that Deeter would recognize him because Deeter had been a customer at his shoeshine stand downtown, so Cameron gave Shipp the gun and ran from the scene before any shooting started.[21] Whether because of his claim of limited involvement or because of the luck of being the third prisoner dragged from the jail on August 7, Cameron was spared the lynchers' rope to face instead the Indiana criminal justice system.

The Grant County Grand Jury heard testimony from Sheriff Campbell, Mary Ball, and other witnesses and proceeded quickly to indict Cameron for murder in the first degree while perpetrating robbery; murder in the first degree, accessory before the fact; rape in the first degree; and first-degree rape, accessory before the fact. In addition, the grand jury also indicted Cameron for another armed robbery committed on August 2 with a young black accomplice, Robert Sullivan.

It was plainly evident that many in Grant County wanted a conviction that included the full penalty of death in the Michigan City electric chair. Who would defend Cameron? Who would see that he got the fair trial that Shipp and Smith never received?

One possible source of defense was the radical left wing in American politics and labor. Soon after the lynching, members of the American Negro Labor Congress in Gary and Indiana Harbor sent telegrams to Governor Harry G. Leslie to "protest the brutal lynching of the two Negro workers Thomas Shipp and Abraham [sic] Smith . . . by a mob incited by false reports and lies spread by the mayor, the sheriff and other city officials." From Chicago 65 delegates of the International Labor Defense (ILD) resolved "to send their indignant working class protest against the lynching of Negro workers Shipp and Smith . . . by the fascist mob."[22]

But the International Labor Defense did more than send a telegram to the Indiana governor. With headquarters in New York, ILD was closely connected to the American Communist Party and had as its purpose providing defense of workers imprisoned in the nation's class wars. In 1930 this leftist organization began a new initiative to reach African American workers. Legal defense efforts by the NAACP were directed against racism and racial injustice; for the ILD the issue was capitalist oppression and class injustice. For the former the goal was to provide racial equality by working through the American legal and political system; for the latter the hope was to overthrow that corrupt system through class revolution.[23]

Two members of the ILD's Chicago office arrived in Marion on August 26 to conduct their own investigation of the lynching. They reported interviews with 13 residents, nearly all African Americans. While all those interviewed condemned the lynching, some were not very sympathetic to a left-wing labor organization: Maggie Fulton, a black cook in the local hospital, had a "petty business outlook," the two organizers lamented, though they were hopeful she might be persuaded to join the American Negro Labor Congress. William Holder seemed more supportive. He was a factory worker and Apostolic preacher with a "proletarian congregation" located on East Third Street in "the most proletarian neighborhood in the city of both white and Negroes." But Holder was "extremely religious" and, in the end, not very sympathetic. Gertrude

Hoovis reported the "colored news" for the local newspaper and knew many people, but she was loyal to the NAACP and therefore should "not be taken into confidence on the matter of the A.N.L.C." Others were more sympathetic, including a Mr. Baker, who was a "very militant foundry worker, very bitter against Campbell and the Republican party."[24]

After talking with Marion residents the Chicago investigators concluded that Deeter, Smith, Shipp, Cameron, and Mary Ball were all members of a highway robbery gang and that a falling out between Deeter and Smith resulted in Deeter's death. There was no rape of Mary Ball; in fact, they reported, she and Smith were "on very intimate terms and wore each other's jewelry." Sheriff Campbell and others spread the false rumors of rape in order to encourage "fascist organizations" to carry out the lynching. There was proof of the "complicity of the police forces" in hanging the bloody shirt from a City Hall window and in directing the mob to the "unlocked" cells. The Chicago investigators also condemned black leaders: Flossie Bailey and Walter White did not push very hard to identify the lynchers and then refused legal assistance to Cameron.[25]

With these findings as rallying calls the ILD planned a series of mass meetings in Marion and across the Midwest to "stress the needs of workers, Negro and white, to organize together for defense against lynching and all other forms of discrimination and exploitation." Black and white workers must understand that lynching was a form of "class persecution." Class, not race, was the issue. ILD organizers "must be able to analyze to the white workers the basic cause of lynching and the necessity of organizing Negro workers into the same unions and other organizations on the basis of full equality."[26]

As part of the ILD effort to use the Marion lynching to explain class differences and encourage workers to unite under their proletarian umbrella, the two Chicago investigators made a special effort to win over James Cameron's family. They talked to his mother, Vera Burden, who lived on West 31st Street, and to Cameron's sister, Marie, and her husband, George Carter, who lived in nearby Anderson. The three promised to attend future International Labor Defense meetings, perhaps to come to Chicago to be interviewed further. But the family refused the key request of the Chicago organizers, to allow the ILD to provide free legal counsel for James. His mother was the key. "Every effort must be made to propagandize her and secure her consent for the I.L.D. to defend her boy," they advised their Chicago office.[27]

James Cameron's family rejected the ILD, as did most workers in Marion and across the Midwest. Even in the depth of the Great Depression, few were prepared to accept such intense class-based analysis of the lynching or of anything else in American life. Few believed that class overrode race as the determining factor in lynchings. Few could see an America in which black and white workers could unite to fight against lynching or anything else. Ultimately, for Cameron's family, the NAACP, dedicated to racial not class goals, seemed to offer a far better chance of obtaining justice for the teenager awaiting trial.

CAMERON'S BLACK LAWYERS

At first the NAACP refused to assist James Cameron. Flossie Bailey wrote Walter White that "the case of the Cameron boy, we have, of course, definitely decided, is not a branch case." White responded in agreement. Cameron had already confessed his guilt. The NAACP could not afford financially or politically to fight losing legal battles. White's treasury was nearly empty; his dues-paying members were blowing away in the storm of the Great Depression. Bailey's warm heart would not allow abandonment of Cameron, however; she helped organize an informal local fundraising to assist Vera Burden in paying legal expenses for her son.[28]

Sometime in the days that followed the NAACP's refusal to defend Cameron, Bailey and White changed their minds. Their reasons are unclear. Perhaps they were moved by the widespread assumption among whites that the 16-year-old should be sent to the electric chair.[29] Perhaps the entry of the International Labor Defense into Marion caused fear that this Communist organization would bleed publicity and support from the NAACP.[30] Whatever the reasons, the NAACP reversed its stand and took up Cameron's case. To the youth's good fortune, perhaps even his survival, the decision brought to the courtroom the full talents of the two best lawyers a black defendant in Indiana could hope for: Robert L. Bailey and Robert L. Brokenburr.

African American lawyers were the key agents of change in the American civil rights movement of the first half of the twentieth century. Increasingly better educated and committed to civil rights, many black lawyers aligned with the NAACP to use the nation's laws and ideals of equality as weapons against the lines of color. Through hundreds of court cases black lawyers gradually blurred some of those lines and helped America move toward realization of its professed commitment to legal equality. Indiana had only a handful of black lawyers, just over 50 by 1940, with about half practicing in Indianapolis. Attorneys Bailey and Brokenburr were among the most prominent in the state and among the new generation of civil rights lawyers that emerged in the 1930s. Many would carry the struggle into the 1950s and beyond.[31]

Robert Lieutenant Bailey was born in Alabama in 1885 but like many other young and ambitious African Americans moved north after graduating from Alabama's Talladega College. In 1912 he received a degree from the Indiana Law School in Indianapolis, where he studied with James Ogden. Ogden became Bailey's patron, sponsoring his admission to the Indianapolis Bar Association, of which Bailey was for many years the only black member. In 1931 Ogden appointed him as his assistant attorney general. The two men were very close professionally, though Ogden never visited the Bailey family home. Hundreds of black friends often did. Many from out of town stayed overnight. The family joked that Mellie Bailey once gave her husband a set of dinner dishes for his birthday because Walter White was coming to stay and the dinner party would be huge.

Everyone knew Robert L. Bailey (no relation to Flossie Bailey), and everyone called him R. L., even his wife. He was a gregarious man, with dark skin and high cheekbones. Often talk around the dinner table was about his work as president of the Indianapolis branch of the NAACP, the activities of the state NAACP Executive Committee, or a case he was trying—all too many of which, his wife thought, brought little or no fee money. R. L. liked to tell stories and jokes, too, sometimes "earthy" in style, and to recite the poetry of Paul Lawrence Dunbar. He drank heavily and smoked cigars, laughing or frowning as his small eyeglasses without earpieces teetered on his nose. He never cared much about his clothing or appearance, but he knew the value of work, often toiling late amidst the cigar smoke and disarray of his Pennsylvania Street office. His wooden rolltop desk was always piled high with papers, and although he could never find anything, neither his secretary nor family was allowed to touch a single thing.

On his office wall was a framed *Chicago Defender* cartoon of him carrying a large briefcase. He died of a stroke working in that office in 1940.[32]

R. L. Bailey shared the Pennsylvania Street office with Robert L. Brokenburr. Brokenburr was born in Virginia in 1886. After graduating from Howard Law School in 1909, he moved to Indianapolis. He became closely connected to Madam C. J. Walker's cosmetics company, one of the most successful black-owned businesses in America, and he served during the 1920s as a Marion County deputy prosecuting attorney. Like R. L. Bailey, he was a Republican, standing in the long line of black Republicans dating back to the days of Abraham Lincoln. And like R. L., he was a member of the Indiana NAACP Executive Board. But Brokenburr was much more serious in demeanor than the man with whom he shared a three-office suite. Tall, lean, and always well dressed, Brokenburr never swore, seldom showed a sense of humor, and loved to listen to classical music. He was "every inch a gentleman, extraordinarily courteous" with a "melodious voice," R. L.'s daughter recalled. Unlike his associate, Brokenburr lived until 1974, long enough to enjoy the accolades that came in the 1950s and 1960s to longtime civil rights activists. Opposites in many ways, Brokenburr and Bailey made a team unmatched.[33]

Flossie Bailey's telephone calls of alarm kept R. L. Bailey awake through much of the night of the lynching. R. L. and Brokenburr traveled to Marion on the Sunday following the lynching and on their own agreed to help Cameron. They were among those who made the unhappy visit to the Indiana governor on August 20. R. L. Bailey led the effort to get and keep his mentor, Attorney General James Odgen, seriously committed to the lynching case, a commitment Flossie Bailey and others thought essential if there was to be any hope of convictions.[34]

Concerned citizens and committed NAACP leaders, the two black Indianapolis lawyers were repulsed by the Marion lynching, but they were also professionals who wanted financial compensation for their legal talent. What to pay them was a source of concern for Flossie Bailey and Walter White, and almost certainly for R. L.'s wife as well. White dragged his feet on legal fees, doubtless because he had so little money, but Flossie Bailey pleaded the lawyers' case in very effective arguments. They had no wish to "charge a regular fee," she wrote White. And she asserted that "the State work could never have progressed as it has in Indiana, had it not been for the very fine help and counsel of both of these attorneys." They worked selflessly. "In the beginning of this trouble, I asked them to do all they could to help us, which they did; nothing was said about recompense by either of us, but they feel that some consideration is due them." White eventually agreed and sent a check for $100 to Mrs. Bailey to support expenses in defending Cameron. It was money well spent.[35]

The first victory for attorneys Bailey and Brokenburr was to win a change of venue for James Cameron. He would never receive a fair trial in Grant County, they believed, where assumptions of his guilt and expectations of his death in the electric chair were widely held. Marion newspapers had reminded readers that the death sentence was mandatory in a conviction of murder while perpetrating a robbery. The change of venue moved the trial and the prisoner to adjacent Madison County and to the courthouse in Anderson. It was Cameron's good fortune. His mother, to whom he was very close, had moved to Anderson and could visit him there more frequently than in Pendleton. In Anderson too he met the county sheriff, Bernard Bradley. Tall and slim, with blue eyes and sandy hair, Bradley often walked around the jailhouse singing "The Old Rugged Cross," a favorite hymn of many Klansmen in the early 1920s. Yet Bradley treated Cameron with a Christian kindness he had never before experienced from a white person and allowed him all manner of special privileges. Decades later Cameron asserted that Sheriff Bradley "was nothing but the Spirit of God walking around with a badge on his bosom." The sheriff's kindness eased Cameron's struggles with nightmares of the lynching of Shipp and Smith and the terror of coming so close to death himself. And there was the wild response of his stepfather, Hezikiah Burden, who several weeks after the lynching went on a shooting spree that wounded Cameron's 18-year-old sister, Marie, and two Marion policemen. Police fired a hundred shots at Burden, including shotgun blasts and machine gun bursts, before wounding and capturing him. As rumors of mob violence flared, police rushed Burden to the Pendleton reformatory where he was safe until his trial and sentencing to one-to-ten years in the Michigan City penitentiary.[36]

James Cameron's trial opened on June 29, 1931, to a packed courtroom. To allow passions to subside, Bailey and Brokenburr had delayed the trial as long as possible by working slowly and carefully. They spent three days selecting jury members, as Bailey carefully questioned potential members and refused to accept many. Finally, with a jury of 12 men sitting, the lawyers made their opening statements. The prosecuting attorney, Grant County's Harley Hardin, vigorously called for a guilty verdict but demanded life imprisonment rather than a death sentence for the teenager.

Sitting through a blistering heat wave, with the temperature topping 100 degrees, the jury heard witnesses that included Mary Ball, Jake Campbell, and Claude Deeter's father, William. Former Sheriff Jake Campbell was first on the stand. He testified that Cameron confessed the night of his arrest that he held Mary Ball while Abe Smith raped her. Marion newspaperman Drysdale Brannon told the jury that he was present to hear Cameron's confession. R. L. Bailey vigorously challenged that alleged confession. Cameron testified that he was threatened and browbeaten by the sheriff that night. R. L. argued vigorously that his client's alleged confession should not be admitted as evidence. After hearing two hours of heated arguments on both sides, the judge eventually ruled that the confession should not be admitted as evidence. A second victory came when Mary Ball took the stand. Although she testified that she was assaulted, she said the summer night was too dark to identify Cameron as one of the rapists.

Bailey and Brokenburr also argued their case on a claim that their client, now 17 years old, was mentally immature. Cameron's mother and younger sister followed R. L.'s lead in testifying to the childlike character of James. Dr. L. A. Lewis, a black physician from Indianapolis and close friend of R. L., testified that there was doubt about Cameron's sanity and mental capacity, but two court-appointed experts testified that he was not insane. Bailey and Brokenburr had spent time carefully coaching Cameron on his dress and demeanor in the courtroom. The young man was in awe of them—"uppity niggers" of a kind he had not seen before, he later said with a big smile. The two black lawyers clearly had the respect of many others in that courtroom, a respect based on their ability and their power.

On July 7, 1931, the jury of 12 citizens retired to deliberate. Two hours later they returned with a verdict that found Cameron guilty of being an accessory to the crime of voluntary manslaughter. Acknowledging his youth, the court sentenced him to not less than two or more than ten years in the Indiana State Reformatory. The other charges of first-degree rape and first-degree murder were dropped, as were the charges of auto banditry and robbery. A jury of 12 white men did not believe all the stories that had circulated in Grant County over the previous 11 months.[37]

It was an unexpected outcome. The NAACP national office issued a press release claming that "the short term given Cameron is a great moral victory" and praising attorneys Bailey and Brokenburr for "their magnificent fight to save the boy from the electric chair." According to Flossie Bailey the two lawyers "were in constant danger during Cameron's trial and had to be guarded every minute in the courtroom by the sheriff's deputies." Thus ended, the NAACP claimed, "one of the most widely discussed cases of recent years and the second time Cameron has been snatched from the jaws of death."[38]

There was, in fact, a coda, a third escape from death for Cameron. On learning of the unexpectedly light sentence given him, some folks in Marion and surrounding areas began to talk of attacking the Madison County Jail and lynching Cameron. Telephone switchboards buzzed again as they had the previous August, but this time not only from potential lynchers. Local black citizens also heard the rumors. They too prepared. The *Indianapolis Recorder* proudly reported that "determined colored Anderson citizens, hundreds of them, armed to the teeth and well organized, stationed themselves at strategic points throughout the city prepared to give the lynchers a really peppery time in the old town." A "bloody race riot" threatened.[39]

Sheriff Bradley's heavily armed deputies whisked Cameron from the Madison County Jail to the Indiana State Reformatory in Pendleton. In a concession to mob rage, they offered to show the jail to any citizen who wished to see that Cameron was no longer there. Thus, the *Recorder* concluded, "Quick action of the local authorities prevented what would have inevitably flared into a bitter race riot the likes of which has never been witnessed in the state of Indiana." A week later the Indianapolis black newspaper commended the "colored men" who saved "Anderson's name from what may have been its first bath in blood. It was a splendid evidence of characteristic patriotism."[40]

That James Cameron lived was a change of large consequence, then and later. But the 1930s in Grant County brought more continuities than changes in the lines of color dividing white and black Americans. As hard as Flossie Bailey, R. L. Bailey, and others worked, they achieved only small concessions toward justice. The rest of the twentieth century lay ahead, to test the validity of W. E. B. Du Bois's prediction of its first-order problem and to see if any seeds of change had been sown.

CHAPTER EIGHT

Remembering

The lynchings of August 7, 1930, created memories and silences. Some folks wanted to tell the stories again and again. Many others in Grant County wanted to forget, to hope that the tragedy would be swept under the carpet like dead spiders.

But the stories would not fade away. The shooting of Claude Deeter, the presumed rape of Mary Ball, and the bloody determination of the lynch mob at the jail and on the Courthouse Square continued to live in tales told and in memories held. Together they constituted the foundations on which people constructed their understanding of the mysteries of race in this ordinary American community.[1]

Two agents in particular prevented forgetting and forced remembering. One was a photograph. The other was an old black man. They not only kept the Marion lynching alive but, by the late twentieth century, had reshaped the stories told.

A FLASH IN THE DARKNESS

Lawrence Beitler flashed his cumbersome photographic equipment sometime after midnight on the morning of August 8, 1930. Later that day, about 2:00

P.M., the Indiana attorney general's investigator, Arthur Bruner, arrived on the Courthouse Square. The bodies of Abe Smith and Tom Shipp were gone, but Bruner reported there were about 60 people milling around the lynching tree:

> One young man about 25 years old was there and had a large picture of the lynching taken by flash light. He was telling every one just how it all happened and pointed out the large stab wounds on the body hanging to the right of the picture, saying he was there in the jail and saw that done. . . . He talked freely at all times to all that asked as people came and went. I tried to purchase the picture. He would not sell it but told me where they were made down the street and selling like hot cakes.

Bruner left the square to interview Sheriff Jake Campbell. When he returned to the scene at 4:30 P.M. the young man with the picture was still there, still showing it to anyone interested. And a block away, at 502 South Adams Street, Beitler was briskly selling his photo.[2]

Lawrence Beitler was a 44-year-old small-town professional photographer. He had taken thousands of photographs in Marion since arriving there in 1917. Most were of wedding couples and babies, of school and church groups, of parades and public events. That special night Beitler lugged his heavy 8-by-10-inch view camera, a tripod, and flash powder to take what eventually became one of the most famous lynching photographs in American history. For Beitler it was a chance less for fame than for fortune. He worked for days making prints and selling them for 50 cents apiece. Some prints had the hand-printed words "Beitler Studio" and "Lynching at Marion, Ind, Aug 1930."[3]

Why people would want to spend 50 cents to purchase one of Beitler's souvenirs is uncertain. But they did, in Marion, and across America, where lynchings often resulted in photographs and even postcards of the gruesome event.[4] Like others, the Marion photograph was a keepsake, of course, a marker of a spectacular occurrence. Perhaps some also wanted to own the photograph as a reassurance of white supremacy and of race solidarity in the face of any perceived black threat, a talisman against murder or rape or inappropriate crossing of the color line. One copy of Beitler's photograph ended up under glass, double matted and framed. Someone inscribed on the inner mat in pencil

"Bo pointn to his niga." And between the mat and the glass were placed locks of hair thought to be either Shipp's or Smith's.[5]

Few if any African Americans bought the photograph. Flossie Bailey was furious that Beitler was selling copies, fearing they would further inflame racial passions. She talked of starting court proceedings against Beitler and eventually convinced the state police to stop his sales. In Terre Haute, Indiana, 140 miles to the southwest, several drugstores and shops sold postcard-sized copies of the picture until protests by that city's NAACP branch produced a stop.[6]

Those who did not own the photograph could see it in newspapers, but not in all of them. Several newspaper photographers took pictures of the two bodies hanging from the tree that night. Within a few hours all the papers in Indiana had copies. The three major Indianapolis newspapers decided not to print them. The *Indianapolis News* said that they were "revolting" and "common decency and good taste" forbade publication. The *Indianapolis Times* had several "closeup pictures" but to print them would have been "catering only to morbid tastes." Marion newspaper editors also decided not to print photographs of the lynching; not in 1930 and not at any time thereafter. Into the twenty-first century the Beitler photograph was kept locked in a safe at the *Marion Chronicle-Tribune*, considered by editors too violent, too graphic, too close to home.[7]

Several other newspapers decided to show readers the visual evidence, almost always selecting Beitler's shot. Those in the nearby towns of Anderson and Muncie ran it the day after. The most frequent and interesting uses were in newspapers catering to African American readers. Doubtless these papers were more eager to print this "morbid" photo in order to make a point about violence and race. Black editors sought to drive home a moral lesson by adding their own captions to Beitler's photo. The *Chicago Defender* ran the full photo with the caption "American Christianity." The NAACP's magazine, *The Crisis*, printed a similarly sarcastic caption, "Civilization in the United States, 1930." This was one of the few lynching photographs the NAACP magazine published in those years. (Indeed, it may have been the Beitler photograph in this civil rights magazine that so haunted Abel Meeropol and led him to write "Strange Fruit.") Some black editors cropped off parts of the photo. The *Indianapolis Recorder*, under the caption "Victims of Savagery Born of Prejudice and Hate," ran a closeup of the two bodies, focusing the eye there, and showed only a small part of the white crowd. The *New York World* cropped the photo to show readers only the white crowd.[8]

One can readily imagine the intense excitement and hurried conversations in newspaper offices as editors struggled with Beitler's photograph, realizing immediately its immense power. Whether or not to publish it, how to caption it, what cropping and size: these were choices first made in August 1930, decisions the photograph demanded again and again over the following decades.

There are really two pictures in Beitler's one. The eye is drawn first to the two bodies hanging from the tree, the two ropes stretched taut over two adjacent limbs. Beitler's night flash powder reflects off the tree's leaves. Someone, perhaps a photographer, has sawed off at least three tree limbs so the bodies of Abe Smith and Tom Shipp are more visible. The bodies themselves hang limp, eyes closed, heads at angles. The faces are of young men, teenagers. Closer inspection shows blood on the faces and clothing, clear even in the black-and-white photograph. The body on the left, that of Tom Shipp, is clothed, sleeves rolled up, shirt open in the front. The body on the right, that of Abe Smith, has a cloth wrapped on the lower half to hide its nakedness after the mob stripped off his pants and shoes. Bare feet and skinny legs suspend five feet in the air.

The lower half of Beitler's photograph is as compelling. Indeed, as James Cameron later told an interviewer, if you cover up the lower half, "you just got a lynching of two blacks," one of dozens of lynching photographs in American history.[9] It's the crowd milling below the two suspended bodies that the eye eventually moves to and stays with, darting back and forth from individuals in the crowd to the two lynch victims.

There are nearly 30 people visible, standing, talking, gesturing. Unlike many lynching photographs, there are women as well as men present.[10] Nine spectators look directly at Beitler's camera. The eye catches first the man with a Hitler-like mustache, his tattooed left arm raised, his index finger pointed toward the bodies, as if the camera lens might miss that part of the scene. To the left is a young couple, holding hands, or rather he is holding her thumb. She is pregnant. Both are smiling for the camera, as if on a picnic along the Mississinewa River. In the front is another young woman, even further along in her pregnancy. Behind her is an older woman; strangely on this hot night, when nearly all the men have their shirtsleeves rolled up high, she wears a coat with a fur collar. To the right

1. Lawrence Beitler took this photograph of the Marion lynching soon after Tom Shipp and Abe Smith died at the hands of the mob. Their bodies and the crowd below combine to make it one of the most famous lynching photographs in American history. (Courtesy Indiana Historical Society C7068A.)

2. People begin to gather outside the massive Grant County Jail on August 7, 1930. In a short time some of them would become the lynch mob. (Courtesy Indiana Historical Society C5077.)

3. The Grant County Courthouse was the center of the community. This photograph, taken around 1900, shows "Lady Justice" on top of the dome, and trees too small for a lynching. (Courtesy Marion Public Library.)

Twenty-Third Annual
OLD FOLKS' DAY
Sixtieth Anniversary Return of Civil War Soldiers
and Martin Boots Centennial
August 25, 1925
Matter Park, Marion, Indiana

THE OCTOGENARIAN

1816
1831

COUNTRYSIDE AND WAYSIDE
BY ROLINDA

ANNUAL REUNION AUG.

PROGRAM
Furnished Through the Courtesy of

Blumenthal & Co.
ESTABLISHED 1865

4. The pioneer log cabin in Matter Park celebrated the achievements of Grant County's early settlers. (Courtesy Marion Public Library.)

5. Marion police pose in front of City Hall, 1922, when they struggled to enforce prohibition and other laws. Jake Campbell, front row, second from left, would be the Sheriff in 1930. Others who testified in the lynching investigations include Lewis Lindenmuth, third row, second from left; and Charles Truex, among the most forthcoming witnesses, third row, fourth from left. The two African American policemen are Harley Burden, middle row, sixth from left, and Fred Mosely, middle row, far right. (Courtesy Marion Public Library.)

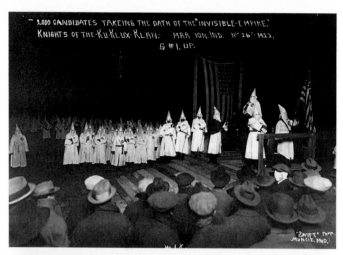

6., 7., & 8. Flags and crosses provide the backdrop as Muncie photographer W. A. Swift took these three photographs of the nighttime initiation of new Ku Klux Klan members in Marion's Goldthwaite Park November 26, 1922. Masked and robed Klansmen face the initiates, dressed in civilian clothes, in figure 6. In figure 7, Klansmen encircle the initiates, and in figure 8, the initiates kneel to take their oath. (Courtesy W. A. Swift Collection, Archives and Special Collections, Ball State University.)

9. Students and teacher, John Will Burden (top right), at Weaver School, ca. 1920. (Courtesy Barbara J. Stevenson and Marion Public Library.)

10. Flossie Bailey, Marion's premier NAACP leader (Courtesy Barbara J. Stevenson.)

11. Policeman Harley Burden, Sr., served for twenty-six years as one of Marion's two black cops. (Courtesy Marion Public Library.)

12. Mary Ball, who claimed she was raped on August 6, 1930.
(Courtesy Todd Gould.)

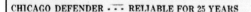

The Wabash Runs Crimson to the Sea

INDIANA

MOB FURY

WHAT THE PEOPLE SAY

13. & 14. The *Chicago Defender* gave its mostly black readers two strong editorial cartoons on August 16 and August 23, 1930. (Courtesy, *Chicago Defender*.)

The Crucifixion

JUSTICE

15. Lawrence Beitler in his commercial photography studio.
(Courtesy Marion Public Library.)

16. Beitler's photograph, framed, mounted and labeled (with locks of hair claimed to be one of the victim's). The label wrongly places the lynching in Joplin, Missouri, 1933. A caption beneath the photo reads, "Bo pointn to his niga." (From the book *Without Sanctuary,* Courtesy Twin Palms Publishers.)

17. The cover of the first edition of James Cameron's *A Time of Terror* (1982), reproducing the Beitler photograph with a third rope drawn in. (Courtesy Ed Breen.)

18. James Cameron tells his story as he leads a reporter through his Black Holocaust Museum in Milwaukee in 1990. (Courtesy *The Post-Crescent.*)

19. The *Indianapolis Recorder* showed its mostly black readers this photograph of one of fifty specially deputized Marion citizens. With gun on hip, he guards the Matter Park pool from African Americans threatening to swim there in June,1954. (Courtesy *Indianapolis Recorder.*)

20. Grant County Sheriff Oatess Archey stands at the east end of the abandoned Grant County Jail, in January, 1999. (Courtesy Jeff Morehead, *Marion Chronicle-Tribune*.)

are four men, one looking at the camera, three gazing at the bodies; two hold fat cigars and wear round-brim hats; another wears a worker's cloth cap and a one-piece coverall with a hole in the sleeve; the youngest man, on the far right, wears bib overalls.

None in the crowd seems angry or embarrassed. All are so ordinary, even banal. Few could have imagined the place in history they earned that night by posing for Lawrence Beitler's camera. It was their shameless faces and everyday gestures as much as or more than the limp bodies of Shipp and Smith that doubtless would keep the photo alive long after they were all dead.

Some thought the ordinary people in Beitler's photograph were the lynch mob. Several newspapers, particularly those with African American audiences, claimed that each person in the photo could be and should be readily identified. Beitler's picture, the *Chicago Defender* claimed, "shows any number of the guilty persons." The *New York World* captioned the crowd as "Spectators and Participants in Killing of Negro Boys" and asserted that it reveals "unmistakably faces of many of the mob." It was, of course, very easy for some Marion residents to put names to faces in the picture, even decades later. Those with guilty bloodstains on their clothing may well have stood there for Beitler's camera, but it is likely that most were curious spectators and that members of the lynch mob had left the scene long before Beitler arrived.[11]

The best evidence of the power of Beitler's photograph is the fact that it appeared in dozens of places over the next decades, reproduced more frequently as time passed. The Acme News Service in New York obtained a copy as early as August 11, 1930, a copy that eventually reached the Bettmann Collection. Years later Magnum Photo Agency also secured a print. From these two major agencies and the Library of Congress, editors, authors, museum exhibit planners, and others readily obtained copies. By the late twentieth century it had become one of America's most well known lynching photographs.

Beitler's photo appeared in all kinds of books, from college textbooks to historical overviews of the twentieth century to a textbook for French students learning the English language. Alistair Cooke's *America* ran it across two pages in 1973; *Life* magazine used it in 1988 to open a special issue devoted to race. It appeared in *Newsweek* twice in one year, 1994; in *The African American Atlas*, published in 1998; and in a 1999 PBS television documentary on photography.

An exhibit of lynching photographs at a New York City gallery attracted wide publicity in early 2000, with exhibit notices often featuring Beitler's photo, including *New Yorker* and Associated Press coverage. In the 1990s museum visitors could see blown-up versions of Beitler's photo at the Birmingham Civil Rights Institute in Alabama, the DuSable Museum in Chicago, and the Museum of Tolerance in Los Angeles. In all three museums as well as in many of the books the photo was unidentified as to time and place. It had become *the* generic lynching photograph, suitable to illustrate the point of white racism and violence without considering when or where. Most viewers likely assumed it was somewhere in the South. The popular documentary *Eyes on the Prize* included it among a sweep of southern lynching images. And a character in the 1996 Hollywood film *The Chamber* opens a book about the South and shows the Beitler photograph, labeled "Lynching in Rural Mississippi in 1936."[12]

Latter-day protesters found the photo useful too. The scheduled execution of an African American death row prisoner in Indiana in 1994 sparked a rally with protesters holding up an enlarged copy of the Beitler photo for press cameras. The rap group Public Enemy reproduced the photo for the cover of its CD single "Hazy Shade of Criminal," released in 1992. On the back of the CD rapper Chuck D explained that boxer Mike Tyson, convicted in Indiana of rape, was "hanged the same Goddamn way" as the "two black men in 1930 Indiana getting hanged for bullshit that they didn't do based on cracker racism, jealousy, envy and greed." The *Indianapolis Star* ran a front-page story on the Public Enemy CD and included a photo of the cover. It was probably the first time the *Star* had shown its readers the Marion photograph, though only as it appeared on a rap album. The Marion newspaper did not show the CD cover, continuing its policy of protecting its readers from Beitler's version of the story. The manager of a record store in Marion's mall refused to tell an out-of-town reporter if his store even carried the Public Enemy CD. Ironically, in the South a few record stores refused to sell the CD, even though it depicted a northern lynching.[13]

As a Marion boy in the late 1940s, James Sutter and a friend were exploring his family's attic and found a copy of Beitler's photograph. More than 50 years later Sutter still vividly recalled that moment of discovery. The memory was as clear to him as the memory of the news of Pearl Harbor was to others of his generation.[14]

The Beitler photograph froze the event in time for all time. It kept the memory alive and the story recoverable long after August 7, 1930. But the story that Beitler told with his camera was really a story with multiple and changing meanings. Over time it depended on what listeners wanted to hear, depended on the present in which the photograph was viewed as much as or more than the events of August 7, 1930.[15]

CAMERON'S STORY BEGINS

Another compelling storyteller emerged in the 1970s, one who used the powerful Beitler image and other tools to fashion his version of the Marion lynching. James Cameron's version became by the century's end the dominant story, overshadowing all others.

Cameron's body was not hanging from the tree in Lawrence Beitler's photograph. The mob roughly forced a rope noose around the teenager's neck, but by a miracle, the devoutly religious man later claimed, he was spared. His life thereafter became a quest for his own personal peace and for healing of racial divisions in his own heart and in his nation. With a stubborn persistence Cameron spent the last decades of the twentieth century forcing his story on Marion and on America. In 1994 he looked back on his life and claimed that the lynching "might have been the best thing that happened to me. God works in mysterious ways."[16]

Cameron's conviction in 1931 of being an accessory to voluntary manslaughter led to four years in jail. As condition of parole, Indiana required him to leave the state, perhaps as a way to help quiet memories. Cameron moved to Detroit, where he lived with his aunt for a time. In 1938 he married Virginia Hamilton, a young woman from Kentucky. They had five children and a long marriage. Cameron first worked delivering milk, then in a drug store. In 1942 the family moved to Anderson, Indiana, where his mother lived and where his trial had been held a decade earlier. Cameron soon became active in the local NAACP. The spark, he said, came when, during World War II, his family was forced to sit in the segregated balcony of the Anderson movie theater.[17]

In nearby Muncie, in early May 1944, a white mob angrily searched for a black man they thought had raped a white woman. The police did not stop several hundred enraged whites as they rampaged through the Muncie jail and the town's black neighborhoods. In response, a few days later, on May 9, two hundred black citizens gathered in Muncie's "Colored YMCA" to organize a new branch of the NAACP. The master of ceremonies and representative from the NAACP branch in Anderson was James Cameron. He brought his own experience to the meeting, speaking about the events in Marion 14 years earlier. He also introduced other speakers, including the coordinator of Negro War Activities of the Indiana State Defense Council, who assured the audience of protection by local and state agencies. A tense moment passed. Marion remained the state's last lynching. James Cameron had made one of his earliest known testimonies.[18]

James Cameron and his family moved to Milwaukee in 1953, where he eventually established a successful air conditioning and refrigeration business. Studying several religions, he finally converted to Catholicism and became a devout practitioner. He and his wife sent their children off to college as they settled into an ordinary middle-class midwestern life. But Cameron continued to be haunted by the events of that August night. While in prison in the 1930s he had begun to make notes; by the 1970s he had the makings of a book.[19]

As part of his effort to remember, Cameron returned to Marion in 1978, only his second visit since 1930. Few people recognized him; Jack Edwards, the former mayor who knew everyone, told an interviewer in 1977 that Cameron had died of tuberculosis. In 1978 Cameron walked the Courthouse Square with a local reporter to find the place where the lynching tree once stood. He climbed to the second floor of the Grant County Jail and stood next to his cell as the local newspaper photographer snapped his camera. And he told his story to the reporter, who featured it in the *Chronicle-Tribune*'s special magazine issue on Grant County's black history. Whether or not the people of the county wished it, Cameron had begun to force their greatest community tragedy back into their collective memory and that of the nation.[20]

SEEKING LISTENERS

Cameron's first success in reaching a broad audience came in 1980, when *Ebony* magazine did a feature article on him. Oriented to black readers, *Ebony* printed the portions of Cameron's book that described how the mob took him from the jail. It was a story Cameron would tell and retell dozens of times in the next 20 years, using the same narrative structure and many of the same words. He told his tale with a powerful, first-person immediacy and with precise details: "Rough hands grabbed my head and stuffed it into a large noose. . . . They began shoving and knocking me closer to the tree and under the same limb weighted down with the half-stripped bodies of Abe and Tommy."

Some of Cameron's details are not corroborated in other extant, firsthand sources, including his memory of a mob leader with a submachine gun and his assertion that there were "several other men dressed in the simpleton dunce-shaped headgear of the Ku Klux Klan." For *Ebony* and in subsequent tellings Cameron always included a mysterious voice that "rang out above the deafening roar of the mob." It was, he asserted, a spiritual voice, an angel's voice, the voice of God who saved him from death. "Hands that had been rough and ready, and willing to kill moments ago, hands that had already committed cold-blooded murder, became soft and tender, kind and helpful."

Accompanying the *Ebony* account were more than a dozen photographs. The largest and most prominent was Beitler's photo of Smith's and Shipp's bodies hanging from the tree and the crowd below. The other photos, taken by *Ebony's* photographer, who met Cameron in Marion, showed the 66-year-old man standing in front of the massive Grant County Jail; sitting in an old cell; meeting with Jack Edwards, mayor in 1930; and visiting on the courthouse lawn with his cousin Tom Wise, now a Marion policeman.[21]

Cameron's full story appeared in book form in 1982, published at his own expense after several years of rejections from publishers. Tom Wise had helped him with the research and in seeking a publisher. *A Time of Terror* told Cameron's life story, centered around the lynching. Beitler's famous picture of the lynching appeared on the cover. But an artist had altered it by drawing a third rope between the two bodies, a rope intended for Cameron. Because it was published by a small vanity press in Milwaukee there was no national publicity or distribution. The book attracted little attention. Milwaukee newspapers and several in Indiana carried stories, all positive. Among the best notices was an essay by Ed Breen, city editor of the *Marion Chronicle-Tribune*. He gave strong praise to Cameron's "account of Marion's most miserable hours," hours that for 52 years "have been the skeleton in our collective closet." Breen ended his piece urging his readers "to listen to him [Cameron] if we are to understand who we are as we stand on the courthouse lawn in September, 1982, trying to come to grips with ourselves and our history." Memories of the lynching in Marion grew.[22]

Cameron had invested $6,000 of his own money to publish *A Time of Terror* and then drove around the Midwest to promote it, often giving away copies. He spoke at schools and community meetings. His story got a big boost in the mid-1980s when he discussed it on Oprah Winfrey's TV show. Invitations to speak increased.[23]

Cameron was tireless. He sent out publicity to universities and other organizations and spoke to dozens of audiences. He was not a slick orator, but he could project a deep honesty and an intense immediacy as he told his story effortlessly, in a calm, quiet voice filled with emotion. Many listeners heard the voice of history, retelling the mundane events of the unbelievable. At times Cameron seemed like an Old Testament prophet, warning of the sins of racism. At points in his dramatic presentation tears would form in his eyes and almost always in the eyes of many in his audience. But Cameron seldom conveyed bitterness. He spoke of his gratitude to God and hope for the future as he condemned the hatred that still existed in Marion and America. Newspaper reporters who interviewed him or covered his speeches were invariably moved and highly sympathetic in the accounts they wrote.[24]

Cameron's first major appearance in Marion came in early 1983, when the Grant County Black History Council invited him to speak at its fourth annual banquet. Before an audience of 250 people at the Sheraton Inn, the former Marion shoeshine boy reviewed the racism of the Ku Klux Klan and the lynching. A Fort Wayne reporter wrote that "many in the crowd, made up of both blacks and whites, were moved to tears during parts of Cameron's speech and during the singing of 'We Shall Overcome' at the banquet's end." The president of the Black History Council, Carlyle F. Gulliford, concluded that "even though it's a dark cloud over our history, it's time to hear the truth out; then we can put it behind us and go forward from here." Cameron had moved the lynching another notch into Marion's memory.[25]

Still, there were many who preferred not to remember. As late as 1988, the executive editor of the *Chronicle-Tribune* felt that "it is one chapter in the community's history that everyone, black or white, would just as soon forget about."[26]

THE BLACK HOLOCAUST MUSEUM

Through the 1980s Cameron continued to expand his efforts as preacher and educator. With his book in print, he shifted to a different podium. After visiting Yad Vashem, the Holocaust museum in Jerusalem, and learning of plans to build one in Washington, D.C., Cameron decided to plan a museum in Milwaukee that would tell the story of black suffering. By 1984 he had organized a nonprofit corporation and begun raising funds. Contributions were meager, but with $5,000 of his own money and by doing nearly all the work himself, including assembling exhibit shelves, he opened the Black Holocaust Museum in Milwaukee on June 19 (Juneteenth, a holiday that celebrates the end of slavery), 1988. Located in a room over the second floor of the Black Muslims' headquarters, the museum would "prick the conscience" of visitors, he said.[27]

Not many people, black or white, wanted what Cameron offered them. During the museum's first four months only a hundred paying visitors showed up. Dozens of applications to foundations and other fund-raising efforts failed. The Black Muslims were sympathetic to Cameron's purposes but wanted rent for the space. Cameron closed the museum several times as he hunted for permanent space and money. At one point he located the museum in what a Dallas reporter called "a dimly lighted former tavern in a crime-ridden neighborhood."[28]

The Black Holocaust Museum was a shoestring operation, kept alive by one person's effort. Yet it was not a failure. From the beginning it attracted media attention. Inquisitive reporters could not resist a place called the Black Holocaust Museum. Cameron certainly risked controversy in the name he chose. "Is 'holocaust' too strong a word?" asked the *Chicago Tribune*. Not for Cameron, who carefully explained his moving experience at the Holocaust museum in Jerusalem and softly spoke of his compassion for those who suffered. America also had a holocaust, he claimed, and it must face its past, just as Germany had. Unsure how to deal with this claim and perhaps fearful of inflaming tender relations between American Jews and blacks, reporters usually moved quickly away from the museum's controversial name.[29]

The reporters who came to this unusual museum in Milwaukee and met Cameron were invariably charmed. He guided them through the exhibits, which focused on lynching and included two black manikins hanging from ropes over a small tree. He showed them the blown-up photographs of America's lynchings, with the Beitler photo at center stage. Often reporters used the words "chamber of horrors" and "gruesome." They described Cameron's collection of Ku Klux Klan robes and hoods, the racist signs, a copy of *Little Black Sambo,* and other artifacts. The museum was emotionally moving, but not as moving as Cameron himself. As a *New York Times* reporter stated, Cameron was not only the museum's founder and curator, "he is also its star exhibit."[30]

Newspaper accounts of the Black Holocaust Museum inevitably focused on Cameron's story. Patiently and with feeling he told it to visitors again and again. Details vividly came to life. An Indianapolis reporter described how "he reaches for a tattered envelope. Inside is a bit of braided rope used to hang his friends nearly 64 years ago." Journalists were impressed with his authoritative voice of immediate experience, so authentic, so real. "You see," he told one visitor, "they don't teach this stuff in school." His eyes twinkled, the reporter wrote: "This is vintage James Cameron. The self-taught author and historian remains a feisty and spirited combatant, capable of arguing history with the proficiency of a learned scholar although his formal education consists of a high school degree and two years in a community college."[31]

The Black Holocaust Museum attracted journalists from as far away as Ireland. It gave Cameron a pulpit from which to preach to the nation and the world. It also helped move his story further onto the Marion stage. The museum pulled a *Marion Chronicle-Tribune* reporter to Milwaukee in August 1992; his piece was similar to others. He wrote about the museum exhibits ("shocking," he said) but focused, as the others had, on Cameron's story, telling it again.

Cameron may have forgiven the Marion mob, but he can't forget, the reporter wrote. An accompanying editorial asserted that "to share in the story of James Cameron is to be reminded of his pain and our community's collective guilt. We believe it's important to do that as we continue to seek ways to address the sins of the past, some of which linger into the present."[32]

"The sins of the past" came home to Marion in another way. As long as the Grant County Jail stood the stories of the lynching would have a symbol towering in downtown Marion. Cameron's first visit to Marion in 1978 included a stop at the jail. In the years to come he would be photographed and filmed there dozens of times. The old jail closed in 1981, replaced by a new one that accommodated six times as many prisoners. The abandoned massive brick building near the Courthouse Square soon became a white elephant.

Cameron tried to get the jail listed as a National Historic Landmark and proposed it as the new location for his Black Holocaust Museum. "It would put Marion on the map," he said. "No other place has a national shrine to the prevention of lynching. People would come from all over the world to see it." Marion residents, the Associated Press reported, "seemed hesitant to embrace the idea." The Historic Landmarks Foundation of Indiana placed the jail on its "Ten Most Endangered" list in 1995 to encourage preservation of the building. As the jail ironwork rusted and the mortar crumbled, the distant voices of the mob of August 7 echoed through abandoned cells. Then, at century's end, workers began renovating the structure to make apartment units, which opened for rent in early 2001.[33]

THE PARDON

In late May 1991, Cameron sat down at his typewriter and composed a letter to Indiana Governor Evan Bayh requesting a pardon for the crime committed on August 6, 1930. With his letter he included a copy of *A Time of Terror*. Cameron's request led to his appearance before the Indiana Parole Board. Once again he told his story and spoke of mercy: he believed "that God has forgiven me for the role I played in the initiation of a crime that resulted in the loss of three human lives." According to the parole board's commissioner, Joe Smith,

"It was absolutely the most emotional hearing before our board." The board approved the request. Governor Bayh signed the pardon on February 4, 1993. The following week Cameron prepared to receive the pardon, not at the state capital, not in Milwaukee, and certainly not in an envelope delivered by the post office, but at the Sheraton Inn in Marion, just a couple of blocks from the old jail. The editor of the local newspaper expressed hope that the public "ceremony might lift some of the collective guilt this community continues to share over the ugliest incident in Marion's history."[34]

At noon on February 11, 1993, in front of television cameras and photographers and an overflow audience of Marion city officials, high school students, and friends, Parole Board Commissioner Smith presented Cameron his pardon. Mayor Ron Mowery gave Cameron a key to the city. All spoke of a new beginning, a new day for Marion. "We can finally say justice has been done," City Councilwoman Shirley Barbour said. Marion School Board member Art Faulkner said the lynching "has been an open sore," but now "the old chapter in our community's history has been closed."[35]

James Cameron stepped to the podium to deliver carefully prepared remarks. He was wearing a black tuxedo that set off his snow-white hair and mustache. Tears stained his cheeks. The 77-year-old survivor delivered a moving and gracious speech filled with lofty rhetoric. More than a dozen times he paused to regain composure. He began: "The African American story has not been told." He quoted from Jerusalem's Yad Vashem: "To remember is salvation. To forget is exile." He told his story, gently and humbly, admitting guilt in the attempted robbery of Claude Deeter. He offered his forgiveness of the mob and his thanks for the state's forgiveness of his long ago crime. He said a prayer for Marion to "set a beacon light for the rest of the state." "I know that the spirit of God is in this building today," the tearful Cameron said. For most of the audience it was a time to share in tears, reconciliation, and hope.[36]

The 1993 pardon ceremony was the key event in bringing James Cameron back home. The ceremony took power from its symbolic "coming home" quality, from its theme of forgiveness, from the extensive media coverage, and from the people who chose to attend. The town's movers and shakers, its white and black leaders, showed up at the hotel conference room that February day. The ceremony, Cameron later thought, was "not an instant healing" but it did "put a salve on the wounds." In the audience were people, recalled local newspaper editor Ed Breen, who 20 years earlier wouldn't talk to each other, now sitting side by side in "a moment of reconciliation." "Years of distrust and fear," Breen reflected, melted in "an emotional catharsis."[37]

The only jarring public note was voiced later to an Indianapolis reporter by Vida Inman. It was a voice seldom heard. Inman was Abe Smith's niece. Happy for Cameron, she was "also saddened that my uncle was not still around to receive a pardon."[38]

THE MEDIA FRENZY

James Cameron became increasingly visible in the two years following the 1993 pardon. Two events sparked the ascent: the appearance of an article in a New York magazine and the reprint of *A Time of Terror*.

On February 1, 1994, the *Village Voice* published a cover story on James Cameron. "The Survivor's Story," the red-ink headline shouted over the top of Beitler's lynching photograph. A smaller photo inset showed a contemplative, white-haired Cameron looking toward the bodies of his long-ago friends. The writer, Cynthia Carr, had stumbled onto one of the many newspaper stories about Cameron, his Black Holocaust Museum, and his book. She knew Marion from visits there to her grandparents. She wrote the lynching story pretty much as Cameron told it in *A Time of Terror* and in the interview she had with him in Milwaukee. Accompanying the essay were photographs of the Grant County Jail and of Cameron's hand holding a piece of the lynching rope. Carr's *Village Voice* account set off a geyser of media attention.[39]

At the same time, in February 1994, a new edition of *A Time of Terror* appeared. *Publisher's Weekly* reported that the front-page story in the *Village Voice* had "prompted a media frenzy around a small press title." Black Classic Press specialized in republishing books that were "out of print and quite often out of memory," ones that "have helped in meaningful ways to shape the Black Diaspora experience." *A Time of Terror* quickly sold its initial printing of five thousand copies; the publisher ordered another ten thousand. So hectic was the small Baltimore publisher's office that it hired a public relations firm to deal with the "feeding frenzy." Calls came to Cameron or the office of Black Classic Press from the nation's leading television and radio shows, including *Good Morning America, CBS Evening News, ABC Prime Time Live, Turning Point, Dateline NBC, Larry King Live, A Current Affair,* the *Donahue Show,* the *Jerry Springer Show,* and National Public Radio's *All Things Considered* and *Fresh Air* programs. From across the Atlantic the BBC and a Dutch broadcaster rang up. *Newsweek,* the *Washington Post,* and other print outlets joined the line of march. In spring 1994 Cameron made several trips to Marion for television crews and reporters, each time posing in the Grant County Jail. James Cameron had more than his 15 minutes of fame.[40]

Cameron's interview on National Public Radio's *Fresh Air* program in March 1994 was doubtless similar to most of the others, though pitched more toward the highbrow end of the audience. The host began by introducing Cameron as "maybe the only living African American to survive a lynching," a lynching by a Ku Klux Klan mob, she said. Several times she referred to her guest as the founder of the Black Holocaust Museum and author of *A Time of Terror.* Mostly she allowed Cameron to tell his story.

In a calm and husky voice well suited to radio Cameron narrated the details of the crime, the arrest, the interrogation, the lynching of Tom Shipp and Abe Smith, and the voice that saved him. Several times he and the interviewer referred to the pardon, which now served as a seal of credibility to his story as well as official forgiveness. Cameron was generous in praising those whites, such as Sheriff Bradley, who treated him kindly. He spoke of forgiveness. On two occasions he lost composure. Although the structure and language were nearly the same as in *A Time of Terror* and dozens of other interviews, Cameron spoke to the NPR audience with a freshness and vividness that caused the sophisticated interviewer to comment how "real" it all was, how powerful it was to hear it now. It was a superb performance.[41]

Following radio and print media came three television versions of Cameron's story. With television Cameron's narrative became visually powerful, reached even larger audiences, and endured on videotape.

Wisconsin Public Television, the Indianapolis Public Broadcasting station WFYI, and the British Broadcasting Corporation (BBC) made documentaries about the lynching. Each documentary maker's camera focused on three primary means of telling the story: the jail, with its powerful brick exterior and its rusted cell bars; the Beitler photo of two bodies and a large crowd (the likely reason two of the documentaries placed a "viewer advisory" caution at the beginning); and James Cameron, the articulate survivor. These icons pulled the film cameras toward them with irresistible force.[42]

On television Cameron's magic was even more powerful than in radio or print interviews. Viewers saw an ordinary old black man, always wearing a coat and tie, telling his story straight, occasionally losing composure. He walked through the abandoned jail, around the Courthouse Square, and along the Mississinewa River crime scene, and he sat in his book-lined study. Each documentary used Cameron as the master storyteller around which other interviewees and the narrator's voice swirled. Other people added moving details, as when the BBC camera recorded Claude Deeter's younger brother, William, now an old man, saying that Claude's "place where he sat at the dinner table was never used" again. Later the camera recorded William Deeter and James Cameron as they met in a Marion church to embrace and pray together for reconciliation. The three documentary directors used music, quick cuts, slow motion, sweeping camera shots, special effects, and old footage of Klan rallies to render Cameron's story even more vivid. Viewers learned the details of the mob's violence, the power of the Klan, the continued memory of the lynching, and the importance of remembering. Two of the documentaries made specific reference to the Holocaust and asserted that Marion people must remember, just as all Germans must remember. Each documentary concluded with Cameron's moving call for equality and justice. "I see my role today as a teacher," he said to the WFYI camera, "to let people know the truth about the past. Once they know the truth, the truth will make them free."[43]

In May 1999 a class of 39 Marion High School students watched the WFYI documentary and then wrote short reaction essays. The students' papers flowed with feeling and thoughtfulness. All harshly condemned the lynch mob and the justice system that failed to convict its leaders. All focused on race as the primary issue, convinced that Shipp and Smith would have lived had they been white teenagers, and all elaborated the horror of racism. Most students concluded that people still remembered, although they thought many adults did not want to talk about the tragedy. "To this day," one student wrote, the people of Marion are "reminded of the horror which occurred on that night each time they drive by the Courthouse Square." Another wrote that the lynching "will forever haunt the inhabitants of Marion." "Haunt" and "shame" were favorite words to describe present-day feelings. All thought that race was still a dividing issue in Marion in 1999. Most agreed that "Marion has come a long way in terms of race relations," though they disagreed on how much progress had been made. Some were very optimistic, some less so.[44]

Through the power of videotape James Cameron, teacher and prophet, had reached into this Marion High School classroom, perhaps even into some hearts. Many students noted with pride the small detail of Cameron receiving the key to their city at the ceremony of pardon. Many evoked his mantra: to forgive, but not forget.

Few could have understood the dominant stories as they had been told in 1930: the claim that it was a "fair mob" that lynched Shipp and Smith; Harley Hardin's reluctance to prosecute mob leaders; the white community's great silences that met Flossie Bailey's calls for justice. These former truths had faded, replaced by Cameron's story. The intended victim had become master prosecutor. The invisible man had become visible, and his story was now the dominant story.

CHAPTER NINE

The Long Lines of Color

Lynching stories and memories helped weave the color line through Grant County's fabric to the end of the twentieth century. There was every reason to believe that W. E. B. Du Bois had been correct in predicting in 1903 that the color line would be the problem of the century. By 2000 the line was certainly more fluid and more ambiguous than at the century's beginning. Some would still see a glass half empty, a color line still too sharp, still too tragic; others would see a glass more than half full, a line weakening to faintness as this ordinary place moved toward fulfilling America's ideals. Few could deny that times had changed.

During the last half of the twentieth century African Americans in Grant County began to struggle more forcefully against the lines of color and to raise their expectations about equality and justice. Fewer whites found it possible to remain silent; more joined the struggle. What would eventually be known as the civil rights movement of the 1950s and 1960s occurred in places like Marion, Indiana, as citizens agonized over such issues as integrating swimming pools. Indeed, what happened in such places as Marion, in the end, was the core of the civil rights movement. That movement let loose a continuing self-examination within communities and between local communities and the nation, a conversation and argument, locally and nationally, about liberty and justice for all. At the beginning of the twenty-first century Grant County citizens would still have memories of the lynching. And as part of their ongoing dialogue about race they would also have an elected black sheriff.

TWO BLACK KIDS AND A SWIMMING POOL

Born in Marion in 1937, Tom Wise and Oatess Archey played together as kids, went on as adults to careers in law enforcement, and, at the end of the century, worked together in Grant County politics. A generation separated them from James Cameron: they became in some ways Cameron's students, their lives crossing with his, affecting their willingness to forgive and their determination never to forget the past.

Wise and Archey grew up in the 1940s and 1950s, when the Courthouse Square was still the town center. Families from town and from Grant County's farms came there on Saturdays, packing the sidewalks in good weather, shopping in the Woolworth's and Penney's stores, buying a nickel Coke, going to hear a touring band such as Artie Shaw or to watch a Hollywood western. In nice weather men would sit and talk, remembering the old days. Former Sheriff Jake Campbell spent lots of time with friends on the square, telling stories. At home people listened to the radio, WOWO from Fort Wayne, WLW from Cincinnati, WLS from Chicago. On summer evenings they sat on their front porches. Few bothered to lock their doors at night.[1]

Tom Wise grew up in South Marion, where black kids learned to negotiate a fluid color line. His family lived on West 34th Street, in a neighborhood of many black families. Most of his friends were also black, though sometimes white kids joined their games. He attended McCulloch Elementary School, a mixed school with more whites than blacks. He belonged to a black Boy Scout troop that met at Allen Temple A.M.E. and went camping and swimming. He played on a black baseball team against white teams in the city's Matter Park and went on picnics there with his Allen Temple Sunday school class. Like nearly all Hoosier boys, Wise played basketball. Games at the YMCA were often with white boys, but after the game only the white kids were allowed to jump in the pool; Wise and his black friends could only play ping-pong.

Tom Wise swam with neighborhood kids in Deer Creek. He learned to swim from Don Hawkins, a tall, athletic black policeman who organized swimming lessons for black children. A bus picked them up every Monday morning in the summer and took them 30 miles south on Highway 9 to Anderson, where they could use the outdoor pool. Often at lunchtime on those summer days Tom would visit and eat with his Aunt Vera Clemens, his mother's sister. Only much later did he learn that Aunt Vera was the mother of James Cameron, that the survivor of the Marion lynching was his cousin. His family held it from him, believing ignorance would protect him from the scars left by the lynching.[2]

Oatess Archey also knew the color line. He grew up on Marion's north side in the 1940s and 1950s. Blacks lived in South Marion, West Marion, East Marion, and Central Marion. A civil rights official visiting the city in 1959 was "struck by the fact that there [were] no well-defined Negro areas in Marion."[3] North Marion was still white, however. All Archey's playmates except his older brother were white. They called him "Odie" and sat with him in the balcony of the movie theater. He remembers that he "fit in mostly," especially if he stayed close to those white neighbors who knew his family. At Washington Junior High School only the Archey brothers were black. Their mother was born in Weaver; their grandfather, Eli Archey, was one of the pioneers of another Hoosier African American community, the Beech settlement. The young Archey boys swam in the gravel pit and the Mississinewa River, but not at the YMCA or at Matter Park Pool.[4]

Matter Park was the city's jewel. Nothing else in this midwestern industrial town was so attractive. Located northwest of the city along the beautiful Mississinewa River, the park contained over 30 acres of tree-shaded space with picnic areas, a zoo, and rides. Kids like Oatess Archey and Tom Wise could also view the pioneer relics and log cabin inside the Octogenarian Museum in the park. Nearby was the statue of Lady Justice that had stood on top of the Grant County Courthouse until 1943. The most attractive place in the park for kids, however, was the huge swimming pool.[5]

Archey and Wise enjoyed all of Matter Park except the pool. There they could only peer through the fence to watch the white kids. In the 1940s and 1950s many whites thought "colored people" were "dirty"; they "didn't want to be polluted by their 'blackness,'" one Marion white woman later sadly recalled.[6] So, each Monday morning in summers, Oatess Archey made his way south across town to Bethel A.M.E. Church at 10th and Nebraska Streets, where Don Hawkins's bus stopped. The bus continued south to pick up Tom Wise and then moved out of town on its 30-mile journey to the Anderson swimming pool.

There were other places where African American citizens of Marion could not go in the years immediately after World War II. The main floor of the movie theaters, many of the restaurants,[7] and the roller skating rink were on the other side of the color line. But it was Matter Park Pool that galled the most. It was a city-owned park and pool, for which they paid taxes just as all citizens did. Going to the park but not the pool rubbed sores and invoked memories that had never healed.

By 1954 there were two civil rights organizations in Marion preparing to integrate the Matter Park Pool. The oldest was the Marion branch of the NAACP, an organization that had lain dormant during the previous 15 years. Flossie Bailey was no longer there. Others had attempted sporadically to revitalize the branch. Finally in 1954 they obtained a new charter from the national office. It was just in time to join the Matter Park Pool case.[8]

The second and stronger civil rights organization was the National Urban League. The Marion branch was organized in 1941 and soon had over two hundred members. The Urban League actively encouraged local companies to hire black workers in the booming war economy. It pushed for fair employment practices through the 1950s, playing a major role in convincing General Motors to hire large numbers of black workers for its new Fisher Body plant in Marion. The Urban League also sought to open housing, recreation, and other public facilities to blacks. While the NAACP's general strategy was to employ political and legal remedies, the Urban League tended to seek cooperation through community dialogue and behind-the-scenes negotiations. The struggle to integrate the Matter Park Pool created the League's largest crisis.[9]

The Urban League had joined with the Red Cross Learn-to-Swim Program to sponsor Don Hawkins's bus that took black kids to Anderson to swim. That bus became the first flash point in the pool fight. Some blacks and a few whites thought it was a cowardly accommodation to the pool segregationists. The executive director of the Marion Urban League, Charles R. Webb, responded to critics in 1953 by using the bus in a public relations campaign, timing stories and pictures about the 60-mile round trip and the cost of $50 per trip with publicity about the learn-to-swim programs at Matter Park to show "the glaring discrimination and segregation."[10]

At the same time, during the summer of 1953, the Marion Urban League began working with the all-white Grant County Council of Church Women. The women had expressed interest in seeing the pool open to all kids; doubtless they were aware of the early calls to unite Christianity and racial justice that were just forming in some churches in America. One of the most courageous of the women, Cecile Moore, headed a committee to call on the mayor and other city officials. Newspaper publicity and pressure put upon their husbands caused some of the women to "reconsider their initial liberal stand." The president of the Council of Church Women resigned and the group split. The Urban League then contacted members of the Indiana Jewish Community Relations Council and the American Friends Service Committee and together moved toward setting up a Human Relations Council of interested community members, consisting of 2 African Americans and 12 whites. Cecile Moore became chairman of the group. Their invitation to the mayor to join did not bring a reply. Similarly, the new Human Relations Council's initiative to the City Park Board failed to produce a response. Official Marion was hunkered down in silence.[11]

By early 1954 the stakes had risen. Executive Director Webb reported to the national Urban League office that pressures were growing on white and black civil rights activists, and some were getting cold feet. A Jewish leader advised sympathetic Jews that "this matter is too hot to handle and that they should withdraw." The head of the local YMCA told Cecile Moore "to drop the matter immediately" and warned that "attempting to better Negro relations should be stopped."[12]

Moore was among those not dissuaded by such pressure. She was in many ways the stereotypical, middle-class, small-town woman of the 1950s. A housewife who never worked outside the home, she was married to a mail carrier and spent much of her time in voluntary organizations such as the American Legion Auxiliary, the Home Economics Chorus, and the Altrusia women's club. She was also active in the United Brethren Church and its women's group. Everyone in town knew and liked her. Forty-five years later, her daughter, Betty

Musser, could hardly imagine "whatever possessed her" to become so interested in matters of race. Her Christianity was one source, she thought. She believed in those tenets of Christian faith that urged justice and equality for all. Another source was her friendship with the Caseys, an African American couple. She met Dr. Joe Casey when foot problems took her to his medical office and then became good friends with his wife, Amy. It was the Caseys who pulled her into the Urban League, where she soon became very active and eventually served as president. Cecile and her husband, Jack, visited the Caseys at their vacation home on Fox Lake in northern Indiana, and they traveled with Joe and Amy to the Urban League national meeting in Miami Beach one year. Cecile Moore had a "strong backbone," her daughter recalled. Neither her husband nor daughter shared her aggressive enthusiasm for racial equality. Nor did some of her white friends who drifted away. This woman—from a background her daughter described as conservative, frugal, and ordinary—became a local pioneer in her community's civil rights movement.[13]

As difficult as it was for white activists, it was doubly so for blacks. Harley Burden, Jr., was among the earliest and most active members of Marion's Urban League, serving a term as president and usually as member of the executive committee. Webb thought Burden "the most able board member we have." Twice Burden went to the City Park Board to complain about treatment his two sons had received in the YMCA day camp. It caused him to have "a rough time in his job" at the Anaconda Wire plant. Indeed, Burden began to talk to Webb about "changing communities because of his family and the pattern of segregation under which this city lives." Webb asked the national office to keep Burden in mind for a job "if his position here becomes untenable."[14]

Eventually joining the Urban League in the Matter Park Pool conflict was the newly organized branch of the NAACP. Its revival in early 1954 caused a crisis for the Urban League. Some Marion League members also joined the NAACP and thought the League should support its fellow civil rights organization. Others believed the NAACP was too radical, too eager to bring legal suit and to challenge directly the lines of color. Webb noted that "our greatest financial support is from a few families of wealthy people, to whom the word 'NAACP' is anathema." To add to fears, he reported, "some board and committee members work for these people." Then, in January 1954, "a white member of the board asked for the resignation of two colored members because of their participation in the NAACP." With his members badly split, Webb wrote the national office asking for advice. Executive Secretary Lester Granger strongly urged cooperation with the NAACP. Leaving behind some of his people, Webb worked out with NAACP leaders a cooperative agreement, under which the Urban League would coordinate publicity and arbitration directed toward opening the pool and the NAACP would be prepared to go to the courts if this moderate course failed.[15]

The opening of the Matter Park Pool in summer 1954 speeded up events. The Urban League organized several meetings with community and church groups, met with the mayor and park board, and circulated a petition, which city officials ignored. By early June the park board was feeling enough heat to offer to construct a separate swimming pool for blacks on Urban League property, an offer, reported Webb, that "threatens to split the board with several contemplated resignations." For many it was too late for a half loaf. Webb, Moore, Burden, Casey, and others in Marion were very much aware of civil rights activity beginning elsewhere in the country.[16]

The modern civil rights movement was taking form in 1954 as grass-roots Americans were questioning and challenging the traditional color line. Black veterans who returned from World War II were more militant and less accommodating, whether the issue was access to jobs or swimming pools. Black parents wanted to buy houses anyplace they could afford to buy and wanted first-class educations for their baby boomer kids. In May 1954 the United States Supreme Court handed down its most important decision of the twentieth century: in *Brown* v. *Board of Education* the Court ruled that segregated schools violated the Constitution's guarantee of equal protection of the law. Rising expectations everywhere caused lessened enthusiasm for half loaves and gave courage in Topeka, Kansas, Montgomery, Alabama, and Marion, Indiana. Thus Lester Granger advised Webb to hold the line and not accept the compromise of a separate-but-equal pool. More direct action seemed necessary.[17]

On June 20, 1954, Webb later reported, "seven well chosen, neat, clean young men went to the park to swim." Orderly and polite, they were refused admittance. Standing between the seven black men and the pool that hot Sunday were dozens of law officers. Rumors had circulated that "mobs of Negroes" from other towns were coming to storm the pool. The mayor and sheriff had cancelled all police leaves and added to their regular officers 50 citizens deputized to keep order. These armed civilian deputies stood alongside the regular police, the patrol wagon parked nearby. The president of the park board had warned that any black person who entered the pool might be shot. The *Indianapolis Recorder* ran on its front page a picture of one of the civilian deputies that gave just that impression—a young man in white tee shirt, a gun in a holster around his waist, looking as though he was defending a fundamental right against the forces of evil gathered at the entrance to Matter Park Pool. It was a kind of defense white Americans would mount frequently in the years to come.[18]

Both sides raised the ante as a heat wave settled over the Midwest. A day after the seven men were refused admission the NAACP filed legal suit. The park board requested bids to lease the pool to a private club, which would maintain a white-only membership, and then announced its closing because of cracks in the concrete. Anger on both sides increased. Cecile Moore continued to advocate integration of the pool, which caused her to receive anonymous threatening letters as well as snubs from some whites. Some city officials warned that pushing for integration would create racial violence. As tensions swelled, the United States District Court of Northern Indiana rendered a decision on July 30, 1954: "All persons," the court said, "shall be entitled to the full and equal enjoyment of the Matter Park swimming pool and all other park facilities, regardless of race or color . . . in accordance with the Fourteenth Amendment to the Constitution of the United States."[19]

Marion officials concluded it was hopeless to challenge the federal court. There would be none of the massive, head-on resistance that was beginning to rumble through the South. The city opened the Matter Park Swimming Pool to all citizens. Don Hawkins was the first black swimmer; his bus trips to Anderson were over. White attendance at the pool fell off sharply that summer, but there were no incidents. Oatess Archey and Tom Wise swam there nearly every day.[20]

The people of Marion survived a crisis that had the potential to explode in violence. Some white folks, including elected leaders, had shown a stubborn insistence on drawing hard lines of color. Blacks had displayed a courage to stand and fight. But the lines of color were not solid. While some blacks argued to go more slowly, some whites, like Cecile Moore, had actively and publicly pushed for integration. Gone was the silence from whites that had followed Flossie Bailey's calls for justice in 1930.

Beneath the ferment over the swimming pool lurked memories of the lynching. Many citizens still preferred silence in hope that the community could hide whatever troubled meanings the lynching might hold. But the memories were very much alive even though the tragic scar was now 24 years in the past. Those memories could be used for two contradictory purposes: to intimidate blacks and keep them in their place or to arouse white feelings of guilt that would encourage movement toward justice. The first purpose was conveyed in the anonymous note sent to one of the young black men who tried to enter the Matter Park Pool that hot Sunday in June: "What do you Negroes want, some more of you Black rats strung up again." The second came in an *Indianapolis Recorder* editorial about the pool: "White citizens of Marion, you have something to atone for." The Urban League's Webb agreed when he pointed to "the guilt complex about the lynching which took place on the public square some years ago." Which purpose was stronger in 1954 is impossible to know, but local NAACP leader C. DeVall Banks was likely correct when he reminded the national office of the lynching and concluded that "the entire community suffers the brunt of the incident, naturally, but most assuredly the Negro citizens."[21]

Success in erasing divisions of color could give courage to white and black citizens, strength to overcome the fears the lynching had created. The victory at Matter Park Pool "was the start of many things," Marion postman and NAACP leader Roger Smith remembered. During the late 1950s and early 1960s some blacks began to push against the color line with a new strength and courage, joined by more sympathetic whites. Central to the changing times in Marion were stirrings of an organized civil rights movement, watched closely and emulated by Marion's African Americans. They knew that as in the Matter Park Pool case the United States federal courts were moving toward legal equality; that NAACP lawyers, led by Thurgood Marshall, had developed sophisticated means of using the Fourteenth Amendment and other legal tools; and that the National Urban League and other groups were there as outside forces of assistance. When one black person was denied service at a Marion restaurant in the late 1950s or early 1960s phones rang across town and a small group soon showed up to request service. Some whites showed new courage too, not only as Cecile Moore had but in small, ordinary ways. When the Marion High School Band stopped for a meal on a trip home from Fort Wayne, the roadside restaurant refused service to the black members. The white bandleader insisted that all students be served or none.[22]

Yet no one thought the color lines had been erased in Marion. Indeed, Urban League official Webb predicted soon after the swimming pool was integrated that despite the "deceptive calm and serenity over all, underneath are the ingredients of a racial atom bomb." In particular, he said, "the public school situation and the police force, candidly, stink!"[23]

TEACHERS AND COPS

The schools were perhaps the most important places where Marion still drew the color line in the 1950s. There were no black teachers, although black and white students attended school together, with one exception—D. A. Payne School. It was an all-black school, located on the west side, just outside the city limits. Nevada Pate, a black woman, taught at this county school attended by many black city kids. When Payne closed in 1953, four years after Indiana finally legislated integration of all schools, Pate lost her job. NAACP leaders attended city school board meetings in the 1950s and at open question time always asked the same question: when would black teachers be hired?[24]

The first African American teacher hired in the city schools was Oatess Archey. He had been a superb athlete for the Marion High School Giants. In 1954 he was named all-state in football; in 1955 he won the Indiana state track championship in high hurdles. In true Hoosier tradition, he played basketball. A Marion Giant of Archey's stature was an unmatched local hero. Archey returned to Marion in 1960 with a degree earned at Grambling State in Louisiana. He sought a teaching and coaching job at his old high school, a common destiny for Indiana high school stars. He later recalled thinking of himself at this time as an "all-American kid," thinking that "the people of Marion loved me."[25]

The only job the Marion schools offered Archey in 1960 was as a janitor. He picked up trash and put lime on the football field but he did not teach or coach. Eventually school officials made him responsible for disciplining unruly students. Only a year later was Archey allowed in the classroom, the first African American teacher. About the same time, in 1961, school officials also hired Nevada Pate, the experienced teacher from D. A. Payne who had to wait even longer than the former Marion Giant. Four decades later Archey talked of "painful" memories and a "lot of scars" from his first return to Marion.

The schools gradually changed in the 1960s. More African American teachers were hired. In 1965 voters elected Dr. Joe Casey to the school board, the first black to serve. Casey was a prominent physician, active in the Urban League, and a proud descendant of Weaver people. He worked hard to add more black teachers to the two then employed by the school system. By 1972, when he was elected school board president, there were one or more black teachers in all of Marion's schools except one.[26]

As black teachers appeared in classrooms, more African American policemen eventually appeared on the city's streets, although the decades-old tradition of two and only two black cops continued through the 1950s. When Quentin Pettiford joined the force in 1955 he and the other black policeman, Cleo Beck, were not allowed to patrol in cars, only on foot. Not until 1960 were they permitted to sit behind the wheel. Gradually the city hired more black cops, including Tom Wise.[27]

Wise was one of 15 new policemen hired in 1970. The rapid jump in hiring was because Marion was in the grip of real and imagined racial violence and, even more important, in the midst of fear about America's changing struggle with race.[28]

HOT SUMMER IN THE CITY

The summer of 1969 was one of the worst in Marion's history, as it was for many American cities. Arson, looting, marches and protests, verbal and violent confrontations between blacks and whites sent anger and shock across the nation. Young African Americans spoke against the moderation of recently assassinated Martin Luther King, Jr., and raised clenched fists and loud voices of "black power." In some places Black Panthers were showing guns and talking boldly of violence.

Marion's time came in July with a series of firebombings, including one at the Meshingomesia Country Club. Whites assumed that "black hoodlums" had caused the damage, though no arsonists were ever charged. One business-man later recalled sitting for three nights, armed with a deer rifle, on the roof of his company, guarding against arsonists. "Old wounds have been opened," the local newspaper lamented, without specifying exactly what those wounds were. Two days after the July firebombings the Marion City Council met to consider purchase of police dogs. NAACP leader Roger Smith asserted it was the wrong time for such a provocative move: "You know what they have been used for in the past in other cities," he warned. But many at the meeting spoke of a "simple breakdown of law and order." The city council approved the purchase of police dogs.[29]

Marion's NAACP leaders that hot summer complained of "racial atroci-ties," including "police brutality" and "unprovoked assaults by white hood-lums" on blacks. Some whites responded by presenting the mayor with three thousand signatures on a petition that defended the police, claimed they needed to work without citizen interference, and denigrated "the overworked police brutality charge." The NAACP organized a protest march. The *Indianapolis Recorder* told its black readers that 3,000 people turned out for the march, which ended with a rally on the Grant County Courthouse Square. The *Marion Chronicle-Tribune* reported the protesters numbered 600 and claimed only 50 were from the city. Carrying signs that read "Lick Police Brutality" and "No Dogs," the marchers made their way peacefully to the courthouse. Milwaukee civil rights priest James Groppi spoke from the courthouse steps. NAACP official Syd Finley reminded the crowd of the 1930 lynching: "I want to serve notice right here and now that they aren't about to ever do that thing again in Marion, Indiana."[30]

The march leaders presented the city with a manifesto. It called for equal employment and educational opportunities, equal housing, more black teachers, and more black history programs in the schools. These were complaints similar to those voiced in other cities in America in the late 1960s. There were also issues specific to Marion. The manifesto asked that the local Fisher Body auto plant clean its house of racist activity among some white workers and suspend the president of the UAW local for his right-wing activities. Even more specifically, the manifesto called for equal access to Idyl Wyld roller skating rink, a local public amusement place. Some time earlier NAACP activist Roger Smith had allowed his daughter to accompany her Brownie Scout troop to a skating party there. Since she was with white leaders, he thought, there would be no trouble. But soon after his daughter left home Smith received a call from the rink. He had to pick her up; she was too young to understand what had happened or why.[31]

Marion's mayor did not respond specifically to the complaint about the skating rink. He did say that "most of the things in the 'manifesto' are just something somebody dreamed up to say. There is really no basis for them."[32] The mayor did hire 15 new police and decided not to appoint members to the city's new Human Relations Commission. Established in 1968 to help enforce laws on discrimination in jobs, housing, and education, the new organization of hope withered. It was the time of white America's backlash on race, of President Richard Nixon's combative rhetoric about law and order, of fears about a bloody war in Vietnam and an ailing economy at home. Americans hunkered down for hard times.[33]

Tom Wise joined the police force in the midst of this great tension. He was 1 of 2 black policemen along with 13 whites hired in 1970. It was a hard time for any cop, particularly a black one. Seeing what was happening in Detroit, Chicago, and other big cities, Marion's police department prepared for race riots. Some police officers had been shot at by unknown persons; they were quite ready to respond with force. On one occasion police filled a South Marion poolroom with bullets because they thought drug dealers—some said Black Panthers— used it as headquarters. Many blacks, including Tom Wise, who was patrolling South Marion that night, thought shooting up the poolroom was a symbolic show of force in a black neighborhood.[34]

The most tragic event of these troubled years was the murder of a black teenager, Robert Johnson, in 1973. The 14-year-old was shot from a moving car as he and several friends walked home from a school skating party at the Idyl Wyld rink, now open to all kids. Johnson's murder sparked protests from black students at Marion High School, who assumed it was a racial crime. Incidents of arson and violence rolled across the city. Angry blacks threw rocks at policemen and firemen; tensions persisted for weeks. Johnson's murderer was never identified. The crime remained a source of racial tension in the city. Some even claimed it was police who shot the black youth.[35]

NEW TIMES AND OLD MEMORIES

The last half of the twentieth century brought rapid changes to Grant County, similar to the transformations occurring in many American communities. Postwar prosperity spurred city growth and eventually a shopping mall on Marion's west side bypass, which left the downtown area around the Courthouse Square neglected and deteriorating. Most important, new people came to town. The executive director of the National Urban League described the changing community and its people in 1954:

> [A] widely diversified, highly industrialized complex is superimposed on a rich agricultural economy, with the result that we have a great number of emigrants from the near and deep south fleeing from their rural poverty in close juxtaposition to a well-to-do and conservative agricultural class. We have a minute number of 'native' Negroes who are acomodated [sic] to the 'system', a growing group of non-native Negroes who are ambitious, a small but powerful coterie of liberal aggressive whites and over all the financial domination of community life by a scant half dozen families representing the most conservative of the agricultural-industrial native element.[36]

Across the Midwest and across America there were many places like Grant County, Indiana. Few, however, carried memories of a lynching.

One frequent comment from Marion blacks in these changing years was about leadership. No black person emerged to take the place of Flossie Bailey. The Urban League and the NAACP branch sputtered, often plagued by squabbles among leaders or would-be leaders. The Rev. J. D. Williams of the Greater Second Baptist Church lamented that "all the power is held by whites." Williams went a step further, however, to comment that "we're unable to get a united front of black adults. We never have been able to," he said, because "the older blacks in Marion still remember August of 1930." Williams, a resident of

Marion for only ten years, complained that "we're not going to get black people together until they forget about that tree on the square." Many older blacks "have a deep-rooted sense of fear that prevents united action to stop disturbances."[37]

Williams's diagnosis is understandable. Flossie Bailey had made similar observations in the 1930s, reflecting her impatience with black fears that contributed to inaction. Jack Edwards, mayor in 1930 and again in the early 1960s, told an interviewer in 1977 that the lynching "scared the colored people to death. We had no trouble with the colored people from that day on until about, oh, I would say in the last ten years." For many older blacks especially, there was a strong desire to forget the lynching and hope that the fears would also go away.[38]

The younger generation of African Americans, such as Oatess Archey, remembered that black adults were "terrified" to talk about the lynching. Adults didn't need to explain to him what the tree on the square and the massive jail represented. He knew they were signs "to stay in your place." He knew he had to be especially careful with white girls when they were overly friendly to him, a handsome black male athlete: "We knew there could be serious trouble" even if the teenage white girls were too innocent to understand.[39]

Sarah Weaver Pate remembered the lynching all her life. She was Dr. Walter Bailey's assistant in 1930. Sixty-four years later she sat in her living room on a hot August night and spoke with warm memories of Dr. and Mrs. Bailey and of growing up in Weaver. But when her guest introduced the subject of the lynching, the lively and sweet 90-year-old woman's face and voice turned troubled and fearful. She lives alone, she says, and she fears talking about it. Marion is "the most racist city" in Indiana, she says. Another older black woman didn't think there would ever be another lynching in Marion, but, she told an interviewer, "we're like the rabbit now; we don't trust the sound of a stick, if you know what I'm talking about, cause people now got their ears open more now than what they had at that time." Memories still had the power to separate black and white into "them" and "us." Nevada Pate, some four decades after she lost her job at the all-black Payne School, said the lynching "was a blight on the city. I hope some day they'll be able to live it down."[40]

Other older residents remembered the lynching as the beginning of Grant County's racism. Before 1930 people got along fine; there was no discrimination before 1930, some recalled. With the lynching, "the prejudice began to rise up," according to Dr. Joe Casey. That's "when the racial thing in Marion started," claimed a white woman who grew up near Weaver.[41] It may have been that this myth that prejudice began with the lynching was linked to a hope that forgetting about the lynching would mean also forgetting about prejudice. Eliminate its origin and the evil is gone.

James Cameron faced these people and these fears as he began to return to Marion to pose for photographers and documentary cameras inside the old Grant County Jail. When his cousin Tom Wise interviewed people to assist Cameron's book project, blacks often told him to "stop digging that up." Forget it, they said. One old black man refused to talk to Wise except to say that "those boys got what they deserved." Even some of Marion's most effective older black leaders, such as Joe Casey and Harley Burden, Jr., resented Cameron's returns. He was now an outsider stirring up bad memories. Casey and Burden had stayed and fought the good fight. Burden was also angry because Cameron was critical of his father, the black policeman sent to Cameron's house on August 6. His book "ticked me off," Burden recalled. It's "just a money-making and ego-building thing for him." He thought Cameron came back to Marion only for his own publicity. "He never suffered at all," Burden said.[42]

Burden and Casey were among the most widely known and respected descendents of the Weaver community. Casey had established a good medical practice in Marion. Like many of the Weaver community, he was light skinned, so light he could have passed for white, as one of his family members decided to do in order to get a better job. Burden, known to friends as "Bud," graduated from Indiana University in 1942 just when Anaconda, one of Marion's big employers, needed to hire black workers to meet the federal government's new standards for war contracts. With help from the Marion branch of the National Urban League, Burden was hired in an office job, the first black at the company. Soon after other African Americans joined Anaconda, including Oatess Archey's father, who was employed as a machinist. Bud Burden moved up to payroll supervisor and then accounting manager, perhaps the first white-collar black person in a Marion industry— a visible sign that black men could hope for something better than the sweaty labor of the foundries.[43]

Looking back in retirement from their northern Indiana lakeside homes in the late 1990s, Bud Burden and Joe Casey both showed the scars of decades of discrimination and exclusion in their hometown. Both recalled their struggles to buy a house in a better neighborhood. By the mid-1950s, for example, Burden was earning enough money to build a nice home. His wife went looking for a building lot and found several, but when the sellers learned that the light-skinned Mrs. Burden was black and married to a black man, even a white-collar black man, negotiations stopped.[44]

Burden and Casey were proud men, proud of their Weaver community heritage and of their personal accomplishments. They were proud also of their long efforts to erase the color line. Both had been members of Flossie Bailey's NAACP Youth Group in the 1930s and served as board members and presidents of the Marion branch of the Urban League from its beginnings in the early 1940s. Each had been a member and president of the school board. Each had worked hard to hire black teachers and make Marion schools more racially balanced. Each had fought the good fight over decades.

The times changed in the last half of the twentieth century. New black families moved to Marion, families who had no knowledge of the Weaver community or of Marion's better traditions. They came simply for jobs in expanding factories. Former Mayor Jack Edwards lamented in 1977 the recent influx of "so many southern colored, the militant type." Joe Casey often referred to the newcomers as the "rushins," people rushing into Marion, invading the city as the Russians might have had the Cold War turned hot. These newcomers, these "rushins," had no direct memory of the lynching, less fear of its meaning, more willingness to push harder, more awareness of changing times. They tended to be Democratic in politics, while Weaver people were generally Republican. They often did not have the light skin color of so many Weaver people. The newcomers tended to be less moderate, less patient with slow change, even less willing to accept such traditional negotiated arrangements as the one that for decades allowed two and only two black policemen.[45]

As the American civil rights movement of the 1950s and 1960s raised higher expectations of racial equality and justice, the gaps between American ideals and Marion realities seemed to widen. Younger, more educated, more aggressive African Americans pushed harder. A few even found older black leaders like Joe

Casey and Bud Burden closer to "Uncle Toms" than pioneers for justice. Some found the community's handful of black leaders tokens, valuing cooperation with the white community more than justice for all. When Cameron came to Marion they heard his message; they saw good reasons to forgive but not forget. They saw reasons to keep the lynching story alive.[46]

Among the most radical of Marion's citizens by the late 1960s was Marcus Cannon. Not a "rushin," Cannon was descended of Weaver people but did not walk the moderate road of most of his relatives. Cannon grew up in South Marion. Born there in 1937, he rode the same swim bus to Anderson that Oatess Archey and Tom Wise did. Returning from military service in Korea in 1957, Cannon was determined that he "wasn't going to take it any more," that he was going to "demand" equality. He "became threatening," deliberately. A tall, muscular black man, he eventually adopted the blunt language of Malcolm X and traveled in the early 1960s to New Jersey to hear him speak. In the late 1960s Cannon joined the Black Panthers. Like Malcolm, he believed that African Americans had to take control of their community by any means necessary. For a time Cannon was not only unwilling to turn the other cheek but willing to use violence. He thought the police were often following him and threatening him. White fellow workers at GM's Fisher Body plant gave him a hard time, even, he stated, on one occasion firing shots at him as he sat in his car. Other young Marion blacks voiced support for Cannon, but only three or four were as radical. Marcus Cannon personified for many in the white community their worst fears. Many Marion blacks were as angry at him as whites were. Three decades later Cannon regretted that he once had such hate in his heart but remained proud that he "got people's attention" and perhaps thereby helped bring some change.[47]

Most blacks were less interested in Cannon's goal of taking control of Marion's African American community than in participating in the full range of Grant County life. Swimming in a pool was no longer an issue; what mattered now was having a real voice in the full community. One of the most important positive features of Marion's history was the dramatic emergence of African Americans in positions of power by the end of the twentieth century—far beyond what had been imagined in the 1950s and 1960s.

The changes in the police department were among the most visible. By the late 1980s 8 of the city's 63 policemen were African American. Amos

Randle, the police chief, was black. The assistant police chief was Tom Wise. To have one black officer among the top two by this time was not unusual in urban America; to have two in a city of 32,618 people in 1990, a city that was 14.8 percent African American, was very unusual. Tom Wise understood his significance as a black cop, as the cousin of James Cameron, and as the leader of a police force that had not done its duty in 1930. Wise and Randle faced harassment, even in the department. On one occasion someone slipped under their office door a hand-drawn cartoon of a bus with crude figures of Wise and Randle drawn as passengers. Printed on the side of the bus was "Niggerville, Ind." Heading from Marion, the bus was drawn on an imaginary road to Africa. The cartoon was captioned "back where they belong." One Christmas a police radio sang out "I'm Dreaming of a White Chief." There was special resentment toward Wise because he was so active in the NAACP. Yet despite these remnants of the past the Marion police department had clearly changed.[48]

FOURTEEN CITIZENS, THE PAST, THE FUTURE

On a Saturday morning in late summer 1998, 14 residents of Grant County gathered to discuss changing times. The panel was not systematically selected but included citizens especially knowledgeable and experienced in matters relating to the challenges of the color line. Seven were African American; seven were white. The meeting lasted two and a half hours and included free discussion that jumped and wove from subject to subject. There were some differences among the panelists, but also a surprising unanimity on many topics.[49]

All panelists agreed that there had been considerable progress in opportunities for blacks in Marion. They pointed with pride to the opening of doors in the 1960s and 1970s and to the relatively good environment late in the 1990s. At the time of the meeting, Marion had a black school board president, a black superintendent of schools, a black head of the city council, an assistant police chief who was black, and a black candidate for county sheriff. One panelist wryly commented that there were so many black faces in leadership positions that he had heard some whites talk of a "black conspiracy" to take over the city, an ironic note that spread easy laughter through the group.

Panelists noted happily the great progress in the Marion police department, now "one of the most progressive of its size," one claimed. There was pride that the west side bypass, which contained the usual shopping mall, chain stores, and restaurants, was to be renamed Martin Luther King, Jr. Drive. There was enthusiasm for recently formed racial healing circles that were bringing small groups of citizens together to talk. There were reports of strategies and plans to speed up the evolutionary process of progress based on a recently conducted survey of attitudes about race.

Overall these 14 citizens expressed a strong sense of a community that had begun to confront effectively its inequalities and fears, a community that was more positive than pessimistic about the future of black and white neighbors in this ordinary American place.

But no one on the panel claimed that the color line had been erased. There were still hate crimes in Grant County. Only a couple of weeks earlier someone had desecrated the black section of the local cemetery and painted swastikas on tombstones. There were reports of discrimination in employment and housing and still some questions of "comfort" for black families living in mostly white parts of the city. One panelist claimed that black kids were advised in schools to have lower expectations for themselves, to look for jobs in factories rather than in professions.

Older black panelists remembered when the Matter Park Swimming Pool was closed to black kids and they had to swim in the creeks or gravel pits. They recalled a time when there were no black teachers or athletic coaches in the public schools, when the first black teacher in 1961 met all manner of resistance, when there were restrictions on where a black family could buy a house. On two occasions the conversation of what it was like in the 1950s and 1960s produced tears and choked voices from members of the panel.

Panelists talked about the racial struggles of 1969 and later. Some remembered the police and fire departments as hotbeds of racism. They recalled how blacks had changed their expectations, how they were no longer willing to accept the boundaries that many in the first half of the century had considered regrettable but inevitable.

Most of the panelists were too young to remember the lynching firsthand. However, all knew about it. They knew who James Cameron was. Most were unsure of the details. Conversation about the lynching revealed the largest differences between memories of black citizens and white citizens. Whites recalled the lynching with embarrassment and regret, as the most tragic episode in Marion's history. For African American citizens the events of 1930 remained an "open wound" that still needed "healing." People wanted to talk about it, several black panelists thought, but didn't know how to do so and sometimes even acted as though the lynching never happened. Thus there was a kind of "hush-hush" approach. There was a sense that it was "hard to close the books if the whole story has not been told." "The lynching still holds us back," one said. There were still white people who had in a desk drawer or attic box a copy of the Beitler photograph of Tom Shipp's and Abe Smith's bodies hanging from the tree, with the crowd gathered below. Few black people had copies of that photo. Some panelists thought there needed to be some way of remembering, some memorial, some marker other than the photo. And, they insisted, there would be no healing until individual hearts were healed.

The 14 citizens sitting together in the Marion Public Library near the end of the century were proud of the progress in their community. There soon was one more sign of that progress. In the fall of that year of 1998, the people of Grant County elected a black sheriff.

A BLACK SHERIFF AND "HISTORIC MOMENTS"

Oatess Archey left his Marion High School teaching and coaching job in 1969 and eventually joined the FBI. He had a good 20-year career in law enforcement. Retirement in southern California was pleasant but not sufficient for an ambitious man. Archey and his wife, Barbara, began to think about moving back to Marion. Archey had an agenda beyond the call of family and friends back home in Indiana, however. He telephoned his childhood friend Tom Wise and asked him to test the political waters along the Mississinewa. Could Archey win election as Grant County sheriff? Wise had spent all his life in Marion and was closely connected to its politics, particularly within the Democratic Party. He asked around and reported back to Archey that there was a chance, a good chance. Soon Wise became Archey's campaign manager.[50]

The Grant County sheriff's election in fall 1998 was closely contested. The Republican candidate was a respected 25-year veteran of the sheriff's department. Republicans had a solid majority in the county and had held the sheriff's office for 20 years. Some people said Archey was "overqualified" for the job; some said he had been away too long. Others feared that Indiana sheriff departments were not very progressive on matters of race or professional law enforcement, that Archey had two strikes against him. But there were all those people who remembered the Marion Giant star athlete and those kids who had sat in his classes during the 1960s. The majority realized the quality of Archey's experience and talent. Enough Republicans crossed party lines to elect Archey the first black sheriff in Indiana's history.[51]

The swearing-in ceremony was one of the most moving events in Marion's recent past. In the Marion High School auditorium before 250 people, Sheriff Archey placed his hand on the Bible and took his oath, his wife by his side. Flash cameras lit up handshakes and warm hugs as well-wishers greeted Archey, wearing his new brown uniform. Among the greeters was James Cameron. The 84-year-old had driven by himself from Milwaukee. Cameron was determined to be there for this man who stood now in Sheriff Jake Campbell's line of succession. Local and out-of-town newspapers included Cameron's story with that of the new sheriff, joining the two in the long line of history.[52]

Sitting in his modern, spacious office in the new Grant County Jail in 1999, Sheriff Archey showed an interviewer the traits that attracted Grant County voters. He was polished and articulate, careful with words, able to tell stories with clear points and an easy smile. At 61, Archey was handsome, tall, with graying hair, still athletic looking, immaculately dressed. His wide desk was carefully organized. Behind him were two large flags, one of the United States, one of the Grant County Sheriff's Department. Turning his head only slightly, the sheriff looked out a large window across an open parking lot to the next block, where the old, abandoned Grant County Jail still stood. It was "a reminder to me to count my blessings—how far Grant County has come," he said. He didn't say how far he had come, though he regarded being an Indiana county sheriff as his most important life achievement. He was happy that Marion's

African American citizens could take special pride in his victory, and was especially proud that he won because of his qualifications, that no one could dare label him a "token."

Sheriff Archey's conversation returned often to the whole community and how much it had changed, how proud he was of his hometown. He did not pretend that the past was dead, however. He was not afraid of it: he wanted people always to remember the night of August 7, 1930. They did remember, he knew; in fact, many told him that they were pleased to have a chance to vote for him because it "helped clear consciences." They wanted "to do the right thing this time," some said. The people of Grant County knew the distance traveled from Sheriff Jake Campbell's time to Sheriff Oatess Archey's.[53]

In May 1999, Oatess Archey and Tom Wise, now retired from the city police force, traveled together to visit James Cameron. During the late 1990s Cameron's Black Holocaust Museum had attracted increased funding, enough to undertake renovation of the building and to hire an executive director. Notables such as civil rights leader Julian Bond and Vice President Albert Gore visited the museum. Milwaukee's mayor proclaimed Cameron's eighty-fifth birthday in early 1999 as James Cameron Day. And that May the University of Wisconsin at Milwaukee awarded Cameron an honorary degree. It was the commencement ceremony that brought Archey and Wise to Milwaukee.[54]

At the banquet following commencement Archey spoke about "the old and the new." He traveled to the ceremony, he said, because Cameron "was the pioneer"; I "stand on his shoulders." "Our lives have crossed in strange ways," said the man who became head of the department that failed to prevent the Marion lynching.[55]

Archey, Wise, and Cameron are all deeply aware of the ironies and twists of history, of the "historic moments," as Archey calls them, that come to all people if they have the eyes to see and the ears to hear. James Cameron had eyes and ears. And he had the voice to speak, not unlike the voice of the Old Testament prophets. The civil rights movement gave that voice amplification, made people more willing to listen, made silences uncomfortable. Oatess Archey, Tom Wise, and many other white and black citizens of Grant County, Indiana, heard.

There were other voices of courage in Grant County's history: Sheriff Orange Holman, who stood up to a lynch mob in 1885; Vennie and Marsha

Burden, who challenged Louis Chochos's laugh in 1917; James Ogden, the Indiana attorney general who wanted lynchers punished; Flossie Bailey, who fought the good fight in the terrible time of the Great Depression; R. L. Bailey and Robert Brokenburr, black lawyers on the front line; Cecile Moore, the ordinary housewife who lost friends because her Christianity included room for African Americans; Joe Casey and Bud Burden, the old generation that faced challenges the next generation could not understand. Their stories faded as James Cameron's grew. The pulpit Cameron so determinedly constructed as the survivor of the lynching meant that by century's end his voice was the one most heard. These other stories were no less important, however, in revealing the shifting lines of color and the changing possibilities of justice.

Some citizens still hoped that people would forget about the lynching; they pretended that the past was past, even that the past was dead. "It makes it worse when people drag it up all the time," one Marion black woman said in 1996. And there was just weariness, for some, such as Sarah Weaver Pate. She still remembered vividly the night of August 7, but "I feel like throwing it over the shoulder," she told an interviewer in 1994. "There's nothing you can do, the boys are dead and buried." "No need stirring up all that stuff, forget it and just try to live life."[56] But more and more there was realization that forgetting was not possible, not even desirable, but that forgiveness, healing, and hope were.

Always there were America's ideals. Lady Justice no longer stood on top of the Grant County Courthouse. After a sojourn in Matter Park she disappeared, ending up in a junkyard. Rescued and restored, she was moved to the new history museum in the Old Carnegie Library building, a block from the square. There were other new symbols to see by the end of the century. Inside the courthouse a wall displayed the "Freedom Shrine," a collection of fundamental American documents, including Lincoln's Second Inaugural and the Declaration of Independence. These noble sentiments of equality and justice were always there to lift spirits in this ordinary place—provided that people had the eyes to see and the ears to hear, especially if they were helped by a few preachers and prophets.

While it may have been an ordinary place, Marion experienced fundamental changes in the twentieth century. The color line that had seemed so natural at the beginning of the century had faded. To many by the century's end that line of division seemed a foolish remnant of a time past. Pioneer versions of democracy, which had once unthinkingly applied to whites only, had evolved to include people of color. But no one in Grant County or America could claim that color lines were extinct, that race no longer mattered, that this nation dedicated to the proposition that all were created equal had transcended race.

No one today can be sure exactly what happened August 6 and 7, 1930. No one can satisfactorily explain why the mob became so incensed, why the sheriff and other community leaders did not stop the beast. No can one fully understand why there was no legal justice, no punishment for the crimes committed. No one can explain why there was so much silence. Most certainly no one can fully understand the mysteries of the color line as they wove through these Marion stories. But those questions, once so important, have receded in significance as the ordinary people of Grant County connected their present to their past, not forgetting, but looking ahead with hope. In this way too they were ordinary people, perhaps walking a little more carefully with the burdens of the past than most of their fellow Americans.

There would always be the memory of the battered bodies of Abe Smith and Tom Shipp hanging from the tree on the Courthouse Square. But becoming more and more haunting as time passed was the white crowd standing below those bare, dangling feet. By the beginning of the twenty-first century that crowd of shameless spectators was no longer just Grant County's memory but all of America's. Americans would continue to decide what to do with that memory and what stories it evoked.

NOTES

CHAPTER ONE

1. The following are the best guides to the events of August 6 and 7, 1930: Walter White to James M. Ogden, August 22, 1930, Lynching File, Harry Leslie Papers, Indiana State Archives, Indianapolis; Testimonies of Thirty Witnesses, Grant County Court of Inquiry, August 13, 14, 15, 1930, Lynching Depositions, Box 20, James M. Ogden Papers, Indiana State Archives; "Interview Turnkey Marion Jail," n.d., Lynching Depositions, Box 20, Ogden Papers; Flossie Bailey to Walter White, August 8, 1930, Papers of the NAACP, Part 7: The Anti-Lynching Campaign, 1912-1955, Series A: Investigative Files, 1912-1953, microfilm reel 11; Larry Conrad, interviews with Orville Scott, William Bernaul, Lowell Nussbaum, Faith Deeter Copeland, Thurman Biddinger, Evelyn Thompson, Don Stewart, Mary Campbell Fuller, Robert F. Myers, 1977, tapes in author's possession; author's interviews with James Cameron, June 10, 1993, Robert W. Newell, June 29, 1992, Mary Campbell Fuller, May 22, 1999; James Cameron, *A Time of Terror* (Milwaukee, 1982, Baltimore, 1994); Merle D. Blue to author, January 18, 1995, in author's possession; Fred Trueblood to H. Dixon and Mark Trueblood, August 11, 1930, copy in author's possession; *Marion Leader-Tribune; Marion Chronicle; Indianapolis Times; Indianapolis News; Indianapolis Star; Indianapolis Recorder; Kokomo Tribune.*

CHAPTER TWO

1. For a good overview of lynching scholarship see W. Fitzhugh Brundage, ed., "Introduction," to *Under Sentence of Death: Lynching in the South* (Chapel Hill, N.C., 1997), 1-20. In addition to the essays in the Brundage collection, see also W. Fitzhugh Brundage, *Lynching in the New South: Georgia and Virginia, 1880-1930* (Urbana, Ill., 1993); Linda Gordon, *The Great Arizona Orphan Abduction* (Cambridge, Mass., 1999), 254-74; Jacquelyn Dowd Hall, *Revolt against Chivalry: Jessie Daniel Ames and the Women's Campaign against Lynching* (rev. ed., New York, 1993), 129-57; Nancy Maclean, "White Women and Klan Violence in the 1920s: Agency, Complicity and the Politics of Women's History," *Gender and History* 3 (autumn 1991), 283-303; Robyn Wiegman, "The Anatomy of Lynching," in John C. Fout and Maura Shaw

Tantillo, eds., *American Sexual Politics: Sex, Gender, and Race since the Civil War* (Chicago, 1992); Trudier Harris, *Exorcising Blackness: Historical and Literary Lynching and Burning Rituals* (Bloomington, Ind., 1984); Charlotte Wolf, "Constructions of a Lynching," *Sociological Inquiry* 62 (February 1992), 83-97; Stewart E. Tolnay and E. M. Beck, *A Festival of Violence: An Analysis of Southern Lynchings, 1882-1930* (Urbana, Ill., 1995); Walter White, *Rope and Faggot: A Biography of Judge Lynch* (New York, 1929); J. William Harris, "Etiquette, Lynching, and Racial Boundaries in Southern History: A Mississippi Example," *American Historical Review* 100 (April 1995), 387-410; George C. Wright, *Racial Violence in Kentucky, 1865-1940: Lynchings, Mob Rule, and "Legal Lynchings"* (Baton Rouge, La., 1990); Paul Finkelman, ed., *Lynching, Racial Violence, and Law* (New York, 1992); Orlando Patterson, *Rituals of Blood: Consequences of Slavery in Two American Centuries* (Washington, D.C., 1998), 169-232; Mark Curriden and Leroy Phillips, Jr., *Contempt of Court: The Turn of the Century Lynching that Launched 100 Years of Federalism* (New York, 1999). Visual evidence is provided in James Allen, Hilton Als, John Lewis, and Leon F. Litwack, *Without Sanctuary: Lynching Photography in America* (Santa Fe, N.M., 2000). For a vivid fictional account see Theodore Dreiser's "Nigger Jeff," in *The Best Short Stories of Theodore Dreiser* (New York, 1956), 157-82.

2. Brundage, *Lynching in the New South*, 8. For challenges of counting and the changing definition of lynching see Christopher Waldrep, "War of Words: The Controversy over the Definition of Lynching, 1899-1940," *Journal of Southern History* 66 (February 2000), 75-100.

3. Ida B. Wells, *Southern Horrors: Lynch Law in All Its Phases* (New York, 1892), 14.

4. Lines from "Strange Fruit"—Lewis Allen © 1939 (Renewed) by Music Sales Corp. All rights outside the United States controlled by Edward B. Marks Music Company. Used by permission. All rights reserved. *Strange Fruit.* Words and Music by Lewis Allan. Copyright © by Music Sales Corporation (ASCAP) International Rights Secured. All Rights Reserved. Reprinted by Permission.

5. Thomas Cripps, *Slow Fade to Black: The Negro in American Film, 1900-1942* (New York, 1977), 41-69; David Margolick, *Strange Fruit: Billie Holiday, Café Society, and an Early Cry for Civil Rights* (Philadelphia, 2000), 20. Lynching was also a central feature of many foreigners' understandings of America, particularly from those seeking to highlight the failure of American ideals. Japanese cartoons during World War II, for example, found in lynching useful images to present to Asians. Lewis A. Erenberg and Susan E. Hirsch, *The War in American Culture: Society and Consciousness during World War II* (Chicago, 1996), 192.

6. Brundage, *Lynching in the New South*, 8. Perhaps a much smaller black population, a tradition of free African Americans rather than slave, a less rigid class system and more fluid society, a culture that allowed women to be a bit

less "protected," the remnants of an antislavery sentiment, and memories of the Civil War all helped keep incidences of lynching fewer in the North than the South.

7. Dennis B. Downey and Raymond M. Hyser, *No Crooked Death: Coatesville, Pennsylvania, and the Lynching of Zachariah Walker* (Urbana, Ill., 1991); Michael W. Fedo, *"They Was Just Niggers"* (Ontario, Calif., 1979); Dominic J. Capeci, Jr., *The Lynching of Cleo Wright* (Lexington, Ky., 1998).

8. Bernard W. Sheehan, "'The Famous Hair Buyer General': Henry Hamilton, George Rogers Clark, and the American Indian," *Indiana Magazine of History* 79 (March 1983), 20-21; Harrison quote in R. David Edmunds, "Justice on a Changing Frontier: Deer Lick Creek, 1824-1825," *Indiana Magazine of History* 93 (March 1997), 48.

9. Brian M. Doerr, "The Massacre at Deer Lick Creek, Madison County, Indiana, 1824," *Indiana Magazine of History* 93 (March 1997), 19-47, quote on 37. See also George Chalou, "Massacre on Fall Creek," *Prologue* (summer 1972), 109-14. For a fictional account see Jessamyn West, *The Fall Creek Massacre* (New York, 1974). The willingness of a white jury and community to punish white murderers of Indians in 1824 was influenced to some degree by white fears of Native American retaliation if the murders of the Seneca families went unpunished. Kurt Vonnegut, Jr., in *Sirens of Titan* (New York, 1959), 315, has his character on his return to earth from Titan decide to land not in sunny Florida but in snowy Indianapolis because "the kind of people who'll hang a white man for murdering an Indian . . . that's the kind of people for me."

10. The discussion of lynching in Indiana draws from the pioneering work of Emma Lou Thornbrough, *The Negro in Indiana: A Study of a Minority* (Indianapolis, 1957), 276-87. See also Clifton J. Phillips, *Indiana in Transition: The Emergence of an Industrial Commonwealth, 1880-1920* (Indianapolis, 1968), 374-78; Richard Maxwell Brown, *Strain of Violence: Historical Studies of American Violence and Vigilantism* (New York, 1975), 21-25, 95-133.

11. Darrel E. Bigham, *We Ask Only a Fair Trial: A History of the Black Community of Evansville, Indiana* (Bloomington, 1987), 104-07.

12. Winfield T. Durbin, "The Mob and the Law," *Independent* 55 (July 30, 1903), 1790-93. For Durbin's counterpart in Illinois, see Stacy Pratt McDermott, "'An Outrageous Proceeding': A Northern Lynching and the Enforcement of Anti-Lynching Legislation in Illinois, 1905-1910," *Journal of Negro History* 84 (winter 1999), 61-78.

13. Gordon, *Great Arizona Orphan Abduction,* 254-74.

14. *New York Telegram,* April 23, 1920; *New York Times,* April 23, 28, 1920; *Indianapolis Star,* April 23, 1920; *New York World,* March 16, 1920.

15. This account is from *Marion Chronicle,* July 17, 24, 1885. See also *Indianapolis Journal,* July 16, 1885.
16. *Indianapolis Journal,* July 16, 1885.
17. *Marion Chronicle,* July 24, 1885; *Indianapolis Journal,* July 16, 1885.
18. *History of Grant County, Indiana* (Chicago, 1886), 569-70.
19. *Indianapolis Journal,* July 16, 1885.
20. See Larry J. Griffin, Paula Clark, and Joanne C. Sandberg, "Narrative and Event: Lynching and Historical Sociology," in Brundage, ed., *Under Sentence of Death,* 24-47; Gail Williams O'Brien, *The Color of the Law: Race, Violence, and Justice in the Post-World War II South* (Chapel Hill, N.C., 1999). There was at least one other averted lynching, in 1902: *Marion Chronicle,* May 26, 1902.

CHAPTER THREE

1. The standard local histories used in this chapter are *History of Grant County Indiana* (Chicago, 1886); *Biographical Memoirs of Grant County, Indiana* (Chicago, 1901); Rolland Lewis Whitson, ed., *Centennial History of Grant County, 1812-1912* (Chicago, 1914); *"Lest We Forget": Reminiscences of Pioneers of Grant County, Indiana* (Marion, [1921]); *A Century of Development: Grant County, Indiana* (Marion, 1937); W. H. McGrew, *Interesting Episodes in the History of Marion and Grant County, Indiana* (Marion, 1966); Steve Bunish, *The Golden Age of Marion* (n.p., 1989). Also important is the collection of local history done under the auspices of the Federal Works Progress Administration in the 1930s. The reports and notes for Grant County are in the Indiana WPA Collection, Indiana State University, Terre Haute. These published and unpublished local histories are similar to their counterparts across the Midwest in structure, format, and interpretation. For the commemoration of midwestern pioneers, see John Bodnar, *Remaking America: Public Memory, Commemoration, and Patriotism in the Twentieth Century* (Princeton, 1992), 113-37; James H. Madison, "Celebrating Indiana: 1816, 1916, 2016," in Robert Taylor, Jr., ed., *The State of Indiana History 2000* (Indianapolis, 2001), 274-96.
2. Stewart Rafert, *The Miami Indians of Indiana: A Persistent People, 1654-1994* (Indianapolis, 1996), 108-13; 179-229; Bunish, *The Golden Age of Marion,* 90.
3. Jacqueline S. Nelson, "The Military Response of the Society of Friends in Indiana to the Civil War," *Indiana Magazine of History* 81 (June 1985), 111.

4. U.S. Census Bureau, *Fifteenth Census of the United States: Population,* vol. 3, part 1 (Washington, D.C., 1932); Daniel Nelson, *Farm and Factory: Workers in the Midwest, 1880-1990* (Bloomington, Ind., 1995), 96-97.

5. Stephen J. Fletcher, "The Business of Exposure: Lewis Hine and Child Labor Reform," *Traces of Indiana and Midwestern History* 4 (spring 1992), 12-23.

6. Errol Wayne Stevens, "Heartland Socialism: The Socialist Party of America in Four Midwestern Communities, 1898-1920" (Ph.D. dissertation, Indiana University, 1978), 173-78, 211-26; Nelson, *Farm and Factory,* 96-98.

7. Mary Campbell Fuller, interview with author, May 22, 1999.

8. Faith Deeter Copland, interview with Larry Conrad, June 23, 1977, Walter G. Fansler, interview with Larry Conrad, August 24, 1977, Larry Conrad Papers, in author's possession.

9. For this tension in Muncie, a generally similar place 36 miles southeast of Marion, see Robert S. Lynd and Helen Merrell Lynd, *Middletown: A Study in Contemporary American Culture* (New York, 1929).

10. *Marion Chronicle,* August 8, 1930.

11. John R. McMahon, "Our Jazz-Spotted Middle West," *Ladies Home Journal,* February 1922, 38; Duncan Schiedt, *The Jazz State of Indiana* (Pittsboro, Ind., 1977), 78; James H. Madison, *Indiana through Tradition and Change: A History of the Hoosier State and Its People, 1920-1945* (Indianapolis, 1982), 329-35. The Lynds concluded that "no two generations of Americans have ever faced each other across as wide a gap in their customary attitudes and behavior as have American parents and children since the World War." Robert S. Lynd and Helen Merrell Lynd, *Middletown in Transition: A Study in Cultural Conflicts* (New York, 1937), 168.

12. Quoted in Fletcher, "The Business of Exposure," 17. As a boy Cole Porter traveled from his hometown of nearby Peru to Marion to take violin lessons, and while waiting for the train home discovered a Marion bookshop that sold naughty books, the source, he later claimed, of some of his lyrics. William McBrien, *Cole Porter: A Biography* (New York, 1998), 15.

13. Conrad interviews with Thurman Biddinger, June 24, 1977, Mary Campbell Fuller, July 6, 1977, Vaughn Treber, March 23, 1977, Roy Marvin, June 23, 1977, Conrad Papers; *Marion Chronicle,* January 5, 1960.

14. *Marion Chronicle,* December 30, 1930.

15. Jack Edwards, interviews with author, July 7, 1992, with Conrad, February 15, 1977, in author's possession, and with Douglas Clanin, March 31, 1984, in Indiana Historical Society Library.

16. *Marion Chronicle,* February 27, March 3, 15, 1930, January 5, 1931.

17. Fred Trueblood to H. Dixon and Mark Trueblood, August 11, 1930, copy in author's possession; Arthur F. Raper, *The Tragedy of Lynching* (Chapel Hill, N.C., 1933), 404-5; Biddinger, interview with Conrad.

18. The best account is Leonard J. Moore, *Citizen Klansmen: The Ku Klux Klan in Indiana, 1921-1928* (Chapel Hill, N.C., 1991). Also useful is Madison, *Indiana through Tradition and Change*, 44-75; M. William Lutholtz, *Grand Dragon: D.C. Stephenson and the Ku Klux Klan in Indiana* (West Lafayette, Ind., 1991); Kathleen M. Blee, *Women of the Klan: Racism and Gender in the 1920s* (Berkeley, Calif., 1991); Dwight W. Hoover, "Daisy Douglas Barr: From Quaker to Klan 'Kluckerss,'" *Indiana Magazine of History* 87 (June 1991), 171-95; and especially Allen Safianow, "The Klan Comes to Tipton," *Indiana Magazine of History* 95 (September 1999), 202-31. A reporter counted the marchers in a Marion Klan parade in 1926 and totaled 538 men, 279 women, and 41 junior members, gathered from half a dozen Indiana towns in addition to Marion. *Marion Leader-Tribune*, August 22, 1926.

19. *Marion Chronicle*, November 27, 1922; *Marion Leader-Tribune*, November 27, 1922.

20. Swift's photographs are in the W. A. Swift Collection, Ball State University Library, Muncie, Ind.; *Marion Leader-Tribune*, November 27, 1922.

21. *Fiery Cross*, February 2, 23, 1923; *Marion Leader-Tribune*, November 30, 1923.

22. Conrad interviews with Treber, Ray Robertson, April 7, 1977, Lowell Nussbaum, May 10, 1977, Biddinger, all in Conrad Papers; James Cameron, interview with author, June 10, 1993; Moore, *Citizen Klansmen*, 46-60, 173; Ku Klux Klan officer lists, 1925, Indiana Historical Society Library, Indianapolis. The 1925 Klan lists indicate that all Grant County government officials were "ok," meaning they were sympathetic to or members of the Klan, except for Edward Hays, the county prosecutor.

23. James Cameron is part of the source for the mistaken belief that the Klan lynched Tom Shipp and Abe Smith. Cameron presents also the wider myth about the Indiana Klan of the 1920s: "Arson, bombings, and lynching of black men were their unholy trinity." James Cameron, *A Time of Terror* (Milwaukee, 1982), 46. These notions of Klan violence and its focus on African Americans are deeply embedded in most popular assumptions about the Klan and in most stories about the Marion lynching. See chapter 8 for further discussion.

CHAPTER FOUR

1. Steve Bunish, *The Golden Age of Marion* (n.p., 1989), 66.

2. Unless otherwise indicated all references to this case are from the transcript and briefs of *Vennie Burden* v. *L. Chochos et al.* and *Marsha Burden* v. *L. Chochos et al.*, no. 10447, Indiana Court of Appeals, Indianapolis.

3. Attorneys for the New York Candy Kitchen objected to Marsha Burden's testimony that Chochos laughed at the two women as they left. They moved to strike her statement from the record. The court sustained their motion, so that the jury was not to decide the case on this level of ridicule and emotion.

4. Emma Lou Thornbrough, *The Negro in Indiana: A Study of a Minority* (Indianapolis, 1957), 259-66.

5. *Chochos et al.* v. *Burden et al.,* 74 Ind. App. 242, 128 N.E. 696 (Ind. Ct. App. 1920), quotation on 697.

6. W. E. B. Du Bois, *The Souls of Black Folk* (New York, 1989), 1.

7. Ray Stannard Baker, *Following the Color Line: An Account of Negro Citizenship in the American Democracy* (New York, 1964).

8. Ibid., 126-28.

9. Charles Kettleborough, ed., *Constitution Making in Indiana: A Source Book of Constitutional Documents with Historical Introduction and Critical Notes,* vol. III, *1916-1930* (Indianapolis, 1930), xviii, 229. In 1936 voters approved an amendment to the state constitution that removed the restriction against African Americans serving in the state militia. John A. Bremer, ed., *Constitution Making in Indiana: A Source Book of Constitutional Documents with Historical Introduction and Critical Notes,* vol. 4, *1930-1960* (Indianapolis, 1978), 63-64.

10. The best general accounts are Thornbrough, *The Negro in Indiana;* and Emma Lou Thornbrough, *Since Emancipation: A Short History of Indiana Negroes, 1863-1963* (Indianapolis, 1963). See also Justin E. Walsh, *The Centennial History of the Indiana General Assembly, 1816-1978* (Indianapolis, 1987), 149, 479; Clifton J. Phillips, *Indiana in Transition: The Emergence of an Industrial Commonwealth, 1880-1920* (Indianapolis, 1968), 400-2. For a regional overview see James H. Madison, "Is There a Black Heartland? Questions of Place and Race in Midwestern History," in Gerald Early, ed., *Black Heartland: African American Life, the Middle West, and the Meaning of American Regionalism* (St. Louis, 1997), 50-64.

11. Emma Lou Thornbrough, "Segregation in Indiana during the Klan Era of the 1920s," *Mississippi Valley Historical Review* 47 (March 1961), 594. See also Lionel F. Artis, "The Negro in Indiana, or The Struggle against Dixie Come North," in Tom Lutz and Susanna Ashton, eds., *These "Colored" United States: African American Essays from the 1920s* (New Brunswick, N.J., 1996), 116-28.

12. Thornbrough, "Segregation in Indiana," 609; Emma Lou Thornbrough and Lana Ruegamer, *Indiana Blacks in the Twentieth Century* (Bloomington, Ind., 2000); James H. Madison, *Indiana through Tradition and Change: A History of the Hoosier State and Its People, 1920-1945* (Indianapolis, 1982), 8-11; Darrel E. Bigham, *We Ask Only a Fair Trial: A History of the Black Community of Evansville, Indiana* (Bloomington, 1987), 136-51; Robert S. Lynd and

Helen Merrell Lynd, *Middletown: A Study in Contemporary American Culture* (New York, 1929), 479; Robert S. Lynd and Helen Merrell Lynd, *Middletown in Transition: A Study in Cultural Conflicts* (New York, 1937), 463. For a later and more personal account of Muncie see Gregory Howard Williams, *Life on the Color Line: The True Story of a White Boy Who Discovered He Was Black* (New York, 1995).

13. Martin Luther King, Jr., "Letter from Birmingham Jail," in Henry Louis Gates, Jr., and Nellie Y. McKay, eds., *The Norton Anthology of African American Literature* (New York, 1997), 1857.

14. *"Lest We Forget": Reminiscences of the Pioneers of Grant County, Indiana* (Marion, 1921).

15. The World War I plaque remained on the Courthouse Square through the twentieth century, to be joined by other memorials to Grant County's war dead, which did not make distinctions of color.

16. See especially by Asenath Peters Artis, "The Negro in Grant County," in Rolland Lewis Whitson, ed., *Centennial History of Grant County, 1812-1912* (Chicago, 1914), 348-57. On Weaver and Liberty Township, see the tapes of oral history interviews conducted by Robert McDonough with Joseph Casey, November 24, 1980, Clayton Jackson, December 23, 1980, Delores Betts, January 6, 1980, Georgia Weaver Jones, March 10, 1981, Valerie Stewart, March 18, 1981, all in the Indiana Historical Society Library; and Sarah Weaver Pate, interview with author, August 2, 1994; Norma Scott Johnson et al., *The Pettiford Family Tree: A Genealogical History* (Los Angeles, 1983); Barbara J. Stevenson, *An Oral History of African Americans in Grant County* (Charleston, S.C., 2000). For black rural communities, see Xenia Cord, "Black Rural Settlement in Indiana before 1860," in Wilma L. Gibbs, ed., *Indiana's African-American Heritage: Essays from "Black History News and Notes"* (Indianapolis, 1993), 99-110; Linda Weintraut, "A Glimpse of a Past: Lyles and Weaver Settlements, 1850-1860," *Black History News and Notes,* no. 77 (August 1999), 1-3; Gregory S. Rose, "The Distribution of Indiana's Ethnic and Racial Minorities in 1850s," *Indiana Magazine of History* 87 (September 1991), 252; and especially Stephen A. Vincent, *Southern Seed, Northern Soil: African-American Farm Communities in the Midwest, 1765-1900* (Bloomington, Ind., 1999).

17. William F. Munn, "Little Glory at Home for Jonesboro Enlistees," *Marion Chronicle-Tribune,* February 9, 1999.

18. Xenia E. Cord, "Indiana Applications to the Cherokee Restitution Appropriation of 1906: A Little-Known Source for Black Genealogy," in Gibbs, ed., *Indiana's African-American Heritage,* 218, 224-28. For doubt about some claims to Cherokee ancestry see Vincent, *Southern Seed, Northern Soil,* 156, 174-75.

19. Joseph Casey, interview with author, September 4, 1998; See also Gunnar Myrdal, *An American Dilemma: The Negro Problem and Modern Democracy,* (New York, 1944), 697-98; Vincent, *Southern Seed, Northern Soil,* 67, 147-48.

20. Jones, interview with McDonough; Stewart, interview with McDonough; Jackson, interview with McDonough; Sarah Weaver Pate, interview with Barbara J. Stevenson, July 27, 1994, copy in author's possession; *Marion Leader-Tribune,* July 4, 1925; *Marion Chronicle,* July 2, 1927.

21. Charlotte Fenstermaker, interview with Barbara J. Stevenson, June 27, 1994, in *Remembering the Past: An Oral and Pictorial History of African Americans in Grant County, Indiana,* vol. 1 (n.p.,1996).

22. "There is nothing left of the little village with the exception of the empty store building and one or two houses," WPA researchers noted in the late 1930s. Grant County, folder 700, WPA Collection, Indiana State University, Terre Haute. In fact, Hills A.M.E. Chapel had been destroyed by lightning in the late 1920s but was later rebuilt and continued to stand into the twenty-first century.

23. *Marion Leader,* September 9, 1900.

24. *Marion Leader-Tribune,* December 26, 28, 1915. It is likely that black teacher and attorney John W. Burden was the leader in organizing the tribute to Booker T. Washington. He served as master of ceremonies at the event.

25. Jerry Miller, "People of Color: Grant County's Black Heritage," *Marion Chronicle-Tribune Magazine,* July 9, 1978, 4-12; Stevenson, *An Oral History of African Americans in Grant County,* 55-57, 65-67.

26. U.S. Census Bureau, *Fifteenth Census of the United States 1930: Population,* vol. 3, part. 1 (Washington, D.C., 1932). For a good analysis of choices African American migrants made see Jack S. Blocker, Jr., "Choice and Circumstance: Destinations Sought and Shunned by African-American Migrants in the Lower Midwest, 1860-1930," paper presented at Organization of American Historians, Toronto, 1999, copy in author's possession; and Jack S. Blocker, Jr., "Wages of Migration: Jobs and Homeownership among Black and White Workers in Muncie, Indiana, 1920," in Isidore Okpewho, Carole Boyce Davies, and Ali A. Mazrui, eds., *The African Diaspora: African Origins and New World Identities* (Bloomington, Ind., 1999), 115-38.

27. Katherine M. Jourdan, "The Architecture of Samuel M. Plato," in Gibbs, ed., *Indiana's African-American Heritage,* 177-85.

28. *Marion Chronicle,* April 5, 1904; Marvin Dulaney, *Black Police in America* (Bloomington, Ind., 1996), 23; Harley Burden, Jr., interview with author, September 4, 1998.

29. Harley Burden, Jr., interview with author; Thurman Biddinger, interview with Larry Conrad, June 24, 1977; William Bernaul, interview with Larry Conrad, May 4, 1977, Larry Conrad Papers, in author's possession.

30. U. S. Census Bureau, *Negroes in the United States, 1920-1932* (Washington, D.C., 1932), 278; Joseph Casey, interview with McDonough, November 24, 1980; Jack Edwards, interview with Conrad, February 15, 1977; Sarah Weaver Pate, interview with author, August 2, 1994; Edmund Casey, interview with author, December 12, 1995; Joe Davis, interview with author, June 28, 1995; Bruce Weaver, interview with author, October 2, 1995.

31. Bernaul, interview with Conrad; Don Stewart, interview with Conrad, June 23, 1977; William F. Munn, Sue Bratton, Terry Lakes, eds., *Rough Times: Oral Histories Collected by Students in Advanced Placement US History and Advanced Placement English at Marion High School, Marion, Indiana, 1997-1998* (Marion, 1999), 11, 50-51; Miller, "People of Color," 4-12; Claudia Polley, "Segregation Creates Hidden Paradise," *Indiana Preservationist,* July-August 1993, 12-13. For a proposal to create three new all-black schools in 1907 see *Marion Leader,* January 25, 29, 1907.

32. *Marion Leader-Tribune,* May 27, 1915, February 11, 1919, November 20, 1923, March 15, 1927. See also Earline Rae Ferguson, "A Community Affair: African-American Women's Club Work in Indianapolis, 1879-1917" (Ph.D. dissertation, Indiana University, 1997); Darlene Clark Hine, *When the Truth Is Told: A History of Black Women's Culture and Community in Indiana, 1875-1950* (Indianapolis, 1981).

33. Thornbrough, *Since Emancipation,* 85-86; August Meier and John H. Bracy, Jr., "The NAACP as a Reform Movement, 1909-1965: 'To Reach the Conscience of America,'" *Journal of Southern History* 59 (February 1993), 3-30.

34. Application for Charter of Marion, Ind., Branch, Group I, Series G, Container 65, NAACP Papers, Library of Congress, Washington, D.C.

35. Lincoln and Roosevelt Memorial Program, February 9, 1919, Group I, Series G, Container 65, NAACP Papers.

36. *Marion Leader-Tribune,* December 8, 1920, April 20, 1921.

37. Violet Rhinehardt to Robert W. Bagnall, June 26, 1927, Flossie Bailey to Bagnall, March 1, 1927, Flossie Bailey to William Pickens, March 28, 1927, Bagnall to Flossie Bailey, March 4, 1929, all in Group I, Series G, Container 65, NAACP Papers.

38. Court of Inquiry, August 13-15, 1930, p. 26, Lynching Depositions, Box 20, James M. Ogden Papers, Indiana State Archives, Indianapolis; Edmund Casey, interview with author, December 12, 1995; James Cameron, interview with author, June 10, 1993; *Who's Who in Colored America, 1933-1937* (Brooklyn, N.Y., 1937), 38.

39. Sarah Weaver Pate, interview with author, August 2, 1994; Harriett Bailey Conn, interview with Conrad, August 23, 1977.

40. *Marion Leader-Tribune,* September 8, 10, 1929.

41. Membership Report Blanks, March 19, March 25, June 17, August 27, October 28, 1930, Group I, Series G, Container 65, NAACP Papers.

CHAPTER FIVE

1. Court of Inquiry, August 13-15, 1930, pp. 40-41, Lynching Depositions, Box 20, James M. Ogden Papers, Indiana State Archives, Indianapolis.

2. Flossie Bailey to Walter White, August 8, 9, 1930, Papers of the NAACP, Part 7: The Anti-Lynching Campaign, 1912-1955, Series A: Investigative Files, 1912-1953, microfilm reel 11.

3. R. L. Bailey et al. to Harry Leslie, April 8, 1930, Lynching File, Governor Harry Leslie Papers, Indiana State Archives, Indianapolis; R. L. Bailey to White, August 8, 1930, NAACP Papers, Part 7, reel 11; White to Leslie, August 8, 1930, Lynching File, Leslie Papers; White to Flossie Bailey, NAACP Papers, Part 7, reel 11.

4. Harley Burden, Jr., interview with author, September 4, 1998; Flossie Bailey to White, August 8, 9, NAACP Papers, Part 7, reel 11.

5. *New York Times,* August 9, 1930

6. *Indianapolis Star,* August 10, 12, 1930; *Indianapolis Times,* August 9, 11, 1930; *Marion Leader-Tribune,* August 9, 1930.

7. *Indianapolis Times,* August 11, 1930; *New York Times,* August 10, 1930.

8. *Indianapolis Recorder,* August 16, 1930; *Indianapolis Times,* August 11, 1930; *Indianapolis Star,* August 12, 1930; *Marion Chronicle,* August 11, 1930; *Muncie Star,* August 9, 1930; Hurley Goodall and J. Paul Mitchell, *A History of Negroes in Muncie* (Muncie, Ind., 1976), 25-26.

9. Walter White, *Rope and Faggot: A Biography of Judge Lynch* (New York, 1929); James Goodman, *Stories of Scottsboro* (New York, 1994), 34-35; Donald L. Grant, *The Anti-Lynching Movement, 1883-1932* (San Francisco, 1975), 149-60.

10. White to Flossie Bailey, August 11, 1930, Flossie Bailey to White, August 12, 1930, NAACP Papers, Part 7, reel 11; White to Miss Randolph, August 12, 1930, Papers of the NAACP, Part 1: Meetings of the Board of Directors, . . . 1909-1950, microfilm reel 25.

11. "Expense Account, Aug. 14-19, 1930, of W.W. to investigate lynchings at Marion," Papers of the NAACP, Part 2, 1919-1939: Personal Correspondence of Selected NAACP Officials, Part 2, reel 13; White to James M. Odgen, August 22, 1930, Lynching File, Leslie Papers.

12. *New York Times,* August 9, 1930; F. C. Steinhauer to Leslie, August 21, 1930, Lynching File, Leslie Papers.

13. "Marion Jail Doors Not Locked," NAACP press release, August 22, 1930, NAACP Papers, Part 7, reel 11; "Lynching Record for 1930," typescript, NAACP Papers, Part 7, reel 4; *Crisis,* October 1930, 353; *New York World,* August 24, 1930.

14. "Report on Marion Situation," [1930], Larry Conrad Papers, in author's possession; Burden, interview with author; Ada Swartz Turner, interview with Conrad, August 24, 1977, Conrad Papers; William Bernaul, interview with Conrad, May 4, 1977; Barbara J. Stevenson, *An Oral History of African Americans in Grant County* (Charleston, S.C., 2000), 103,107,108. At least one white law officer later stated that Mary Ball had been "playing with these colored fellas, acting as a decoy" so they could hold up victims. Vaughn Treber, interview with Conrad, March 23, 1977.

15. Faith Deeter Copeland, interview with Conrad, June 23, 1977; Roy Cox, interview with Conrad, June 23, 1977; C. DeVall Banks to Sirs, April 17, 1954, NAACP Papers, Group II, Box 56, Library of Congress, Washington, D.C.; Evelyn Thompson, interview with Conrad, June 23, 1977. See also Nevada Pate, interview with Barbara Stevenson, June 27, 1994, in *Remembering the Past: An Oral and Pictorial History of African Americans in Grant County, Indiana* (n.p., 1996); *Marion Chronicle-Tribune,* July 9, 1978: Arthur F. Raper, *The Tragedy of Lynching* (Chapel Hill, N.C., 1933), 387-88.

16. *Indianapolis Times,* August 13, 14, 19, 1930; *Marion Chronicle,* August 14, 1930; Treber, interview with Conrad; Mary Campbell Fuller, interview with author, May 22, 1999.

17. Flossie Bailey to White, August 18, 1930, NAACP Papers, Part 7, reel 11.

18. "To His Excellency The Honorable Harry G. Leslie . . . ," August 20, 1930, signed by Flossie Bailey, W. T. Bailey, William Oglesby, H. D. Saunders, Charles S. Brown, A. S. Washington, Marcus C. Stewart, R. L. Bailey, Robert Brokenburr, S. A. Furnis, G. N. T. Gray, Lynching File, Leslie Papers; Flossie Bailey to White, August 23, 1930, NAACP Papers, Part 7, reel 11; L. O. Chasey to George F. Milton, October 15, 1930, and Milton to Will H. Alexander, October 17, 1930, Commission on Interracial Cooperation Papers, 1919-1944, Series VI, microfilm reel 41.

19. Chasey to Everett C. Watkins, August 12, 1930; Chasey to Robert J. Nelson, August 12, 1930; L. D. Ratliff to Leslie, August 11, 1930, all in Lynching File, Leslie Papers.

20. *Indianapolis Times,* August 21, 1930; *Marion Chronicle,* August 14, 21, 22, 1930; *Marion Chronicle-Leader Tribune,* August 17, 1930.

21. *Marion Chronicle,* August 8, 1930. See also editorial of August 12, 1930. The *Chronicle* later did call for investigation of the lynching and punishment of mob members. See editorial in August 13, 1930, issue. *Fairmount News,* August 14, 1930. For another survey of newspaper reporting see Raper, *The*

Tragedy of Lynching, 398-400, and, more generally, Richard M. Perloff, "The Press and Lynchings of African Americans," *Journal of Black Studies* 30 (January 2000), 315-30.

22. Tuskegee Institute News Clipping File, Series II, Miscellaneous Files, 1899-1966, microfilm reel 226; Lynching Clipping Files, Arthur F. Raper Papers, Southern Historical Collection, University of North Carolina Library, Chapel Hill; *Concord (N.C.) Times,* August 14, 1930; *Rome (Ga.) News-Tribune,* August 11, 1930.

23. "Marion Jail Doors Not Locked," August 22, 1930, NAACP Papers, Part 7, reel 11; *New York World,* August 24, 1930; White to Harley Hardin, Odgen, Leslie, R. L. Bailey, Flossie Bailey, Jack Edwards, Jacob Campbell, August 25, 1930, NAACP Papers, Part 7, reel 11.

24. *Chicago Defender,* August 16, 23, 1930.

25. *Indianapolis Recorder,* August 16, 23, 1930. The city's other black newspaper, the more moderate *Indianapolis World,* focused on law and order as much as race in reporting the lynching, though its reports claimed that Mary Ball was not raped. *Indianapolis World,* August 15, 1930.

26. *Indianapolis News,* August 9, 11, 1930; *Indianapolis Star,* August 9, 1930. See also the digest of state comment in *Marion Chronicle-Leader,* August 10, 1930.

27. *Kokomo Tribune,* August 8, 1930.

28. *Indianapolis Times,* August 8, 21, 27, 1930.

29. James H. Madison, *Indiana through Tradition and Change: A History of the Hoosier State and Its People, 1920-1945* (Indianapolis, 1982), 70, 348-49; White to Ransom, August 13, 1930, White to Boyd Gurley, August 25, September 3, 1930, NAACP Papers, Part 7, reel 11.

30. *Indianapolis Times,* August 8, 1930; *Indianapolis News,* August 8, 1930; *Kokomo Tribune,* August 9, 1930.

31. *Indianapolis Recorder,* August 16, 1930; *New York World,* August 24, 1930; White to Edwards, August 19, 1930, NAACP Papers, Part 7, reel 11. To the end of his life Mayor Edwards maintained that Mary Ball was raped by one of the "boys" but that she was not engaged to Deeter and that her character was of the lower sort. Jack Edwards, interview with author, July 7, 1992.

32. Flossie Bailey to White, August 23, 30, 1930, NAACP Papers, Part 7, reel 11; Raper, *The Tragedy of Lynching,* 397.

33. R. L. Bailey to White, August 30, 1930, NAACP Papers, Part 7, reel 11; White to James Weldon Johnson, August 22, 1930, Papers of the NAACP, Part 1: Meetings of the Board of Directors, . . . 1909-1950, microfilm reel 25; Flossie Bailey to White, August 23, 1930, NAACP Papers, Part 7, reel 11.

34. White to F. E. DeFrantz, October 2, 1930, Papers of the NAACP, Part 2: 1919-1939, Personal Correspondence of Selected NAACP Officials, reel 13; "Report of the Acting Secretary for the October Meeting of the Board,"

October 8, 1930, NAACP Papers, Part 1, reel 5; Madison, *Indiana through Tradition and Change,* 75; Donald F. Carmony to Fred Hill, December 18, 1994, copy in author's possession; *Indianapolis Recorder,* November 1, 1930.

35. White to Herbert Hoover, August 15, 1930, Colored Question, Lynching, Presidential Papers, Herbert Hoover Presidential Library, West Branch, Iowa; Walter H. Newton to White, August 20, 1930, Hoover Papers; F. B. Ransom to White, October 8, 14, 1930, NAACP Papers, Group I, Series G, Container 64, Library of Congress; *Indianapolis Recorder,* November 1, 15, 1930; Flossie Bailey to White, August 23, 1930, NAACP Papers, Part 7, reel 11.

36. Flossie Bailey to White, August 9, 11, 18, September 20, 1930, White to Ogden, September 23, 1930, NAACP Papers, Part 7, reel 11.

37. *Marion Chronicle-Tribune,* August 17, 1930; *Indianapolis Times,* September 2, 1930; Hardin to Ogden, August 23, 1930, Ogden to Hardin, August 27, 1930, Box 18, James M. Ogden Papers, Indiana State Archives, Indianapolis; Chasey to Hardin, September 17, 1930, Lynching File, Leslie Papers; Jack Edwards, interview with Conrad, February 15, 1977. Ogden was certainly politically ambitious and in 1932 sought the Republican gubernatorial nomination. He doubtless saw political advantage in courting African American votes, but it is likely that he also had a larger sense of social justice. Certainly few other Hoosier Republicans were so attentive to African American concerns. *Indianapolis Star,* March 28, 1932; Stanley Warren, "The Monster Meetings at the Negro YMCA in Indianapolis," *Indiana Magazine of History* 91 (March 1995), 70.

CHAPTER SIX

1. Court of Inquiry, August 13-15, 1930, Lynching Depositions, Box 20, James M. Ogden Papers, Indiana State Archives, Indianapolis.

2. Harley Hardin claimed that "my efforts in the investigation to identify and punish the lynchers was the direct cause for my defeat as Prosecuting Attorney in this county at the last election." Hardin did suffer an embarrassing defeat in fall 1930. While Grant County went heavily Republican, Hardin won only 8,027 votes compared to his Democratic opponent's 10,887. It is difficult to see that his handling of the lynching cases lost him many white votes, however. As Walter White wrote privately in an angry letter, Hardin "consistently failed to do a single thing to apprehend the lynchers . . . and was negligent and inefficient in gathering information." Harley Hardin to Mrs. Gustav Bachman, November 10, 1930, Walter White to Bachman, November 24, 1930, Papers of the NAACP, Part 7: The Anti-Lynching Campaign, 1912-1955, Series A: Investigative Files, 1912-1953, microfilm reel 11; *Year Book of the*

State of Indiana for the Year 1930 (Fort Wayne, 1930). Hardin himself likely was caught in a classic dilemma between local majority community expectations (to not punish lynchers) and professional legal values and norms (to prosecute to the best of his ability). He chose the former. See Donald D. Landon, "Clients, Colleagues, and Community: The Shaping of Zealous Advocacy in Country Law Practice," *American Bar Foundation Research Journal* 81 (1985), 81-111. I am grateful to Professor Dominic Capeci, Jr., for this reference.

3.   *Marion Chronicle,* August 14, 1930.
4.   "Marion Report of Bruner," n.d., and "Interview with Turnkey Marion Jail," n.d., Box 20, Ogden Papers.
5.   Court of Inquiry, Lynching Depositions, 4, 6.
6.   Ibid., 61, 66.
7.   Ibid., 143.
8.   Ibid., 183.
9.   Ibid., 116.
10. Ibid., 311.
11. Ibid., 281.
12. Ibid., 133.
13. Ibid., 84.
14. Ibid., 144.
15. Ibid., 311.
16. Ibid., 229-30.
17. "Marion Report of Bruner," n.d., Ogden Papers.
18. Court of Inquiry, Lynching Depositions, 35.
19. Ibid., 74.
20. Ibid., 152.
21. Ibid., 228.
22. Ibid., 285.
23. Ibid., 228.
24. Even an intense campaign for elective office did not seem to lessen the solidarity of the witnesses. The fall election had Bert White running as the Republican candidate against Charles Truex as the Democratic candidate for County Sheriff, to replace Campbell, who was not running. White was the victor. *New York World,* August 24, 1930; *Fairmount News,* October 23, 1930.
25. Court of Inquiry, Lynching Depositions, 313.
26. Ibid., 91.
27. Ibid., 218.
28. *Marion Chronicle,* August 14, 1930.
29. Flossie Bailey to Walter White, September 2, 1930, NAACP Papers, Part 7, reel 11; White to Ogden, September 2, 1930, Box 16, Ogden Papers.

30. Grant County Grand Jury Summons, August, September 1930, copies in Larry Conrad Papers, in author's possession.

31. *Indianapolis Times,* September 9, 12, 1930.

32. *Marion Chronicle,* October 9, 1930.

33. *Indianapolis Times,* October 16, 1930. See also *Indianapolis Times,* October 13, 15, 1930; *Marion Chronicle,* October 15, 16, 1930; *State of Indiana* v. *Charles Lennon, [?] Boyd,[?] Praim, Everett Clarke, Arnold Waller, Bob Beshire, Chester Pease* and *State of Indiana* v. *Jacob C. Campbell,* both in Grant County Circuit Order Book, vol. 72, October 15, 1930, Grant County Courthouse, Marion, Ind.

34. *Marion Chronicle,* October 15, 1930. See also *Indianapolis Times,* October 15, 1930; *Indianapolis Recorder,* October 18, 1930.

35. The Indiana Constitution of 1851 guaranteed defendants in criminal cases a jury trial "in the county in which the offence shall have been committed." Only Beshire and Lennon could have requested change of venue, which was not in their interest, of course. Even had Harley Hardin wished, it would not have been possible for him to move the trial from Grant County. Charles Kettleborough, ed., *Constitution Making in Indiana: A Source Book of Constitutional Documents with Historical Introduction and Critical Notes,* vol. 1, *1790-1851* (Indianapolis, 1916), 298. The first Grant County jury to include a woman met in late 1935 following a state supreme court ruling. *Marion Chronicle,* September 17, 1935.

36. *State of Indiana* v. *Lennon et al.,* December 29, 1930, Grant County Circuit Order Book, vol. 72; *Marion Chronicle,* December 23, 24, 29, 30, 31, 1930, January 2, 1931; *Indianapolis Recorder,* November 20, 1930, January 3, 10, 1931; *Kokomo Tribune,* January 2, 3, 1931; *Indianapolis Times,* January 2, 1931; Flossie Bailey to White, December 29, 30, 1930, NAACP Papers, Part 7, reel 11.

37. *State of Indiana* v. *Charles Lennon,* February 16, 1931, Grant County Circuit Order Book, vol. 72; Handwritten notes of Lennon trial testimony, n.d., Box 20, Ogden Papers; Roy Cox, interview with Larry Conrad, June 23, 1977; *Marion Chronicle,* January 16, February 23, 24, 26, 27, 1931; *Kokomo Tribune,* February 28, 1931; *Indianapolis Star,* February 27, 1931; *Indianapolis Times,* February 28, 1931; *Indianapolis Recorder,* February 28, 1931; Flossie Bailey to William Pickens, March 3, 1931, NAACP Papers, Part 7, reel 11.

38. Flossie Bailey to Pickens, March 3, 1931, NAACP Papers, Part 7, reel 11; William Pickens, "Aftermath of a Lynching," *Nation,* April 15, 1931, 406.

39. Flossie Bailey to Pickens, March 3, 1931, NAACP Papers, Part 7, reel 11; Southern Commission on the Study of Lynching, *Lynchings and What They Mean* (Atlanta, 1931), 55.

40. *Indianapolis Recorder,* March 21, 1931. See also *Marion Chronicle,* March 13, 1931; Tuskegee Institute News Clipping File, Series II: Miscellaneous Files, 1899-1966, reel 226.

41. For a succinct discussion of these issues generally see Linda Gordon, *The Great Arizona Orphan Abduction* (Cambridge, Mass., 1999), 254-74.

CHAPTER SEVEN

1. Southern Commission on the Study of Lynching, *Lynchings and What They Mean* (Atlanta, 1931), 54.

2. Flossie Bailey to William Pickens, n.d., Group I, Series G, Container 65, NAACP Papers, Library of Congress, Washington, D.C. Portions of this section appeared in earlier form in James H. Madison, "Flossie Bailey: What a Woman!" *Traces of Indiana and Midwestern History* 12 (winter 2000), 23-27.

3. *Crisis,* March 1931, 91.

4. Harley Burden, Jr., interview with author, September 4, 1998; Joe Casey, interview with author, September 4, 1998; William Pickens to Flossie Bailey, December 19, 1930, Flossie Bailey to Robert Bagnall, June 24, 1931, Group I, Series G, Container 65, NAACP Papers; "Report of the Department of Branches for the April [1931] Meeting of the Board," Papers of the NAACP, Part 1: Meetings of the Board of Directors, . . . 1909-1950, microfilm reel 5.

5. Robert Bagnall to Luella Greer, September 12, 1930, Flossie Bailey to Walter White, May 22, 1934, Flossie Bailey to Juanita Jackson, February 1, 1937, Group I, Series G, Container 65, NAACP Papers; *Marion Chronicle,* February 15, 1934.

6. Flossie Bailey to Bagnall, January 9, 1931, Group I, Series G, Container 65, NAACP Papers.

7. "Speech of James M. Ogden . . . Before the State Convention of the National Association for the Advancement of Colored People," South Bend, Indiana, October 15, 1931, Papers of the NAACP, Part 7: The Anti-Lynching Campaign, 1912-1955, Series A: Investigative Files, 1912-1955, microfilm reel 4. In courting African American votes Ogden was doubtless conscious of the white majority vote as he framed his remarks in contexts of justice and not of race. And he strongly attacked crime and corruption in Marion, an attack that culminated in bringing charges against his old nemesis, former Grant County Prosecuting Attorney Harley Hardin, in November 1931. *Indianapolis Star,* November 7, 11, 1931.

8. Justin E. Walsh, *The Centennial History of the Indiana General Assembly, 1816-1978* (Indianapolis, 1987), 392; Emma Lou Thornbrough, *The Negro in Indiana: A Study of a Minority* (Indianapolis, 1957), 279-87; Donald L. Grant,

The Anti-Lynching Movement, 1883-1932 (San Francisco, 1975), 71-72, 141-60.

9.   "Report of the Department of Branches for the April [1931] Meeting of the Board"; *Indianapolis Recorder,* January 31, February 14, 28, March 7, 14, 1931; *Indianapolis Times,* February 18, 1931; NAACP press release, March 6, 1931, NAACP Papers, Part 7, reel 11. There was considerable partisanship in the legislature, with Republicans opposing and Democrats generally favoring the bill.

10. Flossie Bailey to Pickens, March 3, 1931, NAACP Papers, Part 7, reel 11.

11. *Indianapolis Times,* September 23, 1930; *Indianapolis Star,* August 18, 1930; NAACP press release, December 28, 1930, NAACP Papers, Part 7, reel 4; Harvard Sitkoff, *A New Deal for Blacks: The Emergence of Civil Rights as a National Issue* (New York, 1978), 268-97.

12. Flossie Bailey to White, May 22, 1934, Group I, Series G, Container 65, NAACP Papers.

13. Flossie Bailey to White, August 3, 1937, Group I, Series G, Container 65, NAACP Papers.

14. Thomas D. Clark, *Indiana University, Midwestern Pioneer,* vol. 2, *In Mid-Passage* (Bloomington, 1973), 139; Flossie Bailey to William T. Andrews, May 7, 1931, Flossie Bailey to Pickens, May 7, 1935, Flossie Bailey to Bagnall, January 9, 1931, Flossie Bailey to White, October 6, 1931, Group I, Series G, Container 65, NAACP Papers; "Report of the Department of Branches for the November Meeting of the Board," November 9, 1931, NAACP Papers, Part 1, reel 5. For the tangled theater case see *Bailey* v. *Washington Theatre Co. et al.,* 34 N.E. 2d 17 (Ind. 1941) and *Flossie K. Bailey* v. *Washington Theatre Co. et al.,* Cause No. 11161, Court Docket, Grant County Superior Court, Clerk of Courts, Marion, Ind.

15. *Marion Chronicle,* December 31, 1930; Flossie Bailey to White, May 22, 1934, Pickens to W. T. Bailey, July 13, 1931, Group I, Series G, Container 65, NAACP Papers.

16. Flossie Bailey to Bagnall, January 9, 1931, Flossie Bailey to Juanita Jackson, February 1, 1937, Group I, Series G, Container 65, NAACP Papers.

17. Edmund Casey, interview with author, December 12, 1995.

18. Harley Burden, Jr., interview with author, September 4, 1998; Edmund Casey, interview with author; Sarah Weaver Pate, interview with author, August 2, 1994.

19. Flossie Bailey to White, February 26, 1941, Group II, Box 56, NAACP Papers; White to Verna Barnes, February 7, 1953, Group II, Series C, Container 52, NAACP Papers.

20. Mr. Cameron prefers "James" as his first name, although most records from the 1930s use the name Herbert Cameron.

21. Court of Inquiry, August 13-15, 1930, Lynching Depositions, Box 20, James M. Ogden Papers, Indiana State Archives, Indianapolis.

22. American Negro Labor Congress to Harry G. Leslie, August 16, 1930, International Labor Defense to Leslie, August 30, 1930, Lynching Folder, Harry G. Leslie Papers, Indiana State Archives, Indianapolis.

23. Charles H. Martin, "The International Labor Defense and Black America," *Labor History* 26 (spring 1985), 169-74; Mark Solomon, *The Cry Was Unity: Communists and African Americans, 1917-36* (Jackson, Miss., 1998), 185-206; James Goodman, *Stories of Scottsboro* (New York, 1994), 24-31; David Levering Lewis, *W.E.B. Du Bois: The Fight for Equality and the American Century, 1919-1963* (New York, 2000), 255-65.

24. "Report on Marion Situation" [1930], Larry Conrad Papers, in author's possession.

25. Ibid.

26. Ibid.; International Labor Defense Press Release, September 11, 1930, NAACP Papers, Part 7, reel 11.

27. "Report on Marion Situation," Conrad Papers.

28. Flossie Bailey to White, August 23, 1930, White to Flossie Bailey, August 26, 1930, NAACP Papers, Part 7, reel 11.

29. In the years from 1900 to 1930 Indiana executed 30 convicted criminals; 15 of the 30 were African Americans. Ward Lane, *Brief History of Capital Punishment in the State of Indiana* ([Michigan City, Ind., 1967]).

30. For the intense conflict between the NAACP and ILD see Goodman, *Stories of Scottsboro,* 32-38.

31. J. Clay Smith, Jr., *Emancipation: The Making of the Black Lawyer, 1844-1944* (Philadelphia, 1993), 386-91; J. Clay Smith, Jr., "The Marion County Lawyers' Club: 1932 and the Black Lawyer," *Black Law Journal* 8 (fall 1983), 170-76; Jerold S. Auerbach, *Unequal Justice: Lawyers and Social Change in Modern America* (New York, 1976), 210-16.

32. Harriet Bailey Conn, interview with Conrad, August 23, 1977, Conrad Papers; Stanley Warren, "Robert L. Bailey: Great Man with a Thirst for Justice," *Black History News and Notes,* no. 55 (February 1994), 6-7.

33. Conn, interview with Conrad; Alan F. January and Justin E. Walsh, *A Century of Achievement: Black Hoosiers in the Indiana General Assembly, 1881-1986* (Indianapolis, 1986), 28.

34. Flossie Bailey to White, August 12, 23, September 11, 1930, R. L. Bailey to White, August 30, 1930, NAACP Papers, Part 7, reel 11.

35. Flossie Bailey to White, August 23, September 11, 1930, NAACP Papers, Part 7, reel 11; Report of the Secretary of the June Meeting of the Board, June 5, 1931, NAACP Papers, Part 1, reel 5.

36. *Marion Chronicle,* October 6, 9, 22, December 18, 1930; *Marion Leader-Tribune,* June 30, 1931; Report of the Secretary for the June meeting of the Board, June 5, 1931, NAACP Papers, Part 1, reel 5; *State of Indiana* v. *Robert Sullivan and Herbert Cameron,* Grant County Circuit Court Order Book, vol. 72, October 14, 1930, Grant County Courthouse, Marion, Ind.; James Cameron, *A Time of Terror* (Baltimore, 1994), 129, 108-9. Indiana law allowed defendants to request a change of venue on the basis of "excitement or prejudice in the county." In capital cases the court was required to grant the change. *Indiana Acts 1905,* p. 584. I am grateful to John Martin Smith for assistance in change of venue law.

37. *State of Indiana* v. *Herbert Cameron,* Madison Circuit Court Order Book, nos. 115, 116, 117, 118, 119, Clerk of Madison County Courts, Anderson, Ind.; James Cameron, interview with author, June 10, 1993; *Anderson Bulletin,* June 29, 30, July 1, 2, 7, 11, 1931; *Marion Leader-Tribune,* July 1, 2, 8: *Marion Chronicle,* July 1, 2, 6, 7, 1931; *Indianapolis Star,* July 2, 1931.

38. NAACP press release, July 17, 1931, NAACP Papers, Part 7, reel 11.

39. *Indianapolis Recorder,* July 11, 1931.

40. Ibid., July 11, July 18, 1931.

CHAPTER EIGHT

1. For an introduction to the massive scholarship on memory, see Alon Confino, "Collective Memory and Cultural History: Problems of Method," *American Historical Review* 102 (December 1997), 1386-1403.

2. "Marion Report of Bruner," n.d., Box 20, James Ogden Papers, Indiana State Archives, Indianapolis.

3. *Marion Chronicle-Tribune,* April 3, 1988. Many of Beitler's negatives from a lifetime of commercial photography are now at the Indiana Historical Society, Indianapolis.

4. James Allen, Hilton Als, John Lewis, and Leon F. Litwack, *Without Sanctuary: Lynching Photography in America* (Santa Fe, N.M., 2000). James Allen writes: "The photographic art played as significant a role in the ritual as torture or souvenir grabbing" (204-5). See also John Courtmanche, "Hate in Black and White," *Photo District News,* July 2000, 74-76.

5. Allen et al., *Without Sanctuary,* 177. Also inscribed on the outer mat of this framed photograph are the words "Klan 4th Joplin, Mo. 33'." This is an incorrect identification, of course. The reference to "Bo" is presumably to the man with the tattoo on his raised left arm.

6. Flossie Bailey to Walter White, August 9, 1930, Papers of the NAACP, Part 7: The Anti-Lynching Campaign, 1912-1955, Series A: Investigative Files, 1912-1953, microfilm reel 11; *Indianapolis Recorder,* September 27, 1930.

7. *Indianapolis News,* August 12, 1930; *Indianapolis Times,* August 8, 1930; *Indianapolis Star,* August 9, 1930; *Marion Chronicle-Tribune,* April 3, 1988, May 7, 2000. For Brent Staples's thoughtful argument against public showing of lynching photos, especially without historical context, see *New York Times,* April 9, 2000.

8. *Anderson Bulletin,* August 8, 1930; *Muncie Press,* August 8, 1930; *Richmond Daily Register,* August 11, 1930; *Baltimore Afro-American,* August 30, 1930; *Chicago Defender,* August 16, 1930; *Crisis,* October 1930, 348; David Margolick, *Strange Fruit: Billie Holiday, Café Society, and an Early Cry for Civil Rights* (Philadelphia, 2000), 36-37; *Indianapolis Recorder,* August 16, 1930; *New York World,* August 24, 1930.

9. Fresh Air, National Public Radio, March 8, 1994, tape in author's possession.

10. Allen et al., *Without Sanctuary.*

11. *Chicago Defender,* August 16, 1930; *New York World,* August 24, 1930; Jack Edwards, interview with Larry Conrad, February 15, 1977, Larry Conrad Papers, in author's possession.

12. J. F. Watts and Allen F. Davis, *Generations: Your Family in Modern American History,* 3d ed. (New York, 1983), 117; Orlando Patterson, *Rituals of Blood: Consequences of Slavery in Two American Centuries* (Washington, D.C., 1998), 138-39; Joyce Bourjault, Bernard Moro, James Walters, Jean-Claude Souesme, *New Flying Colours: Classe de Terminale* (Paris, 1997), 126; "French Students Study Marion Lynching," *Black History News and Notes,* no. 81 (August 2000), 1; Alistair Cooke, *Alistair Cooke's America* (New York, 1973), 312-13; Harold Evans, *The American Century* (New York, 1998), 192-93; *Life,* spring 1988, 8-9; *Newsweek,* March 21, August 22, 1994; Molefi K. Asante and Mark T. Mattson, *The African-American Atlas: Black History and Culture* (New York, 1998), 132; "American Photography: A Century of Images," PBS, October 13, 1999; *New Yorker,* February 7, 2000, 17; *New York Times,* February 13, 2000; Allen et al., *Without Sanctuary;* "Eyes on the Prize: Awakening, 1954-1956," videotape, Blackside, 1986; *The Chamber,* Universal Pictures, 1996. The Hollywood makers of *The Chamber* altered Beitler's photograph to insert their main character, played by Gene Hackman, as a youth standing at the front of the Marion crowd and pointing his finger to the two bodies. Alistair Cooke's *America* included the caption "No one now knows who took this picture, or exactly when. But lynch law ruled the South in the years after World War I" (311). *Life* magazine's caption described the crowd as "voyeurs" who "look as placid a rubes at a stock show" (8).

13. *Indiana Daily Student,* December 5, 1994; Public Enemy, "Hazy Shade of Criminal," Sony Music Entertainment, 1992; *Indianapolis Star,* October 2, 1992; phone conversation with Marc Allan, October 5, 1992; *Anderson Herald-Bulletin,* October 3, 1992.

14. James Sutter, interview with author, February 12, 2000.

15. Alan Trachtenberg, *Reading American Photographs: Images as History, Mathew Brady to Walker Evans* (New York, 1989), vii, 288.

16. *Indianapolis News,* March 26, 1994.

17. James Cameron, interview with author, June 10, 1993; *Anderson Daily Bulletin,* October 11, 1982.

18. J. Chester Allen, "Report on Racial Situation at Muncie," May 12, 1944, Box B, Drawer 150, Henry F. Schricker Papers, Indiana State Archives, Indianapolis.

19. Cameron, interview with author.

20. Ibid.; Jack Edwards, interview with Conrad, February 15, 1977; *Marion Chronicle-Tribune Magazine,* July 9, 1978.

21. "Man Who Was Almost Lynched," *Ebony,* April 1980, 148-53.

22. *Marion Chronicle-Tribune,* September 19, 1982. See also *Indianapolis Recorder,* October 23, 1982; *Anderson Daily Bulletin,* October 11, 1982; *Indianapolis News,* September 28, 1982; *Milwaukee Journal,* November 14, 1982; *Milwaukee Catholic Herald,* December 16, 1982.

23. *Milwaukee Journal,* December 5, 1988.

24. *Ball State Daily News,* February 10, 1983; *Purdue University Exponent,* February 23, 1981; *Anderson Daily Bulletin,* October 11, 1982; Form letter to Dear Student Center from James Cameron, copy in author's possession. James Cameron showed this ability to reach audiences in early 2001 when, nearly 87 years of age, a bit more stooped, and battling cancer, he spoke at Indiana University, Bloomington, and received a standing ovation from the 400 students in the lecture hall. *Indiana Daily Student,* January 12, 2001.

25. *Fort Wayne Journal-Gazette,* February 27, 1983; James Cameron, "Address of James Cameron, Delivered February 26, 1983, Sheraton Inn, Marion, Indiana" (Milwaukee, 1983); *Milwaukee Journal,* December 4, 1988.

26. Quoted in *Milwaukee Journal,* December 4, 1988.

27. *Milwaukee Journal,* August 1, 1984; *Milwaukee Sentinel,* May 9, June 13, 1988.

28. *Milwaukee Sentinel,* October 31, 1988, April 20, 1992; *Milwaukee Journal,* December 20, 1989; *Appleton Post-Crescent,* March 4, 1990; *Dallas Morning News* in *Harrisburg (Pa.) Patriot-News,* March 28, 1992.

29. *Chicago Tribune,* February 9, 1993; *Milwaukee Times,* April 12, 1989. In early 2000 a Wisconsin politician challenged Cameron's choice of the word "holocaust." Milwaukee *Journal Sentinel,* January 21, 25, 2000.

30. *New York Times,* July 10, 1995; *Washington Post,* February 23, 1994; *Los Angeles Times,* November 27, 1994. From this point on Cameron was linked to the Beitler photograph, often interviewed when the photo was the subject of a story. See, for example, *New York Times,* February 12, 2000.

31. *Indianapolis News,* March 26, 1994; *Milwaukee Journal,* December 4, 1988.

32. *Irish Times,* August 30, 1989; *Marion Chronicle-Tribune,* August 2, 1992.

33. *Indianapolis Star,* November 18, December 3, 1996; *Marion Chronicle-Tribune,* July 22, 1997, March 19, 2000; *Indiana Preservationist,* May-June 1995, 2-3.

34. *Marion Chronicle-Tribune,* February 7, 12, 14, 1993.

35. Ibid., February 12, 1993.

36. Ibid., February 14, 1993, for text of speech. See also *Indianapolis Star,* February 12, 1993.

37. Cameron, interview with author; Ed Breen, interview with author, May 21, 1999.

38. *Indianapolis Star,* February 12, 1993. Cameron's pardon was based in part on his testimony that he had fled the murder scene before shots were fired. The case for pardons of Smith and Shipp would have been more difficult.

39. C. Carr, "An American Life," *Village Voice,* February 1, 1994; Breen, interview with author.

40. *Publishers Weekly,* February 21, 1994; *Newsletter of Black Classic Press,* spring 1994; *Black Classic Press Booklist '94; Newsweek,* March 21, 1994; *Indianapolis News,* March 26, 1994.

41. Fresh Air, National Public Radio, March 8, 1994, tape in author's possession.

42. "A Lynching in Marion," Wisconsin Public Television, 1994, JoAnne Garrett, producer; "The Marion Lynching of 1930," *Across Indiana,* WFYI, Indianapolis, 1998, Todd Gould, producer; "Unforgiven: Legacy of a Lynching," British Broadcasting Corporation, 1995, Paul Sapin, producer. See also *Independent* (London), June 15, 1995.

43. "The Marion Lynching of 1930," WFYI. There are differences among the three documentaries, with the BBC program particularly focused on the memory of the lynching. There are some different elements in the WFYI documentary partly because the author was involved in its creation. Unlike the other two, for example, the WFYI program does not imply that the Klan was behind the lynching and also gives some attention to Flossie Bailey and the NAACP before and after the lynching.

44. I am indebted to William F. Munn, Marion High School teacher and director of the Marion Community History Project, for sharing copies of the student papers with me and for obtaining necessary permission for me to use the papers. It should be noted that the students were enrolled in an Advanced

Placement United States History class. They are not a scientific sample of Marion youth.

CHAPTER NINE

1. *Marion Chronicle-Tribune,* December 6, 1991; Mary Campbell Fuller, interview with author, May 22, 1999; William F. Munn, Sue Bratton, Terry Lakes, eds., *Rough Times: Oral Histories Collected by Students in Advanced Placement US History and Advanced Placement English at Marion High School, Marion, Indiana, 1997-1998* (Marion, 1999), 21, 42, 79-80, 110, 114, 120, 124.

2. Tom Wise, interview with author, May 21, 1999.

3. Nelson C. Jackson to Administration, August 11, 1959, National Urban League Papers, Series 1, Box 106, Library of Congress, Washington, D.C.

4. Oatess Archey, interview with author, May 21, 1999; Phyllis A. Williams to author [February 1999]. For the Beech settlement, see Stephen A. Vincent, *Southern Seed, Northern Soil: African-American Farm Communities in the Midwest, 1765-1900* (Bloomington, Ind., 1999).

5. Steve Bunish, *The Golden Age of Marion* (n.p., 1989), 88.

6. Private letter to author, January 6, 1999, in author's possession.

7. In 1961 the Boston Celtics played an exhibition basketball game in Marion. Afterward, Bill Russell and several other black players went to a Marion restaurant for a hamburger. They were turned away. Angrily, they rousted Mayor Jack Edwards out of bed and gave him back the keys to the city that he had presented before the game. Terry Pluto, *Tall Tales: The Glory Years of the NBA, in the Words of the Men Who Played, Coached, and Built Pro Basketball* (New York, 1992). The *Marion Leader-Tribune,* October 11, 12, 1961, reports only the game.

8. C. DeVall Banks to Sirs, February 15, 1954, NAACP Papers, Group II, Box 56, Library of Congress, Washington, D.C.

9. Report to the Executive Secretary, April 25, 1944, Minutes of the Race Relations Committee, July 25, 1944, Monthly Report, January 9, 1944, National Urban League Papers, Series 1, Box 105; Jackson to Administration, August 11, 1959, National Urban League Papers, Series 1, Box 106.

10. Charles R. Webb to Lester Granger, January 26, 1954, Webb to R. Maurice Moss, August 26, 1954, National Urban League Papers, Series 1, Box 105.

11. Webb to Moss, August 26, 1954.

12. Webb to Granger, March 20, 1954, National Urban League Papers, Series 1, Box 105. It is likely that Marion's small Jewish community was more supportive of pool integration and other civil rights issues than the white community as a whole. Joe Casey, interview with author, October 13, 1999.

13. Betty Musser, interview with author, October 2, 1999; Joe Casey, interview with author, October 13, 1999.

14. Webb to Granger, March 20, 1954.

15. Webb to Moss, January 15, August 26, 1954, Webb to Granger, January 26, 1954, Granger to Webb, January 19, 1954, National Urban League Papers, Series 1, Box 105.

16. Webb to Granger, June 9, 1954, National Urban League Papers, Series 1, Box 105.

17. Webb to Granger, June 9, August 26, 1954, Granger to Webb, June 15, 1954, National Urban League Papers, Series 1, Box 105; Munn, Bratton, and Lakes, eds., *Rough Times,* 92. For an introduction to the national issues, see Harvard Sitkoff, *The Struggle for Black Equality, 1954-1992,* rev. ed. (New York, 1993), 11-36.

18. Webb to Moss, August 26, 1954; *Indianapolis Recorder,* June 26, 1954.

19. Webb to Moss, August 26, 1954; *Indianapolis Recorder,* July 24, 1954; *Donald Meridith Ward et al.* v. *City of Marion,* No. 795 Civil, U.S. District Court, Northern District of Indiana, Fort Wayne Division, copy in National Urban League Papers, Series 1, Box 105. *Marion Chronicle,* July 1, 7, 13, 1954.

20. Webb to Moss, August 26, 1954, Webb to Granger, July 29, 1954, National Urban League Papers, Series 1, Box 105; Roger Smith, interview with author, September 4, 1998; *Indianapolis Recorder,* July 31, 1954; *Marion Chronicle,* July 23, 26, 30, August 5, 1954.

21. Webb to Granger, June 9, 1954; C. DeVall Banks to Dear Sirs, April 17, 1954, NAACP Papers, Group II, Box 56; *Indianapolis Recorder,* July 3, August 7, 1954.

22. Roger Smith, interview with author.

23. Webb to Nelson Jackson, November 12, 1954, National Urban League Papers, Series 1, Box 105.

24. Roger Smith, interview with author; Nevada Pate, interview with Barbara J. Stevenson, June 22, 1994, in *Remembering the Past: An Oral and Pictorial History of African Americans in Grant County, Indiana,* vol. 1 (n.p., 1996). Nevada Pate was an NAACP activist in the 1954 integration of Matter Park. *Indianapolis Recorder,* July 24, 1954.

25. Archey, interview with author.

26. Joe Casey, interview with author, September 4, 1998; *Marion Chronicle-Tribune,* July 22, 1972. By 1965 at least one Marion High School student was so alert to the civil rights movement and "the prejudice of the mind" that he wrote a long and thoughtful letter to an Indianapolis newspaper: Tony Maidenberg to *Indianapolis Star,* May 4, 1965.

27. *Marion Chronicle-Tribune,* January 17, 1999.

28. Wise, interview with author.

29. *Indianapolis Star,* June 30, 1969; *Marion Chronicle-Tribune,* July 1, 2, 1969; Ed Breen, interview with author, May 21, 1999; James Sutter, interview with author, February 12, 2000. Terry H. Anderson, *The Movement and the Sixties* (New York, 1995), provides national contexts and suggests how much later and more moderate the crises were in Marion compared to larger cities. At the time many folks in Marion would not have taken much comfort in such historical contexts.

30. *Indianapolis News,* July 17, 1969; *Indianapolis Recorder,* July 5, 19, 1969; *Marion Chronicle-Tribune,* July 2, 17, 1969.

31. *Indianapolis Recorder,* July 26, 1969; *Marion Chronicle-Tribune,* July 21, 23, 1969; Smith, interview with author.

32. *Marion Chronicle-Tribune,* July 21, 1969.

33. Ibid., March 27, 1995; Breen, interview with author; Ann Secttor, interview with author, October 2, 1999.

34. Smith, interview with author; Breen, interview with author; Wise, interview with author; Marcus Cannon, interview with author, August 12, 1999.

35. *Marion Chronicle-Tribune,* May 15, 16, 17, 18, 20, 23, June 7, 1973.

36. Webb to Granger, June 9, 1954.

37. Xen Stewart to Roy Wilkins, March 20, 1959, Wilkins to Lavern C. Lett, Jr., July 10, 1975, NAACP Papers, Group II, Box 56; Nelson C. Jackson to Administration, August 11, 1959, National Urban League Papers, Series 1, Box 106; *Marion Chronicle-Tribune,* May 20, 1973.

38. Jack Edwards, interview with Larry Conrad, February 15, 1977, Larry Conrad Papers, in author's possession. See also Edwards's comments in *Indianapolis Times,* August 4, 1963.

39. Archey, interview with author.

40. Sarah Weaver Pate, interview with author, August 2, 1994; Evelyn Thompson, interview with Conrad, June 23, 1977; Nevada Pate, interview with Stephenson.

41. Joseph Casey, interview with Robert McDonough, November 24, 1980, Indiana Historical Society Library, Indianapolis; Charlotte Fenstermaker, interview with Barbara J. Stevenson, June 27, 1994, in *Remembering the Past.*

42. Wise, interview with author; Harley Burden, Jr., interview with author, September 4, 1998; Breen, interview with author; Secttor, interview with author.

43. Burden, interview with author; Casey, interview with author; Munn, Bratton, and Lakes, eds., *Rough Times,* 15, 92-93.

44. Burden, interview with author; Casey, interview with author.

45. Edwards, interview with Conrad; Breen, interview with author; Casey, interview with author; Wise, interview with author.

46. *Marion Chronicle-Tribune,* July 22, 1977; Secttor, interview with author. There was criticism of Joe Casey for being too accommodating to white leaders as early as the 1950s. See Jerome B. Johnson to Moss, April 17, 1950, National Urban League Papers, Series 1, Box 105; Banks to Sirs, April 17, 1954, NAACP Papers, Group II, Box 56.

47. Cannon, interview with author.

48. *Indianapolis Star,* July 31, 1988; Wise, interview with author.

49. The panel met August 29, 1998, at my invitation. I gave the panelists no specific questions but asked them only to provide insights into race relations in the last half century and to indicate the significance of memories of the lynching in those relations. I took extensive notes of the discussion, but to increase frankness I did not tape record comments and promised that no person would be identified with any statement or view. I am most grateful to Richard Simons, Grant County historian, and to Ed Breen, former editor of the local newspaper, for their help in arranging this panel.

50. Archey, interview with author; Wise, interview with author.

51. *Marion Chronicle-Tribune,* November 4, 1998; Archey, interview with author; Wise, interview with author.

52. *Marion Chronicle-Tribune,* January 2, 1999; *Indianapolis Star,* November 12, 1998, January 2, 1999; *Bloomington (Ind.) Herald-Times,* November 8, 1998; *Richmond (Ind.) Palladium-Item,* November 15, 1998; Wise, interview with author.

53. Archey, interview with author. See also *Indianapolis Star,* November 12, 1998; *Marion Chronicle-Tribune,* November 17, 1998; Breen, interview with author.

54. *Milwaukee Journal Sentinel,* August 18, 21, September 23, 1998, February 26, April 18, 1999, January 30, February 18, 2001; Terry Higgins, "Conscience of a Nation," *UWM Today,* vol. 1, no. 2 (1999), 6-7.

55. Archey, interview with author; Wise, interview with author.

56. *Indianapolis Star,* December 3, 1996; Sarah Weaver Pate, interview with Barbara J. Stevenson, July 27, 1994, copy in author's possession.

BIBLIOGRAPHY

ARCHIVES AND MANUSCRIPTS

Commission on Interracial Cooperation Papers, 1919-1944. Ann Arbor, Mich.: University Microfilms International.

Larry Conrad Papers. In author's possession.

Herbert Hoover Presidential Papers. Herbert Hoover Library, West Branch, Iowa.

Ku Klux Klan Papers. Indiana Historical Society Library, Indianapolis.

Harry Leslie Papers. Indiana State Archives, Indianapolis.

National Association for the Advancement of Colored People Papers. Manuscript Division, Library of Congress, Washington, D.C., also Frederick, Md.: University Publications of America.

National Urban League Papers. Manuscript Division, Library of Congress, Washington, D.C.

James M. Ogden Papers. Indiana State Archives, Indianapolis.

Arthur F. Raper Papers. University of North Carolina Library, Chapel Hill, North Carolina.

Henry F. Schricker Papers. Indiana State Archives, Indianapolis.

Tuskegee Institute News Clippings File. Tuskegee Institute, Alabama, microfilm.

WPA Collection, Grant County, Indiana. Indiana State University, Terre Haute, Indiana.

ORAL HISTORY INTERVIEWS

Unless otherwise indicated, the author conducted the interviews.

Allan, Marc. October 5, 1992.

Archey, Oatess. May 21, 1999.

Bernaul, William. Interview with Larry Conrad, May 4, 1977.

Betts, Delores. Interview with Robert McDonough, January 6, 1980.

Biddinger, Thurman. Interview with Larry Conrad, June 24, 1977.

Breen, Ed. May 21, 1999.

Burden, Harley, Jr. September 4, 1998.

Cameron, James. June 10, 1993.

Cannon, Marcus. August 12, 1999.

Casey, Edmund. December 12, 1995.

Casey, Joseph. September 4, 1998, and October 13, 1999. Interview with Robert McDonough, November 24, 1980.

Conn, Harriett Bailey. Interview with Larry Conrad, August 23, 1977.

Copeland, Faith Deeter. Interview with Larry Conrad, June 23, 1977.

Cox, Roy. Interview with Larry Conrad, June 23, 1977.

Davis, Joe. June 28, 1995.

Edwards, Jack. July 7, 1992. Interview with Larry Conrad, February 15, 1977. Interview with Douglas Clanin, March 31, 1984.

Fansler, Walter G. Interview with Larry Conrad, August 24, 1977.

Fenstermaker, Charlotte. Interview with Barbara J. Stevenson, June 27, 1994.

Fuller, Mary Campbell. May 22, 1999. Interview with Larry Conrad, July 6, 1977.

Jackson, Clayton. Interview with Robert McDonough, December 23, 1980.

Jones, Georgia Weaver. Interview with Robert McDonough, March 10, 1981.

Marvin, Roy. Interview with Larry Conrad, June 23, 1977.

Musser, Betty. October 10, 1999.

Myers, Robert F. Interview with Larry Conrad, August 25, 1977.

Newell, Robert W. June 29, 1992.

Nussbaum, Lowell. Interview with Larry Conrad, May 10, 1977.

Pate, Nevada. Interviews with Barbara J. Stevenson, June 22 and 27, 1994.

Pate, Sarah Weaver. August 2, 1994. Interview with Barbara J. Stevenson, July 27, 1994.

Robertson, Ray. Interview with Larry Conrad, April 7, 1977.

Scott, Orville. Interview with Larry Conrad, March 17, 1977.

Secttor, Ann. October 2, 1999

Shrock, Elizabeth. August 29, 1998.

Smith, Roger. October 4, 1998.

Stewart, Don. Interview with Larry Conrad, June 23, 1977.

Stewart, Valerie. Interview with Robert McDonough, March 18, 1981.

Sutter, James. February 12, 2000.

Thompson, Evelyn. Interview with Larry Conrad, June 23, 1977.

Treber, Vaughn. Interview with Larry Conrad, March 23, 1977.

Turner, Ada Swartz. Interview with Larry Conrad, August 24, 1977.

Weaver, Bruce. October 2, 1995.

Wise, Tom. May 21, 1999.

COURT CASES

Bailey v. Washington Theatre Company et al., 34 N.E. 2nd 17 (Ind. 1941).

Flossie K. Bailey v. Washington Theatre Company et al., Cause No. 11161, Court Docket, Grant County Superior Court Clerk of Courts, Marion, Ind.

Marsha Burden v. L. Chochos et al., no. 10447, Indiana Court of Appeals, Indianapolis.

Vennie Burden v. L. Chochos et al., no. 10447, Indiana Court of Appeals, Indianapolis.

Chochos et al. v. Burden et al., 74 Ind. App. 242, 128 N.E. 696 (Ind. Ct. App. 1920).

Donald Meridith Ward et al. v. City of Marion, No. 795 Civil, U.S. District Court, Northern District of Indiana, Fort Wayne Division.

State of Indiana v. Charles Lennon, [?] Boyd, [?] Praim, Everett Clarke, Arnold Waller, Bob Beshire, Chester Pease, Grant County Circuit Order Book, vol. 72, October 15, 1930, Grant County Courthouse, Marion, Ind.

State of Indiana v. Jacob C. Campbell, Grant County Circuit Order Book, vol. 72, October 15, 1930, Grant County Courthouse, Marion, Ind.

State of Indiana v. Robert Sullivan and Herbert Cameron, Grant County Circuit Court Order Book, vol. 72, October 14, 1930, Grant County Courthouse, Marion, Ind.

State of Indiana v. Herbert Cameron, Madison Circuit Court Order Book, nos. 115, 116, 117, 118, 119, Clerk of Madison County Courts, Anderson, Ind.

MAGAZINES AND NEWSPAPERS

Anderson (Ind.) Bulletin

Anderson (Ind.) Herald Bulletin

Appleton (Wis.) Post-Crescent

Ball State Daily News

Baltimore Afro-American

Bloomington (Ind.) Herald-Times

Chicago Defender

Chicago Tribune

Concord (N.C.) Times

Crisis [NAACP]

Dallas Morning News

Ebony

Fairmount (Ind.) News

Fiery Cross [Indianapolis]

Fort Wayne (Ind.) Journal Gazette

Harrisburg (Pa.) Patriot-News

Independent (London)

Indiana Daily Student (Indiana University, Bloomington)

Indianapolis Journal

Indianapolis News

Indianapolis Recorder

Indianapolis Star

Indianapolis Times

Indianapolis World

Kokomo (Ind.) Tribune

Life

Los Angeles Times

Marion (Ind.) Chronicle

Marion (Ind.) Chronicle-Tribune

Marion (Ind.) Leader

Marion (Ind.) Leader-Tribune

Milwaukee Catholic Herald

Milwaukee Journal

Milwaukee Journal Sentinel

Milwaukee Sentinel

Milwaukee Times

Muncie (Ind.) Press

New York Telegram

New York Times

New York World

New Yorker

Newsweek

Publishers Weekly

Purdue University Exponent

Richmond (Va.) Daily Register

Richmond (Ind.) Palladium-Item

Rome (Ga.) News-Tribune

UWM Today (University of Wisconsin, Milwaukee)

Washington Post

MULTIMEDIA

"American Photography: A Century of Images." Public Broadcasting System, October 13, 1999.

The Chamber. Universal Pictures, 1996.

"Eyes on the Prize: Awakening, 1954-1956." Blackside, 1986.

Fresh Air. National Public Radio, March 8, 1994.

"A Lynching in Marion." JoAnne Garrett, producer. Wisconsin Public Television, 1994.

"The Marion Lynching of 1930." Todd Gould, producer. WFYI, Indianapolis, 1998.

Public Enemy. "Hazy Shade of Criminal." Sony Music Entertainment, 1992.

"Unforgiven: Legacy of Lynching." Paul Sapin, producer. British Broadcasting Corporation, 1995.

ARTICLES

Blocker, Jack S., Jr. "Choice and Circumstance: Destinations Sought and Shunned by African-American Migrants in the Lower Midwest, 1860-1930." Paper presented at the annual meeting of the Organization of American Historians, Toronto, 1999.

Cameron, James. "Address of James Cameron, Delivered February 26, 1983, Sheraton Inn, Marion, Indiana." Milwaukee, New World Griots, 1983.

Carr, C. "An American Life." *Village Voice,* February 1, 1994, 31-36.

Chalou, George. "Massacre on Fall Creek." *Prologue* (summer 1972), 109-14.

Confino, Alon. "Collective Memory and Cultural History: Problems of Method." *American Historical Review* 102 (December 1997), 1386-1403.

Courtmanche, John. "Hate in Black and White." *Photo District News,* July 2000, 74-76.

Doerr, Brian M. "The Massacre at Deer Lick Creek, Madison County, Indiana, 1824." *Indiana Magazine of History* 93 (March 1997), 19-47.

Durbin, Winfield T. "The Mob and the Law." *Independent* 55 (July 30, 1903), 1790-93.

Edmunds, R. David. "Justice on a Changing Frontier: Deer Lick Creek, 1824-1825." *Indiana Magazine of History* 93 (March 1997), 48-52.

Fletcher, Stephen J. "The Business of Exposure: Lewis Hine and Child Labor Reform." *Traces of Indiana and Midwestern History* 4 (spring 1992), 12-23.

Harris, J. William. "Etiquette, Lynching, and Racial Boundaries in Southern History: A Mississippi Example." *American Historical Review* 100 (April 1995), 387-410.

Higgins, Terry. "Conscience of a Nation." *UWM Today* 1, no. 2 (1999), 6-7.

Hoover, Dwight W. "Daisy Douglas Bar: From Quaker to Klan 'Kluckerss.'" *Indiana Magazine of History* 87 (June 1991), 171-95.

Landon, Donald D. "Clients, Colleagues, and Community: The Shaping of Zealous Advocacy in Country Law Practice." *American Bar Foundation Research Journal* 81 (1985), 81-111.

Maclean, Nancy. "White Women and Klan Violence in the 1920s: Agency, Complicity, and the Politics of Women's History." *Gender and History* 3 (autumn 1991), 283-303.

Madison, James H. "Flossie Bailey: What a Woman!" *Traces of Indiana and Midwestern History* 12 (winter 2000), 23-27.

Martin, Charles H. "The International Labor Defense and Black America." *Labor History* 26 (spring 1985), 165-94.

McDermott, Stacy Pratt. "'An Outrageous Proceeding': A Northern Lynching and The Enforcement of Anti-Lynching Legislation in Illinois, 1905-1910." *Journal of Negro History* 84 (winter 1999), 61-78.

McMahon, John R. "Our Jazz-Spotted Middle West." *Ladies Home Journal,* February 1922, 38, 181.

Meier, August, and John H. Bracy, Jr. "The NAACP as a Reform Movement, 1909-1965: 'To Reach the Conscience of America.'" *Journal of Southern History* 59 (February 1993), 3-30.

Nelson, Jacqueline S. "The Military Response of the Society of Friends in Indiana to the Civil War." *Indiana Magazine of History* 81 (June 1985), 101-30.

Perloff, Richard M. "The Press and Lynchings of African Americans." *Journal of Black Studies* 30 (January 2000), 315-30.

Pickens, William. "Aftermath of a Lynching." *Nation,* April 15, 1931, 406-7.

Polley, Claudia. "Segregation Creates Hidden Paradise." *Indiana Preservationist,* July-August 1993, 12-13.

Rose, Gregory S. "The Distribution of Indiana's Ethnic and Racial Minorities in 1850s." *Indiana Magazine of History* 87 (September 1991), 224-60.

Safianow, Allen. "The Klan Comes to Tipton." *Indiana Magazine of History* 95 (September 1999), 202-31.

Sheehan, Bernard W. "'The Famous Hair Buyer General': Henry Hamilton, George Rogers Clark, and the American Indian." *Indiana Magazine of History* 79 (March 1983), 1-28.

Smith, J. Clay, Jr. "The Marion County Lawyers' Club: 1932 and the Black Lawyer." *Black Law Journal* 8 (fall 1983), 168-76.

Thornbrough, Emma Lou. "Segregation in Indiana during the Klan Era of the 1920s." *Mississippi Valley Historical Review* 47 (March 1961), 594-618.

Waldrep, Christopher. "War of Words: The Controversy Over the Definition of Lynching, 1899-1940." *Journal of Southern History* 66 (February 2000), 75-100.

Warren, Stanley. "Robert L. Bailey: Great Man with a Thirst for Justice." *Black History News and Notes,* no. 55 (February 1994), 6-7.

———. "The Monster Meetings at the Negro YMCA in Indianapolis." *Indiana Magazine of History* 91 (March 1995), 57-80.

Weintraut, Linda. "A Glimpse of a Past: Lyles and Weaver Settlements, 1850-1860." *Black History News and Notes,* no. 77 (August 1999), 1-3, 8.

Wolf, Charlotte. "Constructions of a Lynching." *Sociological Inquiry* 62 (February 1992), 83-97.

BOOKS

A Century of Development: Grant County, Indiana. Marion, Ind.: Grant County Junior Historical Society, 1937.

Biographical Memoirs of Grant County, Indiana. Chicago: Bowen, 1901.

History of Grant County, Indiana. Chicago: Brant and Fuller, 1886.

"Lest We Forget": Reminiscences of Pioneers of Grant County, Indiana. Marion, Ind.: Marion High School, 1921.

Who's Who in Colored America, 1933-1937. Brooklyn, N.Y.: Thomas Yenser, 1937.

Year Book of the State of Indiana for the Year 1930. Fort Wayne, Ind.: State of Indiana, 1930.

Allen, James, Hilton Als, John Lewis, and Leon F. Litwack. *Without Sanctuary: Lynching Photography in America.* Santa Fe, N.M.: Twin Palms, 2000.

Anderson, Terry H. *The Movement and the Sixties.* New York: Oxford University Press, 1995.

Asante, Molefi K., and Mark T. Mattson. *The African-American Atlas: Black History and Culture.* New York: Macmillan, 1998.

Auerbach, Jerold S. *Unequal Justice: Lawyers and Social Change in Modern America.* New York: Oxford University Press, 1976.

Baker, Ray Stannard. *Following the Color Line: An Account of Negro Citizenship in the American Democracy.* 1908. Reprint, New York: Harper and Row, 1964.

Bigham, Darrel E. *We Ask Only a Fair Trial: A History of the Black Community of Evansville, Indiana.* Bloomington: Indiana University Press, 1987.

Blee, Kathleen M. *Women of the Klan: Racism and Gender in the 1920s.* Berkeley: University of California Press, 1991.

Bodnar, John. *Remaking America: Public Memory, Commemoration, and Patriotism in the Twentieth Century.* Princeton, N.J.: Princeton University Press, 1992.

Bourjault, Joyce, Bernard Moro, James Walters, Jean-Claude Souesme. *New Flying Colours: Classe de Terminale.* Paris: Didier, 1997.

Bremer, John A., ed. *Constitution Making in Indiana: A Source Book of Constitutional Documents with Historical Introduction and Critical Notes.* Vol. 4, *1930-1960.* Indianapolis: Indiana Historical Bureau, 1978.

Brown, Richard Maxwell. *Strain of Violence: Historical Studies of American Violence and Vigilantism.* New York: Oxford University Press, 1975.

Brundage, W. Fitzhugh. *Lynching in the New South: Georgia and Virginia, 1880-1930.* Urbana: University of Illinois Press, 1993.

———, ed. *Under Sentence of Death: Lynching in the South.* Chapel Hill: University of North Carolina Press, 1997.

Bunish, Steve. *The Golden Age of Marion.* N.p., 1989.

Cameron, James. *A Time of Terror.* Milwaukee: T/D Publications, 1982. Reprint, Baltimore: Black Classic Press, 1994.

Capeci, Dominic J., Jr. *The Lynching of Cleo Wright.* Lexington: University Press of Kentucky, 1998.

Clark, Thomas D. *Indiana University, Midwestern Pioneer.* Vol. 2, *In Mid-Passage.* Bloomington: Indiana University Press, 1973.

Cooke, Alistair. *Alistair Cooke's America.* New York: Knopf, 1973.

Cripps, Thomas. *Slow Fade to Black: The Negro in American Film, 1900-1942.* New York: Oxford University Press, 1977.

Curriden, Mark, and Leroy Phillips, Jr. *Contempt of Court: The Turn of the Century Lynching that Launched 100 Years of Federalism.* New York: Faber and Faber, 1999.

Downey, Dennis B., and Raymond M. Hyser. *No Crooked Death: Coatesville, Pennsylvania, and the Lynching of Zachariah Walker.* Urbana: University of Illinois Press, 1991.

Dreiser, Theodore. *The Best Short Stories of Theodore Dreiser.* New York: Cleveland World Publishing Company, 1956.

Du Bois, W.E.B. *The Souls of Black Folk.* 1903. Reprint, New York: Penguin, 1989.

Dulaney, Marvin. *Black Police in America.* Bloomington: Indiana University Press, 1996.

Early, Gerald, ed. *Black Heartland: African American Life, the Middle West, and the Meaning of American Regionalism.* St. Louis: Washington University, 1997.

Erenberg, Lewis A., and Susan E. Hirsch. *The War in American Culture: Society and Consciousness during World War II.* Chicago: University of Chicago Press, 1996.

Evans, Harold. *The American Century.* New York: Knopf, 1998.

Fedo, Michael W. *"They Was Just Niggers."* Ontario, Calif.: Brasch and Brasch, 1979.

Ferguson, Earline Rae. "A Community Affair: African-American Women's Club Work in Indianapolis, 1879-1917." Ph.D. diss., Indiana University, 1997.

Finkelman, Paul, ed. *Lynching, Racial Violence, and Law.* New York: Garland, 1992.

Fout, John C., and Maura Shaw Tantillo, eds. *American Sexual Politics: Sex, Gender, and Race Since the Civil War.* Chicago: University of Chicago Press, 1992.

Gates, Henry Louis, Jr., and Nellie Y. McKay, eds. *The Norton Anthology of African American Literature.* New York: W.W. Norton and Company, 1997.

Gibbs, Wilma L., ed. *Indiana's African-American Heritage: Essays from "Black History News and Notes".* Indianapolis: Indiana Historical Society, 1993.

Goodall, Hurley, and J. Paul Mitchell. *A History of Negroes in Muncie.* Muncie, Ind.: Ball State University Press, 1976.

Goodman, James. *Stories of Scottsboro.* New York: Vintage Books, 1994.

Gordon, Linda. *The Great Arizona Orphan Abduction.* Cambridge, Mass.: Harvard University Press, 1999.

Grant, Donald L. *The Anti-Lynching Movement, 1883-1932.* San Francisco, R and E Research Association, 1975.

Hall, Jacquelyn Dowd. *Revolt against Chivalry: Jessie Daniel Ames and the Women's Campaign against Lynching.* Revised ed. New York: Columbia University Press, 1993.

Harris, Trudier. *Exorcising Blackness: Historical and Literary Lynching and Burning Rituals.* Bloomington: Indiana University Press, 1984.

Hine, Darlene Clark. *When the Truth Is Told: A History of Black Women's Culture and Community in Indiana, 1875-1950.* Indianapolis: National Council of Negro Women, Indianapolis Section, 1981.

January, Alan F., and Justin E. Walsh. *A Century of Achievement: Black Hoosiers in the Indiana General Assembly, 1881-1986.* Indianapolis: Indiana Historical Bureau, 1986.

Johnson, Norma Scott, et al. *The Pettiford Family Tree: A Genealogical History.* Los Angeles: n.p., 1983.

Kettleborough, Charles, ed. *Constitution Making in Indiana: A Source Book of Constitutional Documents with Historical Introduction and Critical Notes.* Vol. 1, *1790-1851.* Indianapolis: Indiana Historical Commission, 1916.

———. *Constitution Making in Indiana: A Source Book of Constitutional Documents with Historical Introduction and Critical Notes.* Vol. 3, *1916-1930.* Indianapolis: Indiana Historical Bureau, 1930.

Lane, Ward. *Brief History of Capital Punishment in the State of Indiana.* Michigan City, Ind.: Indiana State Prison Print Shop, 1967.

Lewis, David Levering. *W.E.B. Du Bois: The Fight for Equality and the American Century, 1919-1963.* New York: Henry Holt, 2000.

Lutholtz, M. William. *Grand Dragon: D.C. Stephenson and the Ku Klux Klan in Indiana.* West Lafayette, Ind.: Purdue University Press, 1991.

Lutz, Tom, and Susanna Ashton, eds. *These "Colored" United States: African-American Essays from the 1920s.* New Brunswick, N.J.: Rutgers University Press, 1996.

Lynd, Robert S., and Helen Merrell Lynd. *Middletown: A Study in Contemporary American Culture.* New York: Harcourt, Brace and Company, 1929.

————. *Middletown in Transition: A Study in Cultural Conflicts.* New York: Harcourt, Brace and Company, 1937.

Madison, James H. *Indiana through Tradition and Change: A History of The Hoosier State and Its People, 1920-1945.* Indianapolis: Indiana Historical Society, 1982.

Margolick, David. *Strange Fruit: Billie Holiday, Café Society, and an Early Cry for Civil Rights.* Philadelphia: Running Press, 2000.

McBrien, William. *Cole Porter: A Biography.* New York: Knopf, 1998.

McGrew, W. H. *Interesting Episodes in the History of Marion and Grant County, Indiana.* Marion, Ind.: Grant County Historical Society, 1966.

Moore, Leonard J. *Citizen Klansmen: The Ku Klux Klan in Indiana, 1921-1928.* Chapel Hill: University of North Carolina Press, 1991.

Munn, William F., Sue Bratton, and Terry Lakes, eds. *Rough Times: Oral Histories Collected by Students in Advanced Placement US History and Advanced Placement English at Marion High School, Marion, Indiana, 1997-1998.* Marion, Ind.: Marion Public Library and Museum, 1999.

Myrdal, Gunnar. *An American Dilemma: The Negro Problem and Modern Democracy.* New York: Harper and Brothers, 1944.

Nelson, Daniel. *Farm and Factory: Workers in the Midwest, 1880-1990.* Bloomington: Indiana University Press, 1995.

O'Brien, Gail Williams. *The Color of the Law: Race, Violence, and Justice in the Post-World War II South.* Chapel Hill: University of North Carolina Press, 1999.

Okpewho, Isidore, Carole Boyce Davies, and Ali A. Mazrui, eds. *The African Diaspora: African Origins and New World Identities.* Bloomington: Indiana University Press, 1999.

Patterson, Orlando. *Rituals of Blood: Consequences of Slavery in Two American Centuries.* Washington, D.C.: Civitas/CounterPoint, 1998.

Phillips, Clifton J. *Indiana in Transition: The Emergence of an Industrial Common-wealth, 1880-1920.* Indianapolis: Indiana Historical Bureau, 1968.

Pluto, Terry. *Tall Tales: The Glory Years of the NBA, in the Words of the Men Who Played, Coached, and Built Pro Basketball.* New York: Simon and Schuster, 1992.

Rafert, Stewart. *The Miami Indians of Indiana: A Persistent People, 1654-1994.* Indianapolis: Indiana Historical Society, 1996.

Raper, Arthur F. *The Tragedy of Lynching.* Chapel Hill: University of North Carolina Press, 1933.

Schiedt, Duncan. *The Jazz State of Indiana.* Pittsboro, Ind.: Duncan P. Schiedt, 1977.

Sitkoff, Harvard. *A New Deal for Blacks: The Emergence of Civil Rights as a National Issue.* New York: Oxford University Press, 1978.

————. *The Struggle for Black Equality, 1954-1992.* Revised ed. New York: Hill and Wang, 1993.

Smith, J. Clay, Jr. *Emancipation: The Making of the Black Lawyer, 1844-1944.* Philadelphia: University of Pennsylvania Press, 1993.

Solomon, Mark. *The Cry Was Unity: Communists and African Americans, 1917-36.* Jackson: University Press of Mississippi, 1998.

Southern Commission on the Study of Lynching. *Lynchings and What They Mean.* Atlanta: n.p., 1931.

Stevens, Errol Wayne. "Heartland Socialism: The Socialist Party of America in Four Midwestern Communities, 1898-1920." Ph.D. diss., Indiana University, 1978.

Stevenson, Barbara J. *Remembering the Past: An Oral and Pictorial History of African Americans in Grant County, Indiana.* Vol. 1. N.p., 1996.

————. *An Oral History of African Americans in Grant County.* Charleston, S.C.: Arcadia, 2000.

Taylor, Robert, Jr., ed. *The State of Indiana History 2000.* Indianapolis: Indiana Historical Society, 2001.

Thornbrough, Emma Lou. *The Negro in Indiana: A Study of a Minority.* Indianapolis: Indiana Historical Bureau, 1957.

————. *Since Emancipation: A Short History of Indiana Negroes, 1863-1963.* Indianapolis: Indiana Division, American Negro Emancipation Centennial Authority, 1963.

———— and Lana Ruegamer. *Indiana Blacks in the Twentieth Century.* Bloomington: Indiana University Press, 2000.

Tolnay, Stewart E., and E. M. Beck. *A Festival of Violence: An Analysis of Southern Lynchings, 1882-1930.* Urbana: University of Illinois Press, 1995.

Trachtenberg, Alan. *Reading American Photographs: Images as History, Mathew Brady to Walker Evans.* New York: Hill and Wang, 1989.

Tsoukas, Liann E. "Uneasy Alliances: Interracial Efforts to End Lynching in the 1930s." Ph.D. diss., Indiana University, 1998.

U.S. Census Bureau. *Fifteenth Census of the United States: Population.* Vol. 3, part 1. Washington, D.C., 1932.

————. *Negroes in the United States, 1920-1932.* Washington, D.C., 1932.

Vincent, Stephen A. *Southern Seed, Northern Soil: African-American Farm Communities in the Midwest, 1765-1900.* Bloomington: Indiana University Press, 1999.

Vonnegut, Kurt, Jr. *Sirens of Titan.* New York: Delacorte Press, 1959.

Walsh, Justin E. *The Centennial History of the Indiana General Assembly, 1816-1978.* Indianapolis: Indiana Historical Bureau, 1987.

Watts, J. F., and Allen F. Davis. *Generations: Your Family in Modern American History.* 3d ed. New York: Knopf, 1983.

Wells, Ida B. *Southern Horrors: Lynch Law in All Its Phases.* New York: New York Age Print, 1892.

West, Jessamyn. *The Fall Creek Massacre.* New York: Harcourt, Brace, Jovanovich, 1974.

White, Walter. *Rope and Faggot: A Biography of Judge Lynch.* New York: Knopf, 1929.

Whitson, Rolland Lewis, ed. *Centennial History of Grant County, 1812-1912.* Chicago: Lewis Publishing Company, 1914.

Williams, Gregory Howard. *Life on the Color Line: The True Story of a White Boy Who Discovered He Was Black.* New York: Penguin Books, 1995.

Wright, George C. *Racial Violence in Kentucky, 1865-1940: Lynchings, Mob Rule, and 'Legal Lynchings'.* Baton Rouge: Louisiana State University Press, 1990.

INDEX